ESSAYS
in tribute to
J. Valentine Rice
1935–2006

J.V. Rice, 8 March 2005 (photograph: Anthony Dawson)

ESSAYS
in tribute to

J. Valentine Rice
1935–2006

edited by
AIDAN SEERY

THE LILLIPUT PRESS
DUBLIN

First published in 2010 by
THE LILLIPUT PRESS
62–63 Sitric Road, Arbour Hill
Dublin 7, Ireland
www.lilliputpress.ie

Copyright © The Lilliput Press and
individual contributors, 2010

Drawing on p. 240 from *Trinity College Dublin
Founded 1591: Thirty-Four Drawings and Descriptions*,
by Alexander Norman Jeffares, with a foreword by
G.F. Mitchell (Dublin: Alexander Thom, 1944)
© The Literary Estate of A.N. Jeffares

ISBN 978 1 84351 178 6

10 9 8 7 6 5 4 3 2 1

All rights reserved. No part of this publication
may be reproduced in any form or by any means
without the prior permission of the publisher.

A CIP record for this title is available
from The British Library.

Set in 11 pt on 15 pt Sabon by Marsha Swan
Printed and bound in the UK by J.F. Print Ltd, Sparkford, Somerset

Contents

Barbara Wright
  Professor John Valentine Rice: A Tribute — 7

Susan M. Parkes
  Centenary of the Chair of Education in Trinity College Dublin, 1905–2005 — 10

Cecily M. Begley
  Nursing and Midwifery Education in Ireland: The Contribution of Professor Val Rice — 35

Padraig de Bhál
  I gCuimhne ar an Ollamh Valentine De Rís — 43

P.J. Drudy
  Val Rice Outside the Classroom: Some Reflections — 47

John Heywood
  J. Valentine Rice, Emeritus Senior Fellow of Trinity College Dublin and the Philosophy of Education — 50

Vincent Alan McClelland
  John Carmel Heenan, the Second Vatican Council and the Rise and Fall of an English Lumen Vitae — 69

Dan Murphy
  International Trends in Denominational Schooling — 98

Michael O'Rourke
  A History of Guidance and Counselling in Ireland: American and European Influences — 116

Michael O'Shea
  *From Psychotherapy to Pedagogy: A Holistic Journey
  Towards Self-Autonomy* 141

Elizabeth Oldham
  *The Status of Mathematical Knowledge and its
  Implications for Mathematics Education* 159

Aidan Seery
  *Knowledge and the Idea of the University:
  Val Rice and John Henry Cardinal Newman* 182

Raymond Topley
  Educating for Consistency in Knowing and Doing 192

Valentine Rice
  Toward an Interpretation of the Work of Art 210

Eileen Doyle
  Resilience: Ordinary Magic 222

Susan M. Parkes
  Professor John Valentine Rice (1935–2006): An Appreciation 236

Professor John Valentine Rice: A Tribute

BARBARA WRIGHT

Imagine. Statistically, the chances are negligible that one would find, in the small community of fellows of Trinity College Dublin, two people born on the same day of the same year, with a son bearing the same first name, also born on the same day of the same year. And yet, that is the first bond that links me with Val Rice, in a strange kind of 'twinning', which made each of us anxiously seek news of the other, knowing that the parallels even ran to our having the same, rather unusual, make of piano.

For me, then, it was not difficult to empathize with this urbane and gracious man, who was appointed to the chair of education at Trinity College, in 1966 – a year after I myself had joined the full-time staff of the College. Our friendship spanned the decades until his unexpected death in Boston on 15 September 2006. In time, as senior fellows, we sat together on the Board of the College and on a variety of committees. Val Rice's commitment to Trinity was total – 'like a love affair', he used to say. That was another point we had in common.

Val Rice's predecessor, Revd Ernest Crawford, also died suddenly while on a visit to the United States. His remains were brought back to Ireland by Raymond Houghton, subsequently to become a great friend of the School of Education at Trinity.

Val Rice's appointment attracted considerable attention. This was the first time, since the creation of the chair of education in 1905, that it had been held by a Catholic – an outcome strongly urged by Professor W.B. Stanford, a pillar of the Trinity establishment, who considered that this was a way in which the College could come out of the isolation that characterized its existence in the 1920s and 1930s, and play its full part in the development of the still-young nation.

In this respect, Val Rice more than fulfilled the expectations of the College. He restructured the course for the higher diploma in education as a full-time programme, an initiative subsequently followed by all the colleges of the National University of Ireland. Having pursued his graduate studies in Harvard in the early 1960s, he used the Harvard model in setting up the MEd programme in Trinity as a means of preparing teachers for positions of responsibility in the Irish education system.

His activities, in terms of outreach, were to make themselves felt throughout the country. The Church of Ireland College of Education had been associated with Trinity since 1924. On Val Rice's watch, and with the active support of the senior lecturer and the deans of the appropriate faculties, these undergraduate courses were expanded into a BEd degree for primary teachers, in association with two other colleges in Dublin: the Froebel College at Sion Hill and Coláiste Mhuire at Marino.

The students of all three colleges took courses together on the university campus, without prejudice to their individual traditions, thus shaping an ecumenical context for the education of Irish primary teachers. This was a major breakthrough. Since independence, the State had been content to maintain the inherited educational structure, with its class-conscious, confessional schools. Now a wind of change rustled in the corridors of power.

Following on the Catholic condemnation of the 'godless' Queen's Colleges (forerunners of the National University of Ireland) in 1850 and of both the Queen's Colleges and Trinity College by the Maynooth Synod of 1875, Dr McQuaid, the Archbishop of Dublin, in 1944 forbade attendance by the Catholic faithful at Trinity. In 1956 the Plenary Council of the Church made the Dublin diocesan regulations applicable throughout the country. Val Rice is said to have been influential in bringing about the relaxation of this ban in 1970, which measure allowed the College to play a central role in the higher education of the nation's young people. Whether or not he was fully conscious of it at the time, Val Rice found himself at the helm when there truly was 'a tide in the affairs of men, which, taken at the flood, leads on to fortune'.

Utterly loyal to his students, who frequently also became his lifelong friends, Val Rice built up a network of contacts spanning great distances and periods of time. Devoted to his family, he also espoused a variety of public causes. He defended the Liffey Valley, persuading Fingal County Council to change its plans for a waterworks extension at Leixlip, so as to preserve a reputed Viking site. In Dingle, he worked for the preservation of Rice House, the property of one of his ancestors, charged with bringing Marie-Antoinette to safety in Ireland, although at the last moment the queen of France decided not to escape without the king.

Above all, he was informed, in all that he did, by Cardinal Newman's *Idea of a University*. The domain of pedagogy is one in which knowledge is apprehended as a whole, with one subject bearing upon another. This is the core of the great 'liberal' tradition advocated by Cardinal Newman: the pursuit of knowledge for its own sake, which Val Rice strove to uphold against all the countervailing forces that threatened, and continue to threaten, its ongoing integrity.

BARBARA WRIGHT is Fellow Emeritus in the Department of French, School of Languages, Literatures and Cultures at TCD. An internationally recognized expert in nineteenth-century French arts and letters, her most recent publications have been on French Orientalist and artist Eugène Fromentin. She was a direct contemporary of Val Rice in TCD for almost forty years.

Centenary of the Chair of Education in Trinity College Dublin, 1905–2005

SUSAN M. PARKES

I cannot doubt the University, in seeking to promote investigation into the philosophy and practice of the teacher's art, is entering on an honorable field of public awareness, and that, under her sanction, future explorers in this field will do much to make the work of honest learning and of noble teaching simpler, more effective, and more delightful to coming generations.[1]

The centenary of the chair of education in Trinity College was celebrated in 2005. The professorship in Trinity was the first chair of education in Ireland, to be followed soon after by chairs of education in the three constituent colleges of the newly established National University of Ireland and in Queen's University Belfast from 1908.[2] Although the study of education has been a pursuit of mankind from ancient times, as an academic university subject education is comparatively young, as can be seen in Trinity, which is over 400 years old.

What is unusual, perhaps, is that in the hundred years of the chair of education in Trinity there have only been four professors, which shows the stability of the School of Education. These were Edward Parnall Culverwell, 1905–16; Robert John Fynne, 1922–50; Ernest Albert Crawford,

1950–65 and John Valentine Rice, 1966–2005, each contributing to the development of the department. Professor John Heywood was appointed to a new chair of teacher education, 1977–96.

However, it is important to note that although the chair of education was a hundred years old in 2005, Trinity had already introduced a diploma in the theory and practice of education even earlier, in 1898. This diploma was the forerunner of the higher diploma in education, now the required postgraduate qualification for secondary teachers. The purpose of this paper is to discuss the background to the founding of the chair in 1905 under Culverwell, and the establishment of the School of Education in 1922 under Professor Fynne.

Education as a university subject

The establishment of the chair of education in TCD in 1905 was part of the broader development of education as an academic subject, worthy of its place in the university. Various factors contributed to this. One was the search for what was called a 'science of education' – that is, a set of fundamental principles and rules that would underpin the processes of teaching and learning.[3] In 1879 Alexander Bain (1818–1903), Professor of Logic at Aberdeen, published an influential book entitled *Education as a Science*, which sought to establish the underlying principles of education.[4] Bain was a member of a new society called The Society for the Development of a Knowledge of Education. Fellow pioneer members were James Sully (1843–1923), a philosopher and psychologist at University College London;[5] James Ward (1843–1925) at Cambridge, sometimes called the 'father of modern British psychology';[6] and Joseph Payne (1808–76), Professor of Education at the College of Preceptors in London. Payne's *Lectures on the Science and Art of Education* was published in 1880. The College of Preceptors had been founded in 1846 to provide lectures and qualifications for teachers. It offered both a licentiate and a fellowship by examination, and Payne had been appointed as the first Professor of Education in Britain in 1872.

Meanwhile in Scotland the first two university chairs of education had been appointed: Professor S.S. Laurie (1829–1909), at Edinburgh in 1876 and Professor J.M.D. Meiklejohn (1836–1902), at St Andrew's in the same year. Both men emphasized the responsibility of universities to support the study of education and the need to provide professional qualifications for both primary and secondary teachers.[8] In 1879 the University of Cambridge agreed to set up a Teacher Training Syndicate, which provided a qualification for secondary teachers and gave a pioneer set of lectures in the history, theory and practice of education, which became the foundation courses for the study of education.[9] The Cambridge Training College for Women, founded in 1885, also played an important role in qualifying women to teach in the growing number of new secondary schools for girls.[10] Oxford University established a Delegacy for Teachers in 1896, which offered qualifications for practising teachers.

Professional training of teachers

However, the academic study of education in universities would not have got very far if it not been closely linked to the demand for professional qualifications for teachers. Traditionally the universities had not been closely connected with the professional training of teachers. The training of primary teachers had developed in separate residential training colleges, while secondary teachers were considered qualified on the completion of a university subject degree. The content of what was being taught was considered more important than the method of delivery. Critics of the narrowness of primary training, however, encouraged the universities to take responsibility for providing a broader education for teachers and this led to the setting up, in England in the 1890s, of day training colleges attached to universities. These institutions provided a joint concurrent degree in art and education, which proved very successful. Many of the new universities in England like Manchester, Liverpool, Bristol and Reading, set up day training colleges that eventually developed into their university departments of education. The most important and largest of them was the London Day Training College, founded in 1902, which eventually became the University of London Institute of Education in 1932, a powerhouse of educational innovation.[11]

Education courses were much influenced at that time by the writing of the German educator, J.F. Herbart (1776–1841), who stressed the importance of the psychology of learning to develop a 'science of education', which would underpin educational theory. His famous 'five steps' became the accepted basis for school lesson-planning and for the logical structure of a lesson into 'introduction', 'presentation', 'assimilation', 'application' and 'evaluation'. Herbart emphasized the importance of the teacher in the construction of this lesson plan, and made a strong argument for the training of teachers in a coherent pedagogy.[12]

Professional status of teachers

The other movement that influenced the establishment of education departments was the demand from teachers themselves. In the campaign to become a recognized and well-paid profession it was essential for teachers to have a system of formal qualifications and registration. There had been a strong movement in the 1890s to introduce the registration of teachers in England but it had not got very far.[13] In Ireland, secondary teachers' registration was not introduced until 1914 when the postgraduate higher diploma in education became compulsory for State recognition, thus providing the small university departments with a welcome number of students.

A hundred years ago, graduate teacher training in Ireland was in its infancy. Primary teacher training took place in teacher-training colleges in Dublin, like St Patrick's, Drumcondra,[14] and Our Lady of Mercy College, Carysfort, Blackrock. There had been no movement for day training colleges such as in England, due partly to the strong denominational nature of primary training and partly to the failure to solve the 'university question' and find an acceptable structure for university education for Catholics. The religious orders involved in secondary education such as the Jesuits, the Carmelites, the Loreto sisters and Dominicans, provided their own system of training within the orders. The Intermediate Board of Education, set up in 1878 to provide public examination schools at second level, played no part in the training and certification of teachers, as recruitment and employment was entirely in the hands of the voluntary schools themselves. A graduate with a good degree was considered adequately qualified to teach: 'Better to have a good historian and a bad teacher, than a poor historian and a good teacher.'

Education in TCD

In Trinity, the first move to provide a professional course for teachers was the introduction in 1898 of a diploma in the theory, history and practice of education. This was the result of the work of two distinguished fellows, Edward Parnall Culverwell (1855–1931) and George Fitzgerald (1851–1901). Culverwell was an able mathematician and a Scholar and prizewinner of the College. He had been elected to fellowship in 1883 and had published a popular book, *Elementary Mechanics*, in 1890, as well as a number of articles including 'The Calculus of Variations'. He also had taught in the engineering faculty of the Royal College of Science. He became best known for his work on Maria Montessori and his book, *The Montessori Principles and Practice* (1913), was widely read.[15]

His brother-in-law, George Fitzgerald, was a distinguished physicist and Professor of Natural and Experiential Philosophy in TCD. He was a man of great energy and drive, who was well known for his work in electro-dynamics and for his strong support of science education. Fitzgerald had been involved in the establishment of Kevin Street Technical School in Dublin in 1877 and he served on the Belmore Commission on Manual and Practical Instruction in the Primary School in 1897.[16] Sadly Fitzgerald died in 1901 and did not live to see the establishment of the chair of education in TCD, which would have pleased him greatly.[17]

Fitzgerald first raised the matter of education as a university subject when he proposed to the University Council in 1891 that it should be made a subject for the fellowship examination. This was not accepted, but in April 1896 the Council agreed to the introduction of a university examination in education.[18] (This would be like the Cambridge Teachers' Syndicate and the Oxford University Delegacy for Teachers.) No lectures would be provided but a reading list was issued and a fee charged for the examination. This was the model that had been used for the examinations for women, introduced in 1869. Fitzgerald; Dr Louis Claude Purser,[19] Professor of Classics; and John Beare, Professor of Moral Philosophy, were appointed examiners, and the first examinations were held in 1898. Alfred Purser, chief of inspection of the Board of National Education in Ireland, was co-opted to act as examiner of practical teaching. The purpose of the examinations was 'to encourage teachers to study the theory of education and to apply the principles to practice'. From the outset the course was seen as being an in-service diploma, as the candidates had to have had at least one year's experience of school teaching before entering for the examinations.

Structure of 1898 diploma in education

The diploma examinations were structured in two parts. The first was in the theory, history and practice of education. The second part, which could only be taken after successful completion of the first part, was in proficiency in practical teaching and was examined in the candidate's school. The reading list for the examinations clearly shows what was to become the accepted structure of education diploma courses. In theory of education the set texts were John Locke's *Some Thoughts Concerning Education* (1693) and Joseph Payne's *Lectures on the Science and Art of Education* (1880). In history of education the texts were Gabriel Compayré's *Histoire de la Pédagogie* and Oscar Browning's *Introduction to the History of Educational Theories* (1888).[20] In addition, the well known sixteenth-century tract *The Scholemaster* (1570) by Roger Ascham, and John Milton's seventeenth-century *Tractate on Education* (1644) were set texts. In the practice of teaching there were two standard books: Joshua Fitch's *Lectures in Teaching* (1895) and Patrick W. Joyce's *A Handbook of School Management*, first published in 1863, which had become the essential manual for primary school teachers.[21] As a set text it was soon to be replaced by a new book, *Principles of Class Teaching* (1902), by Professor J.J. Findlay of Manchester University.[22]

Trial diploma examinations, 1897

A set of trial examinations was held in 1897 and three candidates entered and passed successfully. A trial practical examination was held later at The High School, Harcourt Street, Dublin.²³ It was part prepared and part unseen. Each of the three candidates had to select six subjects in which to present prepared lessons. Then they were asked to prepare three lessons in each and were given twenty-four hours' notice of which ones the examiners would visit. In addition, the candidates were asked to give a short lesson on a selected topic without preparation. The examiners' comments on these lessons included one where a candidate chose to give lessons in Latin and geography and the examiners commented that the lessons were too elaborate. Another was that the teacher lacked animation due to nervousness. The *Irish Independent*, commending this new TCD teacher training course, commented that 'under the grinding despotism of the intermediate examinations there is small room for trained teachers. Our schools require crammers who produce result fees by any method, good or bad, rather than teachers who can awaken the intelligence of children, and can lead them to be eagerly interested in knowledge for its own sake.'

Establishment of the chair of education, 1905

In the first years the numbers taking the new diploma were small, usually two or three a year. However, the number of women taking the examination increased once Trinity began to admit them in 1904. Teaching was one of the careers open to graduate women and they were anxious to improve their professional status; in 1907, eight women qualified with the TCD diploma. Qualified national teachers also showed an interest in the diploma as a form of further education. There was an increasing demand for professional recognition of teachers. In 1897 the Royal University of Ireland had introduced a diploma in teaching examination, which was open to both primary and secondary teachers who were graduates in arts. This diploma was structured in a similar way to the TCD diploma, consisting of theoretical examinations in 'mental and moral sciences in their relation to education', 'the history of education and the lives of eminent teachers', and 'methods of teaching, school management and organization', as well as a practical examination in classroom teaching, along with detailed notes of lesson plans.[24]

In 1905 a government report on secondary education, the Dale and Stephens Report,[25] stressed the great need for the professional training of secondary teachers in order to raise their status and remuneration. The union, the Association of Secondary Teachers in Ireland, was founded in 1909 in an effort to improve the working conditions and status of secondary teachers. Culverwell attended an ASTI conference held in the Mansion House in November 1910 at which he proposed a motion concerning the need to improve the status of Irish secondary teachers. He confessed that, in his opinion, the conditions of teachers were so bad that he 'never advised one of his students to go for a position of secondary schoolmastership in Ireland'.[26] In addition, the Robertson Commission on University Education in 1903[27] had recommended that a chair of pedagogy should be established in the universities. When the National University of Ireland was established in 1908, chairs of education were established in all three constituent colleges (UCD in 1909, UCC in 1910, UCG in 1915 and Queen's University in 1914). The formal registration of secondary teachers dates from 1914 when the Secondary Teachers' Registration Council was established.[28]

Chair of education, 1905

Culverwell, therefore, had much support and backing when he sought to establish a chair of education in 1905. He could show the growing interest in the study of education and the pressing need for professional teacher training. In 1903 he gave a series of public lectures in College on education; College, while granting permission for these, insisted that they should be advertised as personal rather than official university lectures. Therefore, in April 1904, when Culverwell proposed to the Board that Trinity should establish a department of teacher training, the Board agreed to consider it.[29] With the usual due caution, the Board asked Culverwell first to confer with some heads of leading schools and a committee was set up to consider the matter. It consisted of Culverwell, S. Paine Johnston, who was a member of Council and of the Intermediate Education Board, and Mr E.J. Gwynn, the Irish scholar (later

Provost 1927–37). In May 1904 this committee's report presented a strong case for the setting up of an education department. There were three main arguments put forward. Firstly, that knowledge of education would be valuable for all graduates who would later hold important positions in public life:

> The usefulness of the knowledge is surely beyond doubt, unless we assert that an ordinarily intelligent man has in education nothing to learn from the thoughts upon it of the greatest thinkers in the world ... The Primary as well as the Secondary education of the children of one of the great religious denominations is largely controlled by our graduates. As mangers of National Schools, as members of the Education Boards in the country, and as schoolmasters, they are exerting an influence on education of the most far-reaching character; the College might do immense service to education by giving instruction on the subject.[30]

Secondly, the paper stressed that professional qualifications for teachers were becoming essential, in view of the proposed State registration of teachers:

> The question of the training of teachers has become a pressing one. It will be well known that the need for training Primary Teachers has been recognized for many years, with the result that as teachers they are often superior to the better-educated Secondary Teachers. This was because, when the State took charge of Primary education, it adopted, to some extent, at least, the advice of experts, who watched closely the advance of education on the Continent ...[31]

And thirdly, the committee argued that education should be offered as an optional subject in the sophister years of the undergraduate BA degree.

The report stressed that Trinity should act quickly as it was already behind, compared to universities in England, in the introduction of education as an academic subject and in the provision of professional training for teachers. It also stressed the importance of the interface between the university and the secondary schools where TCD graduates taught and from which the College's future students would come.[32]

In May 1905 the Board agreed to the establishment of a chair of education. It was seen very much as a chair for Culverwell and was part-time. The salary was to be £100 per year for a period of five years, after which the matter would be reviewed. Such was the lack of faith in the scheme that a safety clause was added to state that any financial loss incurred would be carried by the university and not by any individual fellow. No department of teacher training was set up and it was left to Professor Culverwell to prove that there was need for one.[33]

Alexandra College education department

The matter was now further complicated by the intervention of Miss Henrietta White, principal of Alexandra College, Dublin. Alexandra had been very disappointed when TCD decided to admit women in 1904. It had hoped to become a recognized women's college of the University of Dublin, but these hopes had been dashed. White, therefore, had decided to establish what were known as the 'extra departments' – one of which would provide teacher training for women, including secondary teaching and a Froebel kindergarten training course.[34] Eventually, after much correspondence and as a gesture of goodwill, the Board agreed that while Trinity would provide the theory courses in education, Alexandra could provide the practical training for secondary women teachers and the fees would be shared.[35]

The arrangement with Alexandra must have been a disappointment for Culverwell, particularly as women students were the main supporters of his course. There were many old Alexandrans among the first women graduates and many of these now chose loyally to return to Alexandra for their teaching training. The loss was Trinity's because many able women took the course at Alexandra, while being awarded a diploma in education from TCD, and this arrangement continued until 1935. Relations between the two departments were not good – the main issue being that while TCD saw the education diploma as an in-service course for teachers with experience, Alexandra regarded their course as an initial training course with a stronger emphasis on practice. At this time the university did not teach methodology but was prepared to examine it, and the diploma was seen as being very theoretical.[36]

Undergraduate BA courses

With Culverwell in his chair in 1905, the diploma course in education was reorganized and three separate grades were now offered: a certificate in elementary education for primary teachers, a diploma in education and a diploma in education with distinction, for which extra academic work was required. There were no lectures provided yet for the diploma examination, and the numbers taking it remained small: in 1906 three students qualified, in 1908 eight students, and in 1916 twelve students – mainly graduate women. Culverwell put most of his energy into establishing the new courses for the BA degree. Education was to be an optional course in sophister years. In those days the BA ordinary degree had to be taken by professional students such as engineers and medical students, prior to the award of a professional degree. Education proved popular among these students as an easy and interesting subject.

The BA education course was designed to cover six terms and consisted of history and philosophy in junior sophister year. The set texts for this year were Paul Monroe's *Textbook of the History of Education* (1905), John Adams' *Herbartian Psychology Applied to Education* (1897) and J. Welton's *Logical Basis of Education* (1899), which also argued for a science of education. In the senior sophister year the course included a study of Newman's *Idea of a University* (1854) and Herbert Spencer's *Education – Intellectual, Moral and Physical* (1861) as well as William Bagley's *The Education Process* (1905).[37] Culverwell was assisted in the undergraduate lecturing by a somewhat eccentric member of College staff, James Maxwell Henry. Henry had a reputation of being able to lecture in almost any subject of which education was but one. He was very entertaining and talkative, and McDowell and Webb have a sharp comment: 'It is difficult see what niche would have suited him in his lifetime, but had he survived he would have made an admirable guru in a Californian commune.'[38] However, he was a popular and entertaining lecturer for education students. He appeared in a satirical play entitled *Patres Conscripts* in *TCD Miscellany* in 1943, which mocked his loquacity:

I talk about Hegel, I talk about Freud, I talk of the age of
   the earth;
And if I feel sure you won't be annoyed, I talk of miraculous
   birth.
I talk about man in the Golden Age, I talk of Tertullian's
   views of the stage,
I talk till my listeners go off in a rage,
Or are quite overcome by their mirth.[39]

Culverwell's own research interest was the educational ideas and methods of the Italian educator, Maria Montessori (1870–1952). The development of her ideas was comparatively new in 1905; her first book, *The Montessori Method*, was not published in English until 1912. Montessori advocated a system of 'auto-education' whereby the child is agent of his own learning and the task of the teacher, or directress as she was called, was to provide a suitably prepared environment and didactic equipment to stimulate the child's learning. Her ideas were gradually spreading, especially in the USA, but in Ireland Culverwell was one of her first disciples. His book, *The Montessori Principles and Practice* (1914), is still read by Montessorians as a useful study. Montessori's ideas at the time were considered by some to be too liberal and to allow the child too much freedom. In particular the new Professor of Education at UCD, Dr T.S. Corcoran, SJ, was very critical of the Montessori method and wrote a number of articles condemning its introduction into Irish schools. Culverwell became well known as a champion of the progressive child-centred approach and his book on Montessori became a set text for the examinations in education in TCD.[40]

Culverwell and the TCD Defence Committee

It was perhaps a pity for the new education department that Culverwell spent much of his time in 1906–7 organizing the TCD Defence Committee in what became known as the 'hands off Trinity' campaign. In an attempt to find a solution to the 'university question' the Irish Chief Secretary, James Bryce, on behalf of the government, put forward a plan to create one single university of Dublin, which would include TCD, UCD and the Queen's Colleges of Belfast and Cork. TCD organized such opposition to the scheme, including rallying its graduates far and wide, that the plan was dropped.⁴¹ The following year Augustine Birrell, the new Chief Secretary, came forward with a new plan to create the National University of Ireland, which did not include TCD and left it alone 'in splendid isolation'. Queen's College Belfast was elevated to become Queen's University.⁴²

Culverwell was so involved in the matter that, in 1907, one of the questions on the senior sophister examination paper related to the university problem in Ireland: 'What criticisms does a reading of Newman's "Idea of a University" suggest about a scheme for including University College, and the Queen's Colleges with Trinity College under an enlarged University of Dublin?' Perhaps the answers could have proved useful to Trinity during the later 1960s' 'merger crisis' when the government proposed to merge Trinity and UCD – a plan that was defeated by opposition from both colleges.

Culverwell's retirement, 1916

Culverwell retired in 1916 without having established a school of education. However, he had laid the solid foundations, so it was only a matter of time. The chair of education was left vacant, but Maxwell Henry was appointed as lecturer in education and kept the subject going, for which we owe him a debt of gratitude. The BA education courses were reduced to five rather than six terms but they held their position as valuable optional courses for the undergraduate degree, and the diploma in education course continued with a small number of graduate students. From the outset, the professorship had been seen as a temporary one for an initial period of five years, renewable during the tenure of the present professor, and there was a serious danger that it might not be continued.⁴³

School of education, 1922

It was, however, in response to an initiative by the Church of Ireland Training College (CITC) that the School of Education and a permanent professorship were eventually established. In 1919 the CITC had been a member of a committee set up by the Board of National Education to examine ways whereby formal links could be established between training colleges and the universities to allow primary teachers to proceed to degrees. Since 1913 an arrangement had been in place whereby qualified students from St Patrick's Training College could attend lectures for an arts degree of the National University of Ireland.[44] CITC then put forward a scheme whereby their students would attend lectures in arts and education in Trinity, while undertaking their professional training at the training college.[45] Professor W.J. Thrift (later Provost 1937–42) was also a governor of CITC, and he took the initiative. Strong links had already been established between the two institutions, which were geographically close to each other, and the new Provost, Dr J.C. Bernard (1919–27), had been Archbishop of Dublin and therefore manager of CITC.[46] The new Archbishop of Dublin, Dr John Gregg, was also a formidable ally.

Undoubtedly it was felt at the time that in view of the difficult political situation and the pending partition of Ireland, Protestant institutions in the south of Ireland should stand together in the difficult days ahead. Indeed CITC was to lose the majority of its students who came from the North and was to be reduced to a small college, serving only the Protestant minority in the south, and it was to be grateful for the support it received from TCD. There had been an established tradition that the education department was involved in both primary and secondary teacher education, and this was to be strengthened by the formal link with CITC.[47]

1921 *scheme*

After lengthy discussions, the scheme was agreed in 1921. Having successfully completed it, they could proceed to the sophister years for a BA degree. This privilege was supposed to apply only to future students but, in December 1921, a former student of CITC, Thomas Spearman, formally requested to be allowed to proceed to degree under the new regulations. The College had grave doubts about granting this privilege, as it was feared that many more past CITC students might apply. However, in the end the Board agreed to allow Mr Spearman to proceed, and he was to be followed later by other former CITC students, who made use of the TCD privilege.[48]

Trinity used the occasion to create a new school of education with a full-time chair. Part of the salary of the new professor (£500) was to be paid by the training college and the professor was to spend some of his time there as well as lecturing the students in Trinity.[49] In 1922 Robert John Fynne was appointed to the chair of education and he began to develop the new School of Education. Fynne was a Trinity graduate who had studied education under Professor J.A. Adamson (1857–1947) of King's College London[50] and was, like Culverwell, an admirer of the Montessori method. In 1924 he published a book, *Montessori and her Inspirers*, which is still used. Fynne was of the new generation of educators who believed in progressive and child-centred education. He was eager and full of enthusiasm to build up the new school but unfortunately did not get on with Kingsmill Moore, the now elderly principal of the Church of Ireland Training College. The underlying disagreement was a fundamental difference between the more open-ended, liberal approach to teacher education of the university and the narrower, more applied methods of the training college.[51] Angry letters on the matter from both of them were sent to Provost Bernard,[52] and eventually Fynne withdrew from the training-college work, but continued to lecture the CITC students when they came to Trinity for education lectures.

Department for the training of secondary teachers

Fynne turned his attention and energies to developing a department of secondary teacher training. He introduced a course of lectures for the higher diploma in education, held in the late afternoons, and the students were now to be supervised, as well as examined, in their schools. Much to the annoyance of Miss White of Alexandra, in 1925 he opened the department to women students of which there were to be many.[53] There is a handwritten register in the Department of Education office, which was begun by Professor Fynne in 1923, and which lists the names and results of all the diploma students. In 1923–4 there were only ten students – five men and five women – taking the course.

By 1932, ten years later, this had increased to twenty-five – fourteen men and eleven women. The register contains the names of most of the future school principals and staff of Irish Protestant schools, and eventually the number grew to about fifty students per year. The School of Education established good relations with the Protestant schools, particularly those in Dublin, which was of benefit to both.[54]

The higher diploma could still be taken by examination only, but in 1937 Fynne made attendance at lectures compulsory, and thus created a full-time course, albeit taught in the late afternoons.[55] Entry to the course could be in October or in January. The undergraduate courses in the BA continued as before and the training-college students had separate classes organized for them. Education was to continue as an optional undergraduate subject until the introduction of the general studies degree in the early 1960s, when it was phased out. After that, the only undergraduates left who were taking education were the students from the training college.

In the 1930s Fynne was joined by other members of staff, including Mrs Anita Little, a modern linguist who was appointed as assistant to the professor, along with scientist and mathematician Mr W.S.E. Hickson. J.J. Auchmuty was a lecturer in the history of education and later published one of the first textbooks on the history of Irish education, which was still in use in the 1960s.[56] Fynne himself lectured in philosophy, psychology and basic principles of teaching, educational administration and English methods. In the 1930s Fynne edited a number of books in the series *Modern Teaching*, which was published by the Educational Company of Ireland. The series was concerned with the methodology of teaching special subjects, and Mrs Little wrote one entitled *The Teaching of Modern Languages*.[57]

Fynne encouraged educational research and introduced a compulsory individual study and investigation essay as part of the diploma in education examinations. He also introduced a higher diploma with honours whereby a student could present a thesis on an approved topic or take a special examination in one of five options: 'new educational movements', 'comparative education', 'adult education', 'technical education' or 'school examinations'. Postgraduate research in education had not developed under Culverwell, unlike in the UCD education department, which, under the leadership of Professor T.J. Corcoran, had been producing higher-degree work since 1911.[58] The first education PhD thesis at Trinity was in 1928 by T.P. Walshe, 'Irish education from earliest times to 1801'. There was another thesis in 1928 by S.J. Willis, 'The principle of individuality in education' and a third by Jacob Weingreen in 1931, 'Ancient Hebrew education'.[59]

Some years ago Professor Fynne's personal library was sent to the second-hand book sale in College. With the support of a grant from the Trinity Trust, the library was purchased and it is now catalogued and housed in the research area in the Church of Ireland College of Education The contents of the library show the breadth of Fynnes's knowledge and reading in education, both in the philosophy and psychology of education, and especially in the measurement of intelligence. He was a great admirer of Sir Percy Nunn, head of the London Institute of Education (1913–36), whose book, *Education: Its Data and First Principles* (London 1920), was one of the most influential education textbooks of the 1920s and 1930s. Nunn's philosophy moved away from the concept of a science of education towards one based on the value and uniqueness of the individual child, and of his or her innate intelligence, which education should nurture and develop.[60]

Importance of the School of Education

The founding of a chair of education a hundred years ago was a very important decision, not only in the academic history of the College, but also in the study of education in Ireland. The TCD School of Education gave leadership in progressive and liberal teacher education, and sought to encourage research into current issues. It was aware of what was happening in the wider world of education outside of Ireland and attempted to bring these ideas to its students. Being involved in both primary and secondary education, the School had a broader vision of the education system and a better understanding of the vital continuum between primary and secondary education. Throughout its existence the School, although small, has served the important function in the university of recruiting able young graduates to enter the teaching profession. It has nurtured and supported them in the difficult initial years of teaching and has encouraged them to return to teach in second-level schools from which the university draws its students. If there are few good science graduates recruited into teaching, then there will be fewer science students entering the university. In this way the School of Education has been, and still is, a very important interface between second- and third-level education.

Conclusion

The vision of Culverwell and Fitzgerald at the beginning of the twentieth century was that the study of education and of teaching and learning were essential subjects for the university to undertake. TCD's lead in founding the chair in 1905 undoubtedly encouraged the founding of chairs of education in the university colleges of the NUI after 1908. The provision of a professional educational qualification for secondary teachers was a vital step in the campaign to establish a well-educated teaching force, who could demand better salaries, conditions of employment, and a fulfilling life career. Ireland has been, and still is, very fortunate in maintaining a high-quality teaching profession to educate the rising generation. This is of vital importance to a society, and it is one of the responsibilities of the university to assist and support it. The Irish education system has had many admirers as well as critics in recent years, but its importance in the growth of the economy and its contribution to the wealth and quality of life of the country, are fully acknowledged. Professional and enthusiastic teachers (and university lecturers) are the lifeblood of an education system, and they deserve the best initial training and in-service education that can be offered.

Last year a dinner was held in honour of Professor Valentine Rice, who retired in 2005 after thirty-nine years in the chair of education. Over 200 past students and staff attended and it was a very enjoyable occasion. What was most impressive was the number of leaders in Irish education in 2005 who were present – many of whom had been students in the School of Education in the 1970s, 1980s and 1990s.

In addition to its graduates, the School of Education has contributed to Irish education through its research and staff expertise. By publishing studies in education, serving on government committees, leading curriculum development, advising on reform of the examination system, working with subject associations like science, mathematics, history and modern languages, offering advice and counselling, providing in-service diplomas, and by assisting with learning and teaching courses in the university, the School has played an important leadership role in Irish education. The School currently offers two concurrent undergraduate courses, two postgraduate higher diplomas, taught MEd and EdD courses, two research centres, as well as higher degrees by research. The School will keep to the forefront of educational change and development in 21-century Ireland.

Overall, Professor Culverwell would be well pleased to know what has been achieved by his innovative chair in education founded in 1905:

> If this Chair can do anything to make the work of the ordinary school instruction more real and vital – to fill the young students of this neglected art and uncultivated science with some strong working-day sense of the high character of its aims and the usefulness of its methods – to prevent a noble occupation from sinking into a monotonous round of dreary labour – to make the schoolroom a place of happy spontaneous activity, and the teacher's work a perpetual blessing and hourly success – the Chair will not have been founded in vain, nor will its work end in barren theory or resultless speculation.[61]

NOTES

1. J.G. Fitch, *Lectures in Teaching* (Cambridge 1881), p. viii.
2. Chairs of education were founded in University College Dublin in 1909; in University College Cork in 1910; in University College Galway in 1915; and in Queen's University Belfast in 1914.
3. Brian Simon, *Does Education Matter?* (London 1985); Peter Gordon (ed.), *The Study of Education*, 3 vols (London 1980; 1985); J.W. Tibble (ed.), *The Study of Education* (London 1966).
4. This book was first published by Kogan Page in a scientific series alongside the writings of T.H. Huxley (1825–95) and John Tyndall (1820–93). Huxley was a science educator and a strong admirer of Charles Darwin. His book of essays, *Science and Education*, was published in 1893. See Richard Aldrich and Peter Gordon, *Dictionary of British Educators* (London 1989). John Tyndall was born in County Carlow but moved to England as a young man where he became a distinguished scientist, working along with Darwin, Huxley and Faraday. His research work was

on the atmosphere (he first explained why the sky is blue), and on the 'light pipe', a forerunner of fibre-optic cables. See Mary Mulvihill, *Ingenious Ireland* (Dublin 2002), pp. 368–9.

5. Sully was appointed to the chair of philosophy and mind and logic at University College London in 1892. His key interests were teacher training and child study and he was a founder member of the British Child Study Association. Two of his influential publications were *The Teachers' Handbook of Psychology* (1886) and *Studies of Childhood* (1895).

6. Ward was appointed to the new chair of mental philosophy and logic at Cambridge in 1897. He also lectured in education and his publication, *Psychology Applied to Education* (1926), was very influential. He was a strong supporter of women's higher education and was one of the first to allow women to attend his lectures.

7. J.V. Chapman, *Professional Roots: The College of Preceptors and British Society* (Epping 1985).

8. Laurie's writings included *On Primary Instruction in Relation to Education* (1867) and *The Training of Teachers and Methods of Instruction* (1901). Meiklejohn's best-known work was his inaugural 1876 address, entitled 'Scottish Education'. See Gordon, *The Study of Education*, i (1980) pp. 1–42.

9. Pam Hirsch and Mark McBeth, *Teacher Training in Cambridge: The Initiatives of Oscar Browning and Elizabeth Hughes* (London 2004). Oscar Browning (1837–1923) was a founder of the Cambridge University Day Training College (1891–1909) for elementary teachers. He was author of *History of Educational Theories* (1881), which became a standard textbook for the history of educational ideas. R.H. Quick, another supporter of secondary-teacher training and the university study of education, gave the first set of lectures on the history of education to students at the Cambridge Teacher Training Syndicate, and his *Essays on Educational Reformers* (1868) also became a well-known textbook for teachers. Another major figure in teacher training in Cambridge was J.G. Fitch (1824–1903), who was formerly chief of Her Majesty's inspectors for training colleges. His book, *Lectures on Teaching* (1902), was widely used as a manual of practical teaching.

10. Elizabeth Hughes (1851–1925) was founder of the Cambridge Training College for Women, later Hughes Hall. See M.V. Hughes, *A London Girl of the 1880s* (London 1978), for a personal record of the early days of the college.

11. See R. Aldrich, *A Century of Education* (London 2002); J.T. Thomas, *British Universities and Teacher Education: A Century of Change* (Lewes 1990); R.R. Rich, *The Training of Teachers in England and Wales* (Cambridge 1933); Lance Jones, *The Training of Teachers* (Oxford 1923);

P.H.J.H. Gosden, *The Evolution of a Profession* (Oxford 1972).

12. Herbart was Professor of Philosophy and Pedagogy at the University of Konigsberg. W. Boyd, *A History of Western Education*, 5th edn (London 1950), pp. 338–49; J.H. Herbart, *Science of Education* (trans. H. and M. Felkin, 1892); John Adams, *Herbartian Psychology Applied to Education* (London 1897).
13. In 1895, the *Report of the Royal Commission on Secondary Education* (Bryce) HC 1895 (c.1862), strongly recommended the training of secondary teachers in the universities and the formation of a teachers' professional register. A teachers' registration bill was introduced in 1898 but was subsequently withdrawn, and no official register was implemented. In Ireland the Palles Commission on Intermediate Education, 1898, made no specific recommendations regarding teacher registration, which it decided was outside its brief. The chairman of the board, Baron Palles, told the Robertson Commission on University Education in 1902 that the lack of higher education for Catholics meant that many teachers in Catholic schools lacked the formal qualifications that a system of registration would demand. See John Coolahan, *The ASTI and Post-Primary Education 1900–1984* (Dublin 1984), pp. 6–10.
14. James Kelly (ed.), *St Patrick's College, Drumcondra: A History* (Dublin 2006).
15. R.B. McDowell and D.A. Webb, *Trinity College Dublin: An Academic History, 1592–1952* (Cambridge 1982), pp. 305–7.
16. *Royal Commission on Manual and Practical Instruction in Primary Schools under the Board of National Education in Ireland*, HC 1897 (c. 8383, 8531, 8532, 8618, 8619), xliii, 1; HC 1898 (c. 8923–5) xliv, 1.
17. McDowell and Webb, *Trinity College*, pp. 305–7.
18. TCD muniments, board register, MUN/V/5/16, 25 April 1896: 'The resolutions of Council respecting the examination in methods of teaching were considered and it was resolved ... that the Board while feeling that great difficulties attach to the proposed scheme of examinations and diplomas in Methods of Teaching, which would be mainly applicable to persons not members of the university, are willing that it should be tried and will join with Council in appointing a joint committee to advise the necessary details.' The board appointed Dr Haughton, Senior Proctor, Dr Ingram, Registrar, and Dr Abbott, Professor of Hebrew, to a committee on the proposed scheme of examinations and diplomas in methods of teaching. The council appointed Dr Mahaffy, Professor of Ancient History, Dr Fitzgerald and Chetwode Crawley to the committee. Chetwode Crawley was headmaster of his own school in St Stephen's Green, which prepared boys for entrance to TCD.
19. McDowell and Webb, *Trinity College*, p. 302.

20. Compayré was head of the Normal School in Fontenoy, France.
21. P.W. Joyce (1827–1914) had been head of the Marlborough Street Model Schools and trained national-school teachers. He was also well known as an Irish scholar and his book, *Origins and History of Irish Place Names*, was published in 1869. His textbook for children, *A Child's History of Ireland* (1898), was very popular.
22. *Dublin University Calendar* (1898), pp. 58–9; Findlay (1860–1940) was Professor of Education at Manchester University, 1903–25. He was much influenced by the educational ideas of Herbart, having studied at the universities of Jena and Leipzig in Germany.
23. CICE archives, newspaper cutting book (1898). Article from the *Irish Independent*, 14 October 1898. The headmaster of the High School was William Wilkins, a TCD graduate. See W.J.R. Wallace, *Faithful to Our Trust: A History of the Erasmus Smith Trust and the High School* (Dublin 2005), pp. 135–69.
24. *RUI Calendar* (1909), pp. 205–7. In 1897, the Ursuline convent in Waterford set up a training course to prepare candidates for the teachers' certificate of the Cambridge Syndicate, as did the Dominican convent in Eccles Street in 1908.
25. *Report of Messrs F.H. Dale and T.A. Stephens, His Majesty's Inspectors, Board of Education, on Intermediate Education in Ireland*; HC 1905 (cd. 2546) xxviii, 709. The report estimated that the average salary of a male secondary teacher was £82 6s 7d and only £48 2s 7d for a female teacher. See T.J. McElligott, *Secondary Education in Ireland, 1870–1921* (Dublin 1981), pp. 87–97.
26. Coolahan, *The ASTI*, p. 21.
27. *Report of the Commissioners on University Education (Ireland)*; HC 1902 (cd. 825–6), xxxi, 21; 1902 (cd. 899–90), xxxi, 495; 1902 (cd. 1228–9), xxxii, 1; 1903 (cd. 1483–4), xxxii, 1.
28. Bill to amend the law relating to secondary education in Ireland, HC 1912–13 (219), ii, 879; 1914 (161), iii, 477. The Registration Council consisted of representatives of secondary teachers, the Intermediate Board and the universities. It was responsible for laying down the professional qualifications required for registered teachers. A university postgraduate diploma in education became the standard entry qualification. The first register, published in 1918, listed the names, registration number and school where the necessary teaching practice was obtained. In the list there were twenty-one teachers who had qualified with the University of Dublin education diploma, of whom nineteen were women and three were men. Coolahan, *The ASTI*, pp. 6–40.
29. 'In reference to the letters and documents submitted by Mr Culverwell re teachers' registration it was resolved that Mr Culverwell be asked to draw up a scheme, on which such as a basis might be instituted a "Trinity

College, Dublin Teachers' Training Department".' Mr Culverwell was advised to invite to a conference certain heads of leading schools. TCD muniments, MUN/V/6/3, companion to the board register, 23 April 1904.
30. TCD muniments, MUN/V/6/3, companion to the board register, 7 May 1904, p. 65.
31. Ibid.
32. Ibid. See John B. Thomas (ed.), *British Universities and Teacher Education: A Century of Change* (London 1990). The chair of education at Cambridge was not established until 1948 and at Oxford not until 1989.
33. TCD muniments, MUN/V/6/5, companion to the board register, 6 May 1905. In June 1905 the board received a letter from Robert Morant (1863–1920), permanent secretary to the Board of Education in London, stressing that the diploma in education must be postgraduate if the new TCD secondary teachers training department was to be recognized formally for registration (MUN/V/6/5, companion to the board register, 23 June 1905, p. 90). Morant was largely responsible for the planning and implementation of the 1902 Balfour Education Act, in England and Wales, which established local authority education committees. See G.A.N. Lowdnes, *The Silent Social Revolution: An Account of the Expansion of Public Education in England and Wales 1895–1965*, 2nd edn (Oxford 1937; 1965); E.J.R. Eaglesham, *The Foundations of Twentieth-Century Education in England 1895–1965* (London 1967).
34. Anne O'Connor and Susan M. Parkes, *Gladly Learn and Gladly Teach: Alexandra College and School 1866–1966* (Dublin 1984).
35. TCD muniments, MUN/V/6/3, companion to the board register, 5 May 1905, p. 84.
36. Susan M. Parkes, *A Danger to the Men? A History of Women in Trinity College Dublin 1904–2004* (Dublin 2004).
37. Monroe was from Teachers' College, Columbia, NYC; Adams was Professor of Education at the London Day Training College, 1902–22; Welton was Professor of Education at Leeds University, 1904–16; Bagley was from Montana Normal School – indicative of the Anglo-American influence on the study of education.
38. McDowell and Webb, *Trinity College*, p. 399.
39. *TCD Miscellany*, 4 Feb 1943, reprinted in D.A. Webb (ed.), *TCD Anthology 1895–1945* (Dublin 1945), p. 94.
40. See E.P. Culverwell, 'The Montessori method of home and school education' in *Irish Review*, ii (December 1912), 541–4; B. Mortimer Standing, 'The Montessori method and Irish education' in *Irish School Weekly*, lxxvii, 34 (21 August 1926); T.S. Corcoran, 'Early training of the senses' in *Irish Monthly*, liii (July 1925), 345. Training for Montessori teachers began in Waterford and at Sion Hill, Blackrock, County Dublin.

41. McDowell and Webb, *Trinity College*, pp. 376–8.
42. *Irish Universities Act 8 Edw. vii*, c. 38, 1 August 1908; T.W. Moody and J.C. Beckett, *Queen's Belfast, 1845–49: The History of a University* (London 1959); Donal McCartney, *UCD: A National Idea: The History of University College Dublin* (Dublin 1999).
43. *DU Calendar* (1906–7), ii, p. 393, stated: 'In June 1905, by a decree of Board, Council and Visitors, a professorship of education was established, at an annual salary during the tenure of the present professor of £100, for a period of five years, with power to discontinue it then or when it shall cease to be held by the present professor, or continue it for successive terms of five years each, so long as it shall be deemed convenient.'
44. Kelly, *St Patrick's College*, pp. 234–5.
45. Susan M. Parkes, *Kildare Place: A History of the Church of Ireland Training College 1811–1969* (Dublin 1984), pp. 128–40. Bernard had been appointed Archbishop of Dublin in 1915.
46. McDowell and Webb, *Trinity College*, pp. 423–5.
47. Culverwell was concerned about the new compulsory Irish language programme in schools, introduced by the Free State government in 1922. He wrote a strong letter of protest to the taoiseach, W.G. Cosgrave, arguing that Irish Studies would be a much better programme. See S. Farren, *The Politics of Irish Education 1920–65* (Belfast 1995), p. 118.
48. The Spearman case was discussed by the board on 10 December 1921, the same day as it passed a resolution supporting the 'Irish Settlement', following the Anglo-Irish Treaty negotiations in London. Dr David Spearman, FTCD, son of Thomas Spearman, has been vice-provost and Professor of Mathematics in TCD.
49. TCD advertised the chair of education in February 1922 at a starting salary of £500. The duties of the professor included 'the administration of his own department, lecturing in the theory and practice of education and in educational psychology to the King's Scholars, both in TCD and at the Kildare Place College, as well as lecturing in the theory of education in the arts course and on the higher diploma in education'. TCD muniments, MUN/V/5/23, board register.
50. John Adamson, a distinguished historian of education, was head of the Education Training Department at King's College London, 1890–1924. His books included *Pioneers of Modern Education 1600–1700* (Cambridge 1905), and *English Education 1789–1902* (Cambridge 1930).
51. For example, the system of 'criticism lessons' had been a feature of training colleges for many years. The student teachers were required to teach a small class in front of the whole student and staff body, who then were invited to evaluate the lesson. It was a real ordeal for students. Kingsmill Moore himself had presided for years over these sessions, but

Fynne regarded them as being quite out of date, positively damaging to the students' self-confidence, and wanted them abolished.

52. J.H. Bernard correspondence. TCD MSS 2388–93/343, 385, 387, 388.
53. O'Connor and Parkes, *Gladly Learn*, pp. 165–70.
54. The 'ban' on attendance by Catholic students at TCD was not lifted until 1970.
55. School of Education minute book, 10 June 1937. The new higher diploma education course was laid down in eight sections: i. philosophy and general theory of education; ii. educational psychology; iii. the basic principles of teaching; iv. educational organization and administration; v. the history of education; vi. educational hygiene; vii. special methods of teaching school subjects; viii. individual study and investigation. Attending the School committee meeting in 1937 were 'Dr A.A. Luce, chairman Mrs Little, Mr Henry, Mr La Touche Godfrey, Dr Auchmuty and the professor of education'.
56. J.J. Auchmuty, *Irish Education: A Historical Survey* (London and Dublin 1937). Auchmuty later had a distinguished academic career in Australia. See K.R. Dutton, *Auchmuty: The Life of James Johnston Auchmuty* (Brisbane 2000).
57. Others in the series included *The Teaching of Elementary Mathematics* and *The Teaching of Arithmetic* by J.S. Strettan, and *The Teaching of Irish* by Anna H. O'Connor, later headmistress of Celbridge Collegiate School. Both Strettan and O'Connor gave special methods lectures in the School of Education.
58. At UCD there were fifteen MA degrees in education awarded by 1914. *ESAI Register of Educational Topics*, pp. 1–2.
59. Jacob Weingreen was appointed Professor of Hebrew in TCD in 1937.
60. Books in the Fynne collection relating to the measurement of intelligence included P.B. Ballard's *Mental Tests* (1934) and *The New Examiner* (1936); Raymond Cattell's *Guide to Mental Testing* (1936); Cyril Burt's *The Factors of the Mind: An Introduction to Factor-Analysis in Psychology* (1940); and C.W. Valentine's *Intelligence Test* (1945).
61. J.M.D. Meiklejohn, Professor of Education, University of St Andrew's, inaugural address, 1876. Gordon, *The Study of Education*, i, pp. 1–42.

SUSAN M. PARKES, MA, M.Litt., FTCD, is an Emeritus Fellow of TCD. A historian of education, she was a member of staff of the School of Education and colleague of Val Rice from 1966–2000, and is author of a number of books including *Kildare Place, A History of the Church of Ireland Training College, 1811–1969* (1984). She is editor of *A Danger to the Men? A History of Women in Trinity College, Dublin, 1904–2004* (2004).

Nursing and Midwifery Education in Ireland: The Contribution of Professor Val Rice

CECILY M. BEGLEY

Professor Val Rice was a champion of nursing and nursing education at a time when it did not feature as a viable entrant into third-level education. His first educational encounter with the profession was when he was invited by the dean of the faculty of nursing, at the Royal College of Surgeons in Ireland (RCSI) to act as consultant for the development of a part-time bachelor in nursing studies (BNS) degree for qualified nurses, 1992–3. At the time, there was only one such bachelor's degree in the country, run by UCD. This course had commenced in 1984 solely for registered nurses and midwives wishing to become qualified as nurse and midwife teachers. However, bedside nurses and midwives in Ireland, not necessarily only those who wished to move into the educational field, were hungry for knowledge. Indeed, the uptake of the short diploma courses at that time in the RCSI faculty of nursing, with 1000 students attending annually, indicated the desire and need for further, more in-depth programmes. UCD therefore had extended their full-time

BNS course into a part-time version for qualified nurses and midwives in 1991[1] and the faculty of nursing in the RCSI wished to follow suit.

Professor Rice read the proposed BNS curriculum and provided advice and guidance on levels of learning required at degree standard, suitable terminology and the outline for curriculum documents. He met with potential contributors to the programme and debated the ratio of the various topics that made up the total content. The possibility of the BNS degree being awarded by Trinity under a validation mechanism, was discussed and initial steps were put in place to explore this idea. However, it was found that, under previous agreements, the degree had to be awarded by UCD so Professor Rice's connection ceased at that stage, but the degree did continue its development and commenced in RCSI in 1994.

His interest in nursing education was by then piqued and his next initiative was to introduce a 'health sciences education' strand into the existing two-year full-time master in education course in Trinity. This well-established and highly regarded programme was usually undertaken by secondary school teachers but his vision was to enlarge the clientele to include members of the health professions and other disciplines. Over a period of years, health professionals were, in fact, choosing to attend the MEd programme and Professor Rice's introduction of the specific health sciences education strand was a welcome one for them. A number of nurses, midwives and physiotherapists undertook the programme annually and many went on to become leaders in the health science education field in Ireland. They, and the author, returned in following years to teach on the course and to supervise the research theses of second-year students.

The undoubted success of this programme was obvious in the numbers of students applying, with up to five people registering each year specifically for the health sciences strand in the decade leading up to 2004, the majority of whom were nurses. The only alternative course available at that time, to prepare nurses and midwives for a teaching role, was the three-year full-time BNS in UCD, which later became a two-year MSc programme, both of which were approved by An Bord Altranais (the Irish Nursing Board), to allow successful candidates to register as nurse or midwife tutors. Professor Rice was determined that the TCD MEd programme (health sciences strand) should also be approved by An Bord Altranais, so that the nurses and midwives undertaking it would not be disadvantaged in terms of being permitted to register as ABA-accepted tutors. He therefore entered into prolonged negotiations with An Bord Altranais and arrived at an agreeable solution, whereby students attending the MEd course, if they undertook an assessed module on nursing or midwifery theory and a specified amount of supervised teaching, would be accepted onto the tutors' register. These modules, accordingly, were designed and incorporated into the MEd programme and students were then able to register as nurse or midwife tutors.

The MEd is a research-based degree and, over the past twenty years, MEd theses have been written on a number of diverse topics in the area of health sciences education. These span the professions not only of nursing and midwifery but also physiotherapy, with topics such as the use of a holistic approach in the treatment of patients by final-year physiotherapy students; the extent of post-qualification physiotherapy-related research in Ireland; and women's health in the physiotherapy curriculum. Midwifery topics include the locus of decision-making in midwifery education and the quality of antenatal education and its influence on women's experience of childbirth. Topics in the nursing field are more varied, encompassing many clinical disciplines as well as covering more generic areas such as leadership styles and ward environments; career guidance and the career-planning needs of student nurses; personal-development planning in the nursing profession in Ireland; and evaluations of management courses by Irish nurses.

In the field of general nursing, studies have been conducted into registered nurses' knowledge of acute post-operative pain assessment, and the role and educational preparation of anaesthetic nurses. Proportionately more students from mental health and intellectual disability fields attended the MEd programme, as these areas appeared to be more willing, or able, to fund the two-year full-time course. Studies in mental-health nursing included a review of mental-health promotion policies and programmes in the Eastern Health Board region; the experiences of Irish student psychiatric nurses and factors enhancing their motivation to learn; attitudes of nurses to people who self-harm;

and an evaluation of education and training needs of staff nurses and care officers working in the Central Mental Hospital, Dublin. Similarly, three studies in the area of intellectual disability included studies of quality-assurance activities in residential centres; self-advocacy and people with learning difficulties; and an examination of the perceived education needs of staff in the area of relationships and sexuality training for people with learning disabilities.

In addition to these clinical topics, many health science students researched educational subjects in their field. Some examples of clinical education themes included 'Effective supervision in the clinical education of physiotherapy students' and 'The place of preceptorship in Irish nurse education'. Three students examined students' perceptions of the pre-registration diploma programme of nurse education, the access to bachelor in nursing studies degree programme and the impact of a bachelor of nursing studies programme on graduates' clinical practice.

More generalized topics around the area of clinical education looked at preceptors' perceptions of benefits, rewards, supports and commitment to the role; nurse tutors' perceptions of their role in the education of student nurses in clinical practice; and the clinical learning environment for post-registration emergency nurse students. A study on the educational background and induction needs of newly immigrant Filipino nurses in the Republic of Ireland demonstrated the changing times, when Ireland, which had always exported nurses to other countries,[2] was now in a position where nurses from overseas were being encouraged to apply for work here, with concomitant educational obligations for health-service providers. In the field of educational theory, research was conducted into critical thinking as an essential component of the pre-registration education of nurses, and the readiness of post-registration student nurses for the teaching strategy of problem-based learning. Work on the development of curricula included theses on the development of a self-directed unit of learning on genetics for the registered general nurse diploma course; the theory–practice gap in a school of nursing in Tanzania; and curriculum development and evaluation of a diploma in practice nursing course.

The number and varied nature of these topics demonstrate the wide influence that the MEd course has had on the development of the nursing and midwifery professions during the late 1980s, through the 1990s and up to 2004. Two issues, however, were working against continued success for the MEd (health sciences strand). Firstly, the economic state of the health services in Ireland at the time and, in particular, the acute shortage of nurses and midwives, was not conducive to permitting experienced qualified staff to take two years' paid leave out of the health services to undertake the course, and numbers dwindled. This occurred because, although Ireland in the past had supplied many other countries with nurses and midwives,[3] from 1990 onwards a sudden reversal in this situation took place. As nurse education moved into third-level institutions, there was a reduction in student numbers from 1800 to fewer than 1400 over the period 1990–2000.[4] In addition, as students were no longer undergoing an apprenticeship training, where they provided a service as part of the paid workforce, large numbers of registered nurses were required to replace their labour in the system; any over-supply of Irish-trained nurses and midwives that had existed in the past was thus rapidly diminished.

Secondly, due to the planned introduction of the four-year full-time BSc in nursing degree throughout Ireland in 2002, there was urgent need for an increased number of qualified nurse teachers. The Department of Health and Children requested the School of Nursing and Midwifery in Trinity to develop a one-year part-time programme to enable nurses and midwives, who held bachelor's or master's degrees, to undertake a 'top-up' course in educational theory and practice that would qualify them to register with ABA as tutors. This course was designed in partnership with the School of Education and consisted of five modules: theory and practice of health sciences education; quality improvements in health sciences education; curriculum issues in health sciences education; clinical teaching skills; and the psychology of education. It was first offered as a postgraduate diploma in clinical health sciences education in October 2000. The generic title left the programme open to all health professionals and a small number of non-nurses and midwives applied each year.

Professor Rice supported the development of the postgraduate diploma and championed it through TCD's systems, despite the fact that it could have been seen as being in competition with the long-established MEd. Staff from the School of Education taught the module on psychology of education on the programme, just as staff from the School of Nursing and Midwifery taught the health sciences and nursing theory modules on the MEd. The synergies between the education and health professions, at the level of academic staff and students, led to interesting discussions and debates, and contributed to making both courses more open and diverse in their focus.

Since its inception in October 2000 this programme has graduated almost 100 nurses and midwives, many of whom have continued in careers as academics in third-level institutions. This course has now been incorporated into, and largely superseded by, the MSc in nursing and MSc in midwifery (education strand), but a small number of students each year apply to take the stand-alone course because they have completed a different MSc and now need to develop skills and knowledge in teaching and learning. The education modules of the two programmes are taught together, thus ensuring sufficient student discussion opportunities.

The course was evaluated very positively at the end of its first year, with eighteen students (95 per cent) stating that it met their objectives and expectations; seventeen (90 per cent) that it was well organized and co-ordinated; sixteen (84 per cent) that it was intellectually challenging; seventeen (90 per cent) that it was practically challenging; and nineteen (100 per cent) that it encouraged student interaction. The majority of students felt that it improved their classroom teaching skills (n=18, 95 per cent); clinical teaching skills (n=13, 68 per cent); their skills in assessment (n=17, 90 per cent); and in curriculum development (n=19, 10 per cent). Overall, eighteen students (95 per cent) would recommend the course to other students.

Qualitative comments written on the feedback form supported the above ratings and included comments such as: 'Overall a very good course, very well co-ordinated, very good standard of lecturers'; 'The change for me has been awesome. It has had a profound effect on me professionally and personally, for the better I hope'; 'I really learned a great deal, the idea of skill-teaching, pace, learning outcomes and the aims of your session are so important'; 'More analytical in my ability to assess the overall teaching and learning achieved rather than identifying one specific issue to the detriment of other environmental, political factors'; and 'I feel I have moved from [being] a behavioural-focused teacher to a broader teacher – I feel I am still on the journey'.

Throughout the development of the postgraduate diploma programme, Professor Rice continued to take an interest in its formation and willingly provided advice and guidance on any queries. He and his team joined in the teaching and organization of the curriculum, attending course committee meetings and contributing to discussions on its expansion and progress. Similarly, staff from the School of Nursing and Midwifery were involved in teaching and supervising on the MEd, with very positive relations developing among the staff of both schools. It was unfortunate that, as a result of the commencement of the postgraduate diploma in clinical health sciences education, coupled with the severe shortage of nurses and midwives, enrolment into the MEd (health sciences strand) dwindled around 2004.

Professor Rice had other, more far-reaching effects on developments in nursing and midwifery education. I had the pleasure and privilege of undertaking doctoral studies in the School of Education with him and Elizabeth Oldham as my supervisors from 1994 to 1997. In 1996, I was appointed director of the School of Nursing and Midwifery in Trinity, so it could be said that many of the developments of that school had their seeds in the School of Education and, in particular, in my two supervisors. The combination of Elizabeth Oldham's kindly advice and deep knowledge of empirical research with Professor Rice's attention to philosophical depth and grammatical detail improved my research skills, output and writing to doctoral level. I am unable, to this day, to permit a split infinitive to lurk unnoticed in any document emanating from our School, due to his early influence on my work. However, I cannot say that I enjoyed the stipulation that Turabian's referencing convention[5] be used in all theses; while it is a very useful system for supervisors and examiners, I did not find it user-friendly for the student!

Professor Rice was an admirable mentor, and academic friend. His deep knowledge and love of education shone through in all his efforts, and nothing short of high quality was ever acceptable to him. He has left his mark on the postgraduate diploma in clinical health sciences education, a lasting tribute to his interest and enthusiasm for nursing and midwifery education in Ireland.

NOTES

1. J. Chavasse, 'Nursing education' in J. Robins (ed.), *Nursing and Midwifery in Ireland in the Twentieth Century* (Dublin 2000).
2. P.H. Troy *et al.*, 'Nurses' experiences of recruitment and migration from developing countries: a phenomenological approach' in *Human Resources for Health*, 5, 15 (2007).
3. *Ibid.*
4. J. Buchan and J. Sochalski, 'The migration of nurses: trends and policies' in *Bulletin of the World Health Organisation*, 82, 8 (2004).
5. K.L. Turabian, *A Manual for Writers of Term Papers, Theses, and Dissertations*, 6th edn (Chicago 1996).

CECILY M. BEGLEY holds the chair of nursing and midwifery at TCD. She completed her MEd and PhD in the School of Education under Val Rice. She has published extensively on midwifery research and is a member of a number of international professional institutions.

I gCuimhne ar an Ollamh Valentine De Rís

PADRAIG DE BHÁL

Teach Solais

Buachaill Béasach
As dúthaigh ó Dórna
Mac múinteora
Múinte sibhialta
Ag fás is ag forbairt
I dtalamh torthúil

Tré staidéar dian
Agus fiosracht chíocrach
Ag dreapadh suas go barr na haille
Ghlac le gach dushlán
Dar tháinig sa tslí
Ag diúl feasa i ngach áird

Ceaptha ina ollamh léannta
Scoláire staidéartha críonna gaoismhear
Léachtóir i bhfealsúnacht an tsaoil
Comhairleoir ag iliomad coistí
Bhláthaigh sé i measc scoláiri TCD

I gCUIMHNE AR AN OLLAMH VALENTINE DE RÍS

Bhfuil rian ar bith
Den laoch seo ar fáil
An gcloistear caint faoi
Cá bhfuil a cháil?

I seomraí scoile ar fúd na tíre
I measg lucht cheannais agus lucht riartha
I measg scoláirí agus saoithe
Sa bhaile is í gcéin
Faightear a chuid mac léinn

Daoine ar thug sé seans blathú doibh
Ar chaith sé dian-chúram leo
Le linn dóibh bheith faoina stiúir
Go raibh sé ann dóibh mar aoire

Is iontu siúd anois is mó
Atá a scáil, a thionchar beo
Ba cháirde leis iad le linn a réime
Anois is dual dó gach ard-chéim

Ar mbuíochas duit, a threoraí caoin
ár meas ort choíche, a ollaimh mhín
Go dtuga Dia dhuit go síorraí
An fhís dar shantaigh tú
Le linn do shaoil

Go raibh do chroí corraitheach séimh
Faoi shuan anois I mbaclainn Dé

In Memoriam D.J. Murphy

We drank in the beauty of old town square
As by my side you spoke learnedly
Of the people and ideas which shaped its history –
Of its Slavic civilization
Long suppressed, now reawakened
Out of its Marxist oppression

You spoke of Havel
Of your love for his philosophy
His literature, his plays
His depth of longing
For his people's release
From the brutal grasp of empire

I knew that your years of toil
in unveiling the richness of the
East European mind
had made you a lover and a propagator
of its noble inspiration

The quiet streets of Prague,
each building – church, monument
bridge, castle or theatre
provided a stream of interweaving times and meanings
which you slowly unveiled

We paused near the castle
To taste the native goulash
To drink the local brew
To plan further quests

At evening time
We went to the National theatre
Where for a pittance
We savoured a magnificent performance of Aida.

I gCUIMHNE AR AN OLLAMH VALENTINE DE RÍS

Dan

D'fhág tú sinn
Gan fiú seans againn
Slán a fhágail leat
Shleamhnaigh tú uainn
Gan choinne, gan rabhadh
Mar cheo ag scaipeadh

Leag tú do cheann uaibhreach liath
Don uair dheiridh ar an talamh seo
Stad d'intinn ghéar ag meilt gaoise
Mar a stadfadh ineall ríomhaire

Ba dheacair glacadh
Le do chomhluadar aerach
Do chuid scéalta, do chuid léinn
Do chúram dod cháirde
Do dhíograis don chuardach
I ndiaidh na feasa
A bheith thart go deo
Agus tusa ag dreo sa chré

Maireann cuimhne ort
Maireann do chuid leabhar
Maireann an eagna
Síol curtha agat go fairsing

PADRAIG DE BHÁL was previously lecturer in research and Irish education, Irish language methodology and Irish in the School of Education, TCD. He has also lectured in philosophy and the philosophy of education in Carysfort College, Dublin. He has published a number of poetry collections and essays and edited two books. A colleague and friend of Val Rice, they shared many interests.

Val Rice Outside the Classroom: Some Reflections

P.J. DRUDY

The contributions in this book focus on concerns, challenges and policies relating to education and it was in this critical field that Professor Val Rice made his major contributions. Val often stressed that one of his key responsibilities in education was that of teacher, tutor, mentor and adviser, always encouraging students to realize their full potential in a whole range of academic and other activities. However, Val's role as adviser and mentor extended well beyond the walls of the classroom and the College. I can give only a brief flavour of his legacy in this short piece.

One of Val's early contributions during the 1970s was to the merger proposal by the then minister for education. The proposal was to merge Trinity College with University College Dublin on the grounds that there was no need for two universities in the Dublin area. The idea was misguided in that it failed to recognize the distinctive contributions being made by the two universities and that there would be virtually no savings resulting from the merger. In any case, Val was strongly opposed to it and wrote a remarkable critique of it for the Irish Federation of University Teachers, of which he was an active member. Val's contribution was undoubtedly influential and played a key role in both the removal of the ban on Catholics entering Trinity and the abandonment of the merger proposal.

Val served for many years on the Board of the College, most recently as a senior fellow. I had the good luck to be on the Board at the same time, first as senior dean and later as bursar. His quiet, reasoned, carefully crafted contributions were always taken seriously, whether they related to the plans and designs for lecture theatres or new buildings, or proposals for faculty course changes.

When I first met Val he was chairman of a group established to save Cooldrinagh – an early Viking settlement and a unique rolling landscape, formerly an estate, near Leixlip in County Kildare. In view of its importance, the area was zoned 'amenity' in the county development plan. As commonly occurred, a property developer had purchased the land and proposed to demolish the large residence (which also had a range of unique features) and to build a large volume of housing, quite inappropriate for this special environment. In order to achieve this, the developer had to persuade a majority of the elected representatives to allow a 'material contravention' of the county development plan. This he was determined to do, despite the unique status of the area and significant opposition from the local community. At several meetings, I was to witness Val's remarkable knowledge of the Irish planning system and of the legislation, and his vision for 'balanced and sustainable development', which would cater for current needs without compromising the needs of future generations. It was undoubtedly because of Val's leadership, tenacity and attention to detail that successive attempts to contravene the development plan and compromise Cooldrinagh were defeated. The proposed construction of a water treatment plant at Cooldrinagh was also abandoned and relocated by Fingal County Council due to Val's detailed research on the history and significance of the site.

I recall one oral hearing in particular. Presided over by a senior planning inspector from An Bord Pleanála (the Planning Appeals Board), the developers had employed two of the most experienced and distinguished planning consultants in Ireland. They presented a most detailed and convincing case for substantial construction on land (again zoned 'amenity') in the Liffey Valley. It seemed certain that Val would, on this occasion, suffer an ignominious defeat. However, in one of the most remarkable presentations I have ever witnessed, he clinically undermined all of their arguments. When An Bord Pleanála issued its decision, Val had won the day. The Liffey Valley was to remain under serious threat from speculative construction in subsequent years and Val worked tirelessly in his spare time to curb its worst excesses. It was largely through his efforts and influence that many sensitive sites have been preserved for posterity.

Val gave generously of his time and expertise to many organizations throughout the country. In Dublin alone these included the Liffey Valley Alliance, the South Dublin Environmental Policy Committee, the County Community Forum, the Leixlip Planning Alliance and Lucan Planning Council. He was also an adviser to Leixlip Town Commissioners. His advice and recommendations were invariably adopted.

These are only a few of Val Rice's contributions outside the classroom. There were many more. I recall in particular his generosity and hospitality and that of Ellen, his wonderful wife, who supported all his endeavours. I recall his pride and love of his wife and children; the teacher and musician; the philosopher with a remarkable breadth of learning in the arts and sciences, a true 'Renaissance man'. I fondly remember a good friend and a gentleman.

P.J. DRUDY took his PhD degree at Cambridge University where he was formerly a Fellow of St Edmund's College and a lecturer at the Department of Land Economy. He is a Fellow Emeritus, former associate professor of Economics and co-director of the Centre for Urban and Regional Studies at TCD. He has published extensively on urban and regional policy and housing and is co-editor of the series 'Dublin: Economic and Social Trends'. He was a long-time friend and colleague of Val Rice.

J. Valentine Rice, Emeritus Senior Fellow of Trinity College Dublin and the Philosophy of Education

JOHN HEYWOOD

The man

Until baggage weight restrictions began to make life somewhat tedious, I used to spend some time and money in the bookshops of American airports before flying home. Sometimes I purchased several items and other times none. On one occasion, I came across a third edition (1993) of a book by one Michael Novak. Perusal of the blurb, as well as the preface, suggested that *Belief and Unbelief: A Philosophy of Self-Knowledge* would be of interest and might be readable in the six or seven hours of the journey. I had no idea who Michael Novak was. The cover told me that he held the George Jewett chair in religion and public policy at the American Enterprise Institute. Later I was to learn that he was a distinguished commentator, winner of the Templeton Prize, and had written substantial texts before and after *Belief and Unbelief*.

I cannot remember if I completed the book there and then, but at some stage on the journey I decided to read the preface to the first edition. At the end, where it is customary to put acknowledgments, I read that one of those who had made helpful comments on the manuscript was a Valentine Rice. There was only one person that could be for both were at Harvard when the book was written in 1964. It was our Valentine Rice and he acknowledged this to me some days later.

Valentine Rice died four years ago. He received a massive send-off, testimony to his many friends and the activities he had undertaken during his life. At the time the point was made, as implied in Michael Novak's brief expression of debt, that he was a great adviser, especially of his students; Professor Rice is thanked for his help at the beginning of many theses. Another testimony of this was the dinner that his former students held to mark his retirement.

A decade or so ago, *The Times*, when recording the obituaries of many an Oxbridge don, recalled the importance of the advice they gave their students; this was often the reason the deceased merited an obituary although they had published little. Teaching was rated highly: today it is the number of publications that matters. That was Valentine's lot – he published little because he found it extraordinarily difficult to write. Why that should have been, I do not know, for when he did write he demonstrated a masterly prose. One reason might have been that he was particularly sensitive to stylistic criticism. Another possible reason, and I am sure this was the case, was that he was a perfectionist. Several of his secretaries would testify to this because his letters had to be typed, reconsidered, retyped and retyped again in what they must have thought was an endless iteration.

Student theses suffered likewise but to the benefit of those students. He was a good editor. No one who has read his introduction to the essays and studies of Christopher Butler can doubt Valentine's editorial skills.[1] Butler, who was Abbot of Downside and later auxiliary Bishop of Westminster, had made a significant contribution to the Second Vatican Council. He was well known to the British public through radio and television. Prior to that book, Valentine had contributed a study of Bishop Butler in the University of Notre Dames series, *Men who Made the Council*.

It is worth a digression to note that Butler's essay on belief and reason in science and religion remains highly relevant to the debate caused by Richard Dawkins' *The God Delusion*.

He wrote very little else. However, in 2001, he was forced by illness to provide his students with notes about the areas of the course that he would not be able to complete. They were preceded by a resumé of what had gone before, apparently based on recordings of these lectures that had been made in earlier years. It was clear, from the copy he gave me, that these notes constituted an admirable book in the making on the philosophy of education. Unfortunately, I could not persuade Valentine to undertake such a task. I am not even sure that he recognized the potential of the work for this purpose. It should have been easy, for the notes given to the students were in chapter form and coherent. But, as I mentioned earlier, he found writing extremely difficult and only did so under certain kinds of pressure, in this case, the perceived needs of his students.

Unlike many distinguished scholars before him he did not see his lectures as a vehicle for preparing a book. In his own field, Alisdair MacIntyre, with whose work he would have had some empathy, wrote his Gifford Lectures with a book in mind.[2] A striking feature of the last chapter of that work is a discussion of the development of the lecture and an appeal for a return, in universities, to the lecture disputation of the medieval universities.

Over the years I have heard students testify to the brilliance of Valentine's lectures. Some undoubtedly saw them as a commentary and, perhaps, a few understood them to be, as MacIntyre put it, 'commentary and a prologue for disputation'. I don't think, however, that he entertained the view that a university is a 'place for constrained disagreement'.[3] His notes show that he 'hoped that he had been able to offer a coherent set of answers' from arguments that were set out in detail. I doubt very much if he saw his role as initiating students into conflict, yet, in an age of individualism and disagreement, surely his idea of liberal education as 'an education that seeks to produce the internal freedom that is the freedom of autonomy'[4] is facilitated by that approach.

Be that as it may, there is no doubt that he was controversial, usually in defence of a tradition that culminated in the status quo. If he wanted, or did not want, something to happen, he had a remarkable persistence that could extend over a period of years. He could be equally persistent with scholarship as, for example, in a search to unravel the story of the person in a portrait that he had bought.

Although he had inspired change at the beginning of his career in Trinity, Valentine found many subsequent changes difficult and many of them unacceptable. All change is difficult. A balance has to be kept between the perceived need for security of those involved in change and the perceived need for change. There is always a tension in innovative processes and conflict is inevitable. How that conflict is resolved determines the outcomes of the change. It is no secret that Valentine and I had serious conflicts over departmental policies. From my perspective they were resolved, and in responding to the arguments against my proposals, the outcomes were undoubtedly changed and I think for the better.[5] I cannot say that he took a similar view.

I am aware that, in the outside world we were seen as two professors who were always at loggerheads, and who did not speak to each other. That is not so. True, we did play all the games that people play to get their own way in the introverted, sometimes insular and often even bitter world of a university. Inevitably we complained about each other to colleagues. But – and I emphasize the *but* – we remained friends throughout and continued to dine, if irregularly, together. It is a matter of regret among his circle of friends that he remained embittered towards the university for the division of the School into two departments. His friends and I would point out to him that, in the UK and the US, the demands on schools of education were such that they had to be divisionalized or departmentalized. We had some difficulty in persuading him that he had created an important legacy in his treatment of students, and the development of their learning. In other words he had met what he conceived the aim of education to be, namely 'the personal development of every individual in the community'.[6] I want to suggest that there is even more to his legacy than that.

I conceive this legacy to have been his insistence that the philosophy of education should be a component of all the mainstream education courses taught in the School of Education in Trinity, and to have taken this insistence to the registration council that governed the higher diploma.

The philosophy of education in the education and training of Irish teachers

When Valentine Rice came to Trinity, the higher diploma was very much part-time and needed to be revamped. Its professional purpose was to prepare teachers for secondary schools. They were required to be registered by the Secondary Teacher Registration Council, a statutory body that controlled training requirements. There were five professors of education, one each at the four constituent colleges of the National University of Ireland, and the professor from Trinity College, and each of them was a member of the registration council.[7] They undoubtedly influenced the regulations and were supported by the representatives of management and the unions. The regulations required study in the foundations of education, and importance was attached to the study of philosophy and the history of Irish education. These requirements remained until the duties of the council were taken over by a newly created Teaching Council for all teachers in 2005.[8] Some interpretation of the regulations was allowed and, sometimes, necessary. Professor Rice ensured that substantial courses in philosophy were provided in the higher diploma and master's programmes. My overriding purpose is to argue that it was important that students of education should, as a matter of course, be exposed to the issues raised by the philosophy of education.

The philosophy of education in 1966 in England, Ireland and the United States

I am not competent to give a picture that is other than impressionistic. Although I was engaged in education, it was in higher education and, prior to that, in technological education.[9] It seemed that the philosophy of education, as a subject of study, was going through something of a heyday. R.S. Peters, a philosopher in the analytic tradition, had joined the London Institute of Education from Birkbeck College, and had made educational philosophy hum. At Harvard, another educational philosopher in the analytic tradition, Israel Scheffler, who had been one of Valentine's advisers, was also prominent. An American commentator wrote of them that they:

used the tools of linguistic analysis on a wide variety of educational concepts ... and investigated their interconnections: does teaching entail learning? Does teaching inevitably involve indoctrinating? Etc. This careful, subtle and philosophically sophisticated work has made possible a much needed conceptual precision in educational debates, though the debaters who most influence public and opinion have rarely availed themselves of that precisification.[10]

It seems that Peters had, at least, made himself felt in the upper echelons of the civil service.[11] A mile or so down the road, at King's College, Paul Hirst had begun the work that culminated in his substantial treatise on the 'forms of knowledge', and had engaged in debate with the American educational philosopher, J. Phenix, about his 'realms of knowledge'. Hirst was concerned with the education suitable for a liberal society.[12] There were other philosophers of education in the UK, the most notable of whom was, perhaps, G.H. Bantock, who stood outside the traditions being developed in London.[13] The American commentator, referred to above, pointed out the all-pervasive influence of the American philosopher, John Dewey, on educational thinking at this time. All this is to say that there was a thriving group in the UK devoted to the philosophy of education. Those philosophers of education that were listened to seemed to be associated with the London group.

In Ireland, there was a very different tradition in which the influence on philosophy was that of Thomism. Many of those who entered teaching had received their education at the seminary, but had not pursued the priesthood. Beyond that, Celtic culture is very different to the Anglo-Saxon, which is pragmatic and does not entertain philosophical thinking. It prides itself in being practical and not theoretical. Celtic culture is, on the other hand, a high culture that more readily accepts theory and it was a return to this culture that Valentine proposed. There seems to be little doubt that he benefited from the Anglo-American precision. He was fond of demanding rigour in thinking from his students, and believed that he brought rigour to his own thinking. There is also little doubt that the Harvard experience enabled him to build and broaden the philosophical base he already had. It seems that it was at Harvard, from Novak's description, that he found Lonergan. Novak considered the Catholic tradition to be that of Aristotle-Aquinas-

Newman and Lonergan, and admitted a debt to Maritain.[14] So Valentine became enthused by Lonergan and Maritain, and brought this enthusiasm to a yearly audience of a hundred or more graduates.

There has certainly been a decline in interest in the philosophy of education in the UK. Many politicians believe that the training of teachers is best accomplished through experience – 'sitting next to Nellie' as it sometimes called. They believe, without reference to Dewey, that anything they can call 'progressive' is to be condemned as the source of 'low' standards. There is, in Ireland, a similar loss of interest in the philosophy of education, but to a much lesser extent. So why should the philosophy of education be taught, and how does it relate to the general education and training of teachers?

Why the philosophy of education should be a component of the teacher education curriculum

R.S. Peters offered a defence of the study of the philosophy of education in teacher-education programmes. In his article, 'The place of philosophy in teacher education programmes', he wrote:

> Education no longer has agreed aims, procedures are constantly under discussion and vary according to what different people conceive themselves as doing in teaching the various subjects; fundamental questions concerned with the principles underlying school organization, class management and the curriculum are constantly being raised, and in the area of moral education the task is made more perplexing by the variations of standards that characterize a differentiated society. The question is not whether a modern teacher indulges in philosophical reflection about what he is doing: it is rather whether he does this in a sloppy or rigorous manner.[1]

An American, R.E. Fitzgibbons, who set out to show how the philosophy of education can help make educational decisions, was absolutely scathing about the poor quality of educational decision-making. Such quality would not be expected in any other area of human activity, he argued. Primarily, this was due to the fact that most people, including educational administrators, know little of education and, I would argue, wilfully don't want to know anything about it: 'And the less we know of education, the less our chances of making sound educational decisions.'[16] Much the same can be said about management, as applied in education:

> At the same time it must be recognized that, with or without the appropriate knowledge, educational decisions must be made ... Just as these decisions cannot be avoided, they must be made more or less intelligently. Educational decisions that are based upon sound, relevant evidence are made more intelligently than those based upon weak or irrelevant evidence. In other words, educational decision-making can be viewed as ranging over a continuum. At one end of the continuum are those decisions made on the basis of virtually no evidence at all – 'irrational' or 'uninformed' decisions; at the other end are 'intelligent', 'fully informed' decisions. The important point to recognize here is that since educational decisions can be made more or less intelligently, how intelligently they are made depends upon a person's knowledge and how it is used. The more intelligently a decision has been made, the greater has been the consideration of that which is relevant. And this, of course, requires that the person making the decision actually knows what is relevant.[17]

Of course some people, who do not have a capacity for making decisions, will consider the issue but to the point of procrastination. Fitzgibbons fails to recognize that a group of persons, who have the knowledge available to them, may ignore it, or override it, and make decisions that follow some ideological or political belief.

Decisions are the result of our beliefs and, for both Fitzgibbons and Rice, the beginnings of understanding the issues facing education lay with beliefs and the value judgments we make. Valentine was concerned with the issues thrown up by the deschoolers and the rapidly developing technology of communications (he loved gadgets). Because of the prominence of value judgments in 'educational discourse it becomes a matter of critical importance to determine whether the value judgments are merely subjective statements or whether they can aspire to objectivity in the same way that we consider that statements in science, mathematics or history can be objective'. Valentine argued that 'value judgments can be objective provided they are grounded in an accurate understanding of things as they are'. Clearly this is a demand that the educator should be well informed about education. But he entered the caveat that the 'achievement of objectivity sometimes requires that account be taken of information that can be known only to the acting person'. This is not a trite point given the difficulties that teachers sometimes experience in dealing with issues of child abuse and protection.

These quotations come from the summary he prepared for his 2001 course of lectures. He went from that point to establish a defensible hierarchy of aims in education, which dealt with the conflicting claims of the State, the culture, vocational specialization and personal fulfilment. The need to screen and rank aims was highlighted as long ago as 1958 by E.J. Furst,[18] one of the authors of the famed *Taxonomy of Educational Objectives*.[19] But Valentine's discussion went far beyond the illustrations given by Furst, who was simply intent on making the case for screening because many aims of education were contradictory. Unfortunately, many administrators and policy makers came to regard aims, rather like mission statements, as pious platitudes that are required to be placed in a prominent position in schools, so that no further notice need be taken of them. The demand, by those who authored the *Taxonomy*, for statements of measurable outcomes further eroded belief in the value of aims.

Yet, at the heart of the educational language, that is, the language–thought process that creates action, are broad and often not thought-through views about the intelligence of students and desires to motivate. That there is serious discussion to be had about aims is illustrated by Colin Wringe in a substantive treatise.[20] Would that those who blame modern teaching methods and progressive education for the ills of British education had some knowledge of these ideas. Is it not a contradiction to advocate project methods in higher education as a means of integrating knowledge, and, at the same time, to condemn progressive education the leading light of which, John Dewey, advocated project methods?

Of course there is a debate to be had about the role of schools in a democratic society, and the extent to which they should be democratic institutions. It is not a trivial debate and should not be swept under the carpet. That aims are not considered important may be illustrated by the fact that the Curriculum and Examinations Board did not think it necessary to write a statement of aims. It was only under duress that the chairman allowed a small group to write a statement of aims in fifty words. The situation is no different in higher education. In Britain neither the Dearing nor Robbins committees on higher education paid much attention to aims. It was assumed that higher education was to the economic benefit of the nation, and it is clear that this is the model that pervades thinking about higher education in the English-speaking countries of the Western world. It is against performance in producing scientists, technologists, nurses, teachers and so on, that the criteria for higher education are measured. Scant attention is paid to the social benefits of such an education, what these might be, or the education that might bring them about. No attention is given to the individual benefits of higher education, except in so far as it brings monetary rewards. The idea that it has something to do with the personal development of every individual, in the community, that Valentine had at the top of his hierarchy of aims, is really only recognized at the level of lip service.

Universities have become the home of the specialized technique, promoting the spread of numerous professional organizations that require the universities to supply programmes to qualify students for membership of these organizations. This was recognized by T.H. Marshall as long ago as 1939. He called them semi-professions and said of them that they 'are really subordinate grades placed in the middle of the modern business organization. The educational ladder leads into them but there is no ladder leading out.'[21] At the time, Marshall considered that social structure, in so far as it reflected occupational structure, was frozen as soon as it emerged from schooling. When he wrote, it was only an elite that went to universities, but now there is mass entry and what happened in schools is now happening in universities: 'Mobility between generations is increased but mobility during the working life of one generation is diminished.'[22] Competitiveness begins in education and, for some, that is where it remains.

Let me illustrate. In the United States, IBM announced some time ago that a very large slice of its research money would be devoted to meeting the needs of those working in what it loosely called the service industries. The essence of a very short article that described this development, with the intriguing title, 'Think ... about how others think', was that IBM had created a 'new academic discipline, called "services science and management engineering" '.[23] One immediately wondered if they had come to an agreement with a university department of engineering to provide some kind of new hybrid degree that was different to, say, engineering and management. But no! It related to the employment of the 'many anthropologists, sociologists and economists' that it had hired, in support of that part of its research and development expenditure on 'services', which amounted to about half its total R and D expenditure. The title had been invented for this particular group. The reason for this development was that, historically, technology had given its first boost to the farm, its next boost to the factory, and now it had to boost services. The author highlighted the fact that 80 per cent of jobs in the United States and Europe are filled by 'barbers, teachers, doctors, lawyers, closet re-organizers and their like'. Given that their productivity lags behind agriculture and industry, engineering ought to be devoting more time to seeing how it can help these professionals. That is, it 'should devote more time to figuring out how people think, work, and think about their work'.

The important thing to notice is that IBM did not expect engineers to try and understand other people's modes of thinking, which is what it is presupposed that a person who has received a liberal education can do. Rather, specialists in those disciplines should advise the company, but, given the difficulty specialists have in talking to each other, it could be a recipe for disaster. This is reminiscent of the education of engineers in the 1960s. Crudely speaking, those receiving a university education in engineering saw themselves as being able to pursue the heights of management. They thought that practical engineering should be accomplished by those being trained in diploma of technology sandwich courses. To an extent, some of the diploma students believed this was the case, while others wanted to pursue careers in research and management. It was certainly the government's view that this division should happen. The argument here is that a broad general education transfers the competitiveness to what might be called post-higher education, and transfers the obligation in training, in very specialized techniques, to those who currently have need of such techniques. It is facing up to the cliché that knowledge outdates in five years from graduation.

This view promotes questions about the purpose of higher education. In Britain, in the 1990s, government listened very much to industrialists' views about education. In so far as higher education is concerned, they said that graduates of all disciplines did not have the skills and dispositions necessary for the workplace. Attention was focused on what has loosely been called skills in the 'affective domain', that is, skills that helped people to communicate and to deal with other people. A major inquiry into the demands of employers supported this view and there was a drive to develop what were called 'personal transferable skills'.[24] In Valentine's language, it meant that the specialized education that graduates were receiving was not releasing their full potential. It was argued that these demands, and demands such as those made by MIT in a major report on American competitiveness, were consistent with the concept of liberal education conceived by Newman and others.[25] It was this view of liberal education that inspired the innovative approach to the higher education of women developed by Alverno College in Milwaukee.[26] There are many ways of creating a 'learning that lasts'. The Alverno College curriculum is a challenge to higher-education institutions to do just that.

It was argued at the beginning of this text that educational decisions are often made in the absence of knowledge. Such knowledge can, of course, be false and this can lead to less reliance on knowledge in the future. Sometimes knowledge that is far from complete is used, and such is the knowledge of manpower planning and beliefs about manpower upon which economic models of higher education are based. When the market intervenes, it often leads to temporary shortages in subject areas deemed to be necessary for the future of a nation. For many reasons, in the UK the number of students studying science and technology has fallen dramatically over the years. One reason is that the demand for students in these subjects is less than it is perceived to be. More generally, graduates are criticized by industry and commerce for not having skills in the domain of the affect. Such behaviour reinforces the need for a good general education, which embraces the needs of students in both the cognitive and affective domains.

Thus far it has been argued that, from the perspective of employment, what is required is a good general education. It has not been specified how this might be achieved: that is intentional. There are a variety of approaches, and those used must grow from the particular culture that is intent on change. But Valentine's goal of the 'personal development of every individual in the community' requires a societal dimension and an understanding of the benefit of higher education, not merely to the economy, but to society in general. He linked these themes together in his secondary aims, 'the welfare of the State, the transmission and enhancement of the culture, together with vocational preparation'. He argued that the achievement of these secondary aims would go a long way to achieving the primary aim.

Valentine attempted to clarify the notion of personal fulfilment. In his summary of his argument, he wrote that he had pointed to the long tradition in Western education that affirmed an intimate connection between freedom and the human person. He investigated the relationship and 'confronted the complex issue of human freedom'. He argued that:

> [O]n the basis of our reflex self-knowing, human beings possess a unique freedom that is free will or the freedom of choice. [W]hile freedom of choice is a given and in consequence of our reflexivity, there can be a progressive enlargement of our ability to achieve consistency between our knowing and our doing in the exercise of freedom of choice ... the ideal state of that internal freedom involves the achievement of autonomy, by which one is in full control of oneself. In that context ... the traditional notion of liberal education can be usefully restated, in terms of our own time, as an education that seeks to produce the internal freedom that is the freedom of autonomy.

This, it seems, casts a somewhat different, and complementary, light on the commonly spoken-of goal of education to produce 'autonomous learners'. I am aware that reflexivity has a precise meaning in mathematical philosophy, but I do not think Valentine ascribes it that meaning here. Rather, I think his concept of reflexivity has some affinity with the idea of reflective practice that has grown up since Schön published his influential work on reflective practice.[27] In parallel, but intimately linked, has been the development of the idea of meta-cognition, through which we come to understand better our own thinking processes and develop skill in what King and Kitchener have called 'reflective judgment'.[28] 'True reflective thinking pre-supposes that individuals hold epistemic assumptions that allow them to understand and accept real uncertainty',[29] and it is only when individuals engage with ill-structured or novel problems, that they engage in reflective thinking as defined by King and Kitchener. They hold that a student has to go through eight stages to acquire the ability of reflective judgment, and that each of these stages has its own view of knowledge and concept justification. Moreover, the curriculum, that is the instructional processes and assessment procedures, to which the student is exposed, can impede or encourage that development. This suggests that individuals do not just arrive at Valentine's freedom of autonomy, but develop towards it, and that the educational process may impede or enhance that development.

King and Kitchener were not the first to advocate a relationship between the curriculum and development in higher education. Twenty-four years earlier, William Perry had published his model of intellectual development, based on studies of Harvard students.[30] He defined nine stages of development. In the first stages the students come to the university expecting to be told the truth, that is, that which is right and that which is wrong, or true or false. Thus in stage one, all problems are seen to have right answers and authority must be followed, so it is that the best teachers provide the right answers. By stage three it is apparent that *authority* is 'seeking the right answers' and only in the future will we know what is right. Perry calls these first three stages 'dualism'. From dualism, the student moves into the phase of scepticism, for now it is clear that not only does the authority not have the right answers, but everyone, including the student, has the right to hold his or her own, and some of these can be supported by evidence.

Thus, by stage five, some answers are found to be better than others, and everything has to be considered in its context. It is a stage of relativism. The student perceives that good choices are possible and that commitments have to be entered into. By stage nine (acting on commitment) decisions are made with relative ease, a sense of identity and personal style is obtained and one is now able to take responsibility for one's actions. It seems clear that this model has relevance to Valentine's explanation of freedom of choice.

I would like to end with two points and then consider the implications for teacher education. My first point is to reinforce the argument that educational decision-making needs to be based on knowledge. That is to say, it needs to be evidence-based. It is clear, from the research that has been done, that there is a substantial case to be made for the concept, behind the Perry and King and Kitchener models, that students develop through what are loosely called stages. Research in the United States[31] in subjects as diverse as English and engineering suggests that many students do not get beyond stage four or five in the Perry model. It is also evident that the curriculum, as it embraces instruction and assessment, and how it is organized, can impede or enhance development. Therefore, it has been argued that, when institutions seek to change curriculum structures, they need to take into account the likely effect of the changes on student development. More often than not, issues such as this are ignored and, in some cases, it would appear that the consequences for student-learning are profound.

... *and the education and training of teachers*

My second point is that, while philosophy, as applied to education, can lead us to a hierarchy of aims and even rank the 'personal development of every individual in the community', it is not by itself enough. The internalization of such an aim, in an institution, requires not only knowledge of how individuals develop, but of the culture that surrounds that development. While the screening of aims begins with philosophy, psychology (as it applies to development and instruction), and sociology (as it applies to our understanding of the sub-systems of education). The responses of these disciplines to the pressures from the social system in which they reside must also be considered. This is particularly the case for the foundation subjects in the education and training of teachers.

Taught in isolation, they cannot be expected to achieve that goal, yet that is how they were organized in my day. I hoped that they would be brought together in curriculum studies but, for all my effort, I doubt they were. The problem we faced was that the socialization of intending teachers into the teaching fraternity begins when they first go to school. By the time they graduate and enter a university school of education they believe they know what teaching is and many reject the attempt to provide a theoretical framework that will enable them better to teach and, of more importance, to participate more generally in the educational debate. They remain restricted professionals, seeking only that knowledge that will help them immediately in the classroom. Having to study the foundation subjects of education should go some way to completing the circle of knowledge that Newman thought a liberally educated person should acquire. I venture to suggest that education departments should be a bastion of liberal education, but they must learn to stand outside the disciplines, in order for them to help students develop the capacity of seeing all things in relation to each other. Valentine wrote:

> John Henry Newman pointed out many years ago that human knowledge in any field essentially involved a grasp of certain facts, together with a grasp of the relationship between these facts. This point can be restated in terms of insight. Any subject, any course, any lecture, any class, involves two associated levels of content. Firstly, there are facts, data, experiences; secondly, there are insights into relationships between the data. If one considers any particular field of knowing such as History, Botany or Medicine, one recognizes that there is a range of data which must be grasped – the historical dates and events, the flora of a particular island, the symptoms of a particular disease. But the study of history, for example, requires not merely a comprehensive knowledge of the dates and events; it involves, above all, an understanding of the connections and relationships between them. These two levels of knowing require two different pedagogical approaches. Data may be communicated in a variety of ways, through conventional classes or lectures, through required reading, through programmed instruction, through television or other media; in certain circumstances they can be acquired through behavioural conditioning. The grasp of the relationship between data, however, requires the achievement of insight. And there is a natural movement of the human mind from one level into the other: we are curious about the data of our experience.[32]

The problem of this approach is that it treats of single subjects and what happens within them. Newman saw it differently. It was as much about the relations between the material of different subjects, as with the material within subjects, and that is the problem of teaching the foundation subjects in education in isolation of each other. It is finding out how to do this that should be the goal of education departments.

NOTES

1. B.C. Butler, *Searchings: Essays and Studies* (London 1975).
2. This seems to be a condition of the lectures. A. MacIntyre, *Three Rival Versions of Moral Enquiry: Encyclopedia, Genealogy and Tradition* (Indiana 1990).
3. *Ibid.* 'Such reformers as those who propose some version of a Great Books curriculum ignore the fundamental character of our present disagreements and conflicts, presupposing possibilities of agreement of a kind which do not presently exist. What then is possible? The answer is: the university as a constrained disagreement, of imposed participation in conflict, in which a central responsibility for higher education would initiate students into conflict ...'
4. From a document dated 30 April 2001 addressed to students who attended the philosophy of education course in the Michaelmas and Hilary terms. The notes are held in the archive of the School of Education, Trinity College Dublin.
5. Val Rice had created the first full-time MEd programme in Ireland. It differed in two important respects from the MEd degrees in England. In the first place it was two years long in comparison with the one-year courses in England. This meant that the dissertation was one year in length (compared with three months in England). This made the Trinity MEd an altogether different and superior vehicle for learning. The theses, several of which were upgraded to PhD, were a major source of research. It is a tragedy that so little publication emerged from them or from those PhDs produced in the other universities who followed this route.

    The problem was that the numbers coming forward to participate in these degree programmes were relatively small. They were also extremely costly. Moreover, they were degrees with a strong scholarly orientation, which Valentine thought all higher degrees should be. Yet in the real world of teaching there were numerous teachers who hungered for programmes that were less costly and not full-time. So while Valentine went along with the development of a national programme of part-time in-service education, with some difficulty, he would not bless proposals that would have enabled in-service diploma holders to qualify for a degree through action research in their own institutions. In other words a 'professional' programme that integrated theory with practice. He believed that such degrees would not, indeed could not by their very nature, be of high quality or have high standards.
6. From a document dated 30 April 2001 addressed to students who attended the philosophy of education course in the Michaelmas and Hilary terms.
7. When the School of Education was divided into two departments, the

Professor of Teacher Education became the representative of the University on the Council.
8. The Teaching Council for all teachers was an idea that was first generated in the Secondary Teacher Registration Council in the 1970s and Professor Rice took a lead role in its preparation.
9. I had had to read the philosophy of education in the only qualification that was open to a technical college teacher, the Licentiate of the College of Preceptors. While in industry, I had pursued an extra-mural diploma in logic, epistemology and the history of philosophy, in London, where I was introduced to Copleston's history of philosophy.
10. D.M. Senchuk, 'Philosophy of Education' in R. Audi (ed.), *The Cambridge Dictionary of Philosophy* (Cambridge 1995). R.S. Peters (ed.), *The Philosophy of Education* (Oxford 1973).
11. In an interview for a chair of curriculum, a distinguished civil servant asked me for my thoughts on Peters' view that 'education was the initiation of worthwhile activity'.
12. P. Hirst, *Knowledge and the Curriculum* (London 1974).
13. See for example, J.H. Bantock, *Freedom and Authority in Education* (London 1952).
14. *Ibid*. p. 8.
15. R.S. Peters, 'The place of philosophy in the training of teachers', *Paedagogica Europaea*, 3 (1967), 153.
16. R.E. Fitzgibbons, *Making Educational Decisions: An Introduction to the Philosophy of Education* (New York 1981), p. 7.
17. *Ibid*. pp. 7–8.
18. E.J. Furst, *Constructing Evaluation Instruments* (New York 1985).
19. B.S. Bloom (ed.), *The Taxonomy of Educational Objectives*, vol. 1, *Cognitive Domain* (New York 1956).
20. C. Wringe, *Understanding Educational Aims* (London 1988).
21. T.H. Marshall, 'Professionalism in relation to social structure and policy' in T.H. Marshall, *Sociology at the Crossroads and Other Essays* (London 1963).
22. *Ibid*.
23. 'IBM's new motto: think … about how others think.' *IEEE Spectrum* (December 2006).
24. For a summary see J. Heywood, *Assessment in Higher Education: Student Learning, Teaching, Programmes and Institutions* (London 2000).
25. *Ibid*.
26. The innovative curriculum of Alverno College and the results of two decades of longitudinal research on student college learning is described in Marcia Mentokowski *et al.*, *Learning that Lasts* (San Francisco 2000).
27. D.A. Schön, *The Reflective Practitioner* (New York 1983).

28. P.M. King and K.S. Kitchener, *Developing Reflective Practice* (San Francisco 1994).
29. *Ibid.*
30. W.G. Perry, *Intellectual and Ethical Development in College Years: A Scheme* (New York 1970).
31. In respect of English, R.J. Kloss, 'A nudge is best: helping students through the Perry scheme of intellectual development' in *College Teaching*, 42 (4) (1994), 151–8; M. Pavelich and W.S. Moore, 'Measuring the effect of experiential education using the Perry Model' in *Journal of Engineering Education*, 85 (1996), 287–92.
32. J.V. Rice, 'Rational knowledge' (unpublished lecture notes, TCD 2000), p. 13.

JOHN HEYWOOD is a Professorial Fellow Emeritus of TCD and former professor and head of the department of teacher education in the School of Education where he worked with Val Rice for many years. He is a Fellow of the Chartered Institute of Management. In 2007 he was elected to the Academy of Fellows of the American Society for Engineering Education, and in 2008 was named a Paul Harris Fellow of the Rotary Foundation of the Rotary International.

John Carmel Heenan, the Second Vatican Council and the Rise and Fall of an English Lumen Vitae

VINCENT ALAN McCLELLAND

Perhaps the most significant date in the calendar of events leading to the establishment of what was to become Corpus Christi College, as a centre for catechetical renewal and training in London, is that of 30 October 1964.[1] It was on that date, only a year or so before the effective end of the Second Vatican Council, that Mgr Maurice Kelleher, president, since Easter 1964, of the Westminster Diocesan Seminary at Ware, wrote to his new archbishop in some exasperation at what he deemed the deleterious influences upon young seminarians of the teaching and attitudes of a group of professorial staff. Archbishop John Carmel Heenan, not created cardinal until February 1965, had been translated from the metropolitan see of Liverpool, to Westminster, in September 1963, following the death of Cardinal William Godfrey, and most of his first year in office in Westminster had been occupied by attendance at the Council in Rome, and matters connected with it. His busy schedule necessitated a reliance upon advice from London for the efficient conduct and management of his new diocese, although this was tempered by the daily meetings in Rome of the resident English bishops at the Venerabile, enabling an informal exchange of episcopal views on matters of common concern to be both regular and open.[2] Heenan certainly found this helpful and, it can be maintained, never was camaraderie among English bishops so noticeable as during this period of conciliar exchanges in Rome. Nothing like it was to be achieved again until the subsequent development of the episcopal conference.

The immediate stimulus of Kelleher's letter to Heenan of 30 October 1964 was the appearance, in *The Catholic Herald* a week earlier, of an anonymous article strongly critical of the modus operandi of seminary training in England. While three priests were at the centre of the president's anguish – Charles Davis, Peter de Rosa and Hubert Richards – he considered de Rosa as the likely writer of the article. When challenged by the president as to the article's paternity, apparently de Rosa appeared non-committal or evasive. Kelleher alleged that other members of staff at St Edmund's resented the tone of the article and, especially, its appearance at a time when seminarians were already in a state of insecurity, not least because of reports from Rome about the Council and its imagined implications. Hubert Richards, Kelleher maintained, did not disassociate himself from the ideas of the offending piece of journalism but, rather, commended the writer for publishing it.

Kelleher's charges against the three staff members, Davis, de Rosa and Richards, were somewhat vague but he argued that the close relationship of the trio was giving rise to division in the college, which had become 'very obvious to the students'. On an earlier occasion, Kelleher had expressed disquiet at the influence of Charles Davis on the younger priests of the diocese, and he now formally asked Heenan to remove all three men from the staff of the seminary. While expressing sorrow for burdening the archbishop with seminary issues while he was busy with the Council, the matter had assumed a degree of urgency. Kelleher added that, while he would 'not deny the work of Father Davis in his particular field', he pointed out that the work of professors is not simply in the lecture hall 'but with the whole formation of future priests'.[3]

The letter from the president did not touch upon other possible reasons for the unrest and dissatisfaction of students in the seminary. Kelleher had assumed direction of the institution at a very stressful time. In July 1963, his predecessor, Mgr Reginald Butcher, who had provided lengthy but strong and autocratic leadership to St Edmund's, had suffered a severe stroke and it soon became evident he would be unlikely to function as president again. Over six months elapsed, however, before the selection of Maurice Kelleher for the office. Butcher's style of firm leadership had suddenly been followed by a régime of a less-controlled nature, which gave rise to a period of growing student unrest. When the time arrived for Kelleher to assume the presidency in 1964, he realized he was confronted by a hornet's nest for which his previous experience as a kind, effective and popular parish priest had not entirely equipped him. He was aware, as Heenan was also quickly to appreciate, that there was a lack of adequate personal, spiritual and academic guidance within the college. The ecclesial stance assumed by Davis, de Rosa and Richards was thus only one exacerbating element in an already explosive situation.

Part of the difficulty, as Kelleher saw it, was that Charles Davis and Bert Richards were men of similar age, training and educational background, who had been appointed to St Edmund's in the same year, 1949, who were intellectually attuned to each other and were teaching in key areas of dogmatic theology and scripture. Neither had held permanent parochial appointments, which Kelleher, from his own substantial pastoral experience, considered a major handicap in the work of training priests, the greater part of whom would be destined for a lifetime of parochial duties. De Rosa, on the other hand, had served in a parish, the Holy Redeemer in Chelsea, before his appointment to teach philosophy at St Edmund's in 1956. Ten years junior to Davis and Bert Richards, Kelleher regarded him as largely influenced by the two senior men.

It was evident to the archbishop that if some action was not taken, fairly quickly, to remedy the situation, then the president of St Edmund's himself would seek to resign and return to parish work. Heenan informed Kelleher that, in order to arrive at a measured view for himself, he would visit the seminary as early as possible in the new year, that is after a further period of about two and a half months. Meantime, he would give some preliminary thought to the situation. With hindsight, it was not an unreasonable delay: Charles Davis, for instance, was not to defect until 1966. Heenan would have some time to meet the teaching staff and student body and be able to form a view as to the spirit prevailing within the institution. Before the visitation could take place, however, events were to unfold, indicating how the formation of a catechetical institution in England might fulfil a post-conciliar need as well as possibly solve the domestic difficulties at St Edmund's.

The idea of establishing a catechetical institution in London began to germinate in Heenan's consciousness in January 1965, some three months after receiving Kelleher's letter. This was the immediate result of a proposal from the then Provincial of the Daughters of Sion to Fr John McCoy, working in the archdiocese of Westminster's Schools Commission, to make available part of the nuns' property at Chepstow Villas in Bayswater as a base for such new development.[4] The property had become available as the outcome of the merger of the sisters' grammar school, operating on the site, with the Cardinal Manning secondary school in Bayswater. The day following the receipt of Sr Marie Loreto's offer, Heenan, who had been created cardinal a few days previously, declared, 'I would give my red hat to have an English Lumen Vitae.'[5] There was certainly a perceived and urgent need to secure suitably qualified Catholic teachers to become heads of religious education departments in new secondary schools throughout the country, and it was attractive to think that an English Lumen Vitae might be established to meet the need. A meeting was thus hurriedly arranged between the Cardinal and Sr Marie Loreto to consider the details.

Precipitate by nature, the alacrity of Heenan's response surprised even David Konstant who, at the time, was directing school chaplains for the archdiocese from his residence at the Cardinal Vaughan School. In March 1965 Konstant had returned from Brussels where he had visited Lumen Vitae and been much impressed by what he had seen, although he criticized the predominantly theoretical nature of the course. He wished to send two or three school chaplains from the diocese to take the Brussels programme. They would need to be selected carefully and possess a reasonable facility in French. A greater knowledge of that language would be needed if any priests were to be sent to the catechetical institute in Strasbourg, which he had also visited, finding it more concerned with second-level teaching than was the case at Lumen Vitae.[6] Heenan told Konstant that, in only six months' time (by September), he hoped to have 'a Lumen Vitae of our own in London'. He was to see the premises for the first time that day, he wrote, and would appoint the first director before the end of the week. Konstant's chaplains would thus be better off attending a course in English and 'our course will be more practical than any of the Continental ones'.[7] Konstant was surprised, to put it mildly, at how this could be taking place without his having been made aware of it.

It can be maintained that the breakneck speed with which Heenan moved was to be considerably influenced by the restive situation he found on his visit to St Edmund's, which confirmed him in his initial appraisal of the Kelleher complaint. He felt it was imperative, as a first step to solving the difficulties of the seminary, that alternative employment for the three priests identified by Kelleher should be found. Charles Davis had already begun to take things into his own hands. When he wrote to Heenan to ask for permission to prepare and give the Maurice Lectures at King's College London, in regard to the academic session 1965–6, Heenan expressed delight but added the remark, 'I am sure that the value of your work would be far greater if you had some time in a parish', a hint not received with much favour in view of the academic future Davis had envisioned for himself.[8]

Early in 1965, Charles Davis was in his early forties and eager to develop his talents on a wider canvas than could be provided by a seminary. He toyed with the idea of joining the Downside Centre of Religious Studies and of lecturing at Bristol University. It was an area of the country that appealed to him – he had been born in Swindon and had attended the Irish Christian Brothers College in Bristol. He knew he would be welcomed at the Centre, and he approached the Cardinal for permission to seek or pursue an appointment there. From Heenan's position, it seemed preferable to have Davis located in a religious métier, rather than freelancing in a secular ambiance. His response to the Davis request, therefore, was to discuss with the Jesuits the possibility of finding a niche for him, with an attractive title, at Heythrop College. Although Davis would have preferred a Bristol engagement, he was not averse to the Heythrop suggestion, was perhaps flattered by a title of Professor of Theology and was certainly pleased to have new opportunity for fruitful academic work.[9]

A similar arrangement was arrived at for Bert Richards, who was requested to accept a temporary one-term appointment from Archbishop Beck of Liverpool, to provide some teaching support at Christ's College of Education in Liverpool. While Richards may have suspected there was a ploy at work to remove him, albeit temporarily, from St Edmund's, he decided to accept Beck's invitation, provided he could still retain some of his other academic commitments in London.[10] The cardinal hinted to him also that he had 'plans' for him for the next academic year, which, he asserted, 'I think you will find ... attractive and exciting.'[11] No immediate scheme was devised for the redeployment of Peter de Rosa, and it looked as if a return to parish work might be what Heenan envisaged.

In the first week of March 1965, the cardinal saw Fr Hubert Richards and suggested to him that he become director of the new Catechetical Centre in London. It was a typical Heenan manoeuvre, of course, by which he wished to show confidence in Richards' ability to establish the new project, while enabling him to retain his scholarly interest in scripture studies. He would have a small team of lecturers to assist him and, to boost the new foundation, the catechetical work, in the ambit of the Catholic Education Council (CEC), would be transferred to the newly titled Corpus Christi College. Archbishop Beck, who had responsibility for the CEC, agreed to this development, which was facilitated by the approaching retirement of Fr Nigel Larn from the work of the Education Council, where he had hitherto enjoyed responsibility for the catechetical commitment.

The CEC would give financial help to the catechetical work, after it had been transferred to Richards's jurisdiction. It was expected that this financial support would continue over a number of years. A press release was issued on 11 March announcing that the first English Catholic College of Catechetics would open in London in September 1965. It paid tribute to the generosity of the Daughters of Sion, and announced the name of the first principal. The college would expect to accommodate about 120 students annually, on a one-year course, and preference would be given to applicants with teaching experience.[12]

One of the future seeds of difficulty was planted almost immediately. Fr Richards agreed to accept the new appointment and leave St

Edmund's, on condition that Fr Peter de Rosa was also appointed to Corpus Christi as his first assistant. While acceding to this request might ease the situation further at the seminary, from the cardinal's viewpoint and that of the president of St Edmund's, Heenan feared it might also lead to the transferring of existing problems from the seminary to the new college. He was conscious that allowing Richards and de Rosa to work together was a gamble, but there were advantages in the idea. Richards would have a heavy stake in making the new institution into a success story and, in that regard, he might be a salutary influence on de Rosa, in view of their long-standing personal friendship. Even so, some of Heenan's doubts found a place in the letter of invitation to de Rosa when he told him, 'We can consider later what preparation you will need before taking over. I don't know what special training or qualifications you have for catechetical work. I shall be coming down to the College shortly and I can discuss this question with Father Richards and yourself.'[13] Sr Marie Aloysius, OLS, was to be cirector of Practical Training and Sr Marie Ambrosius, OLS, the librarian.

Bert Richards quickly put together an impressive draft syllabus of studies for the first year of the programme, with a list of visiting lecturers likely to attract media attention. The syllabus was arranged in three parts, labelled theology, anthropology and methodology. The initial printed programme itself was innocuous, if somewhat uninformative, about content. The names of the permanent staff were soon to be augmented by Fr John Perry and Fr Peter Wetz of the White Fathers as well as by other religious sisters. Visiting lecturers included some who had gained experience at Lumen Vitae or elsewhere abroad, such as Charles Davis from Heythrop on the theology of the Christian life; Michael Gaine from Christ's College, Liverpool, on religious sociology, an area he was to share with Anthony Spencer from the Cavendish Square Training College in London; Clifford Howell, SJ, on liturgy; Enda McDonagh from Maynooth on the theology of morals; and Michael Richards from St Edmund's on church history.

The list was eye-catching, containing well-known names and experienced presenters, although the emphasis seemed to be heavily theological rather than pedagogical. The latter area was firmly devolved to the hands of two nuns, with the exception of visual aids, which was the responsibility of Desmond Brennan from the CEC. That the initial programme was approved by Heenan assured that he would not interfere with Richards's freedom of action, although he must have been aware of the strong St Edmund's influence. Peter de Rosa's main brief was to teach philosophical anthropology and, perhaps more controversially, the theory of group dynamics, which was then fashionable in many secular pedagogical institutions, not least in the work of Elizabeth Richardson at Sheffield University. Bert Richards himself retained the scripture portfolio.[14]

There were, of course, difficulties in producing a wide-ranging programme of study to be encompassed within a maximum period of thirty teaching weeks. One of the main criticisms of the initial Corpus Christi programme was, perhaps, not unrelated to its diffuse and eclectic nature, the components of which were in danger of attracting superficial or idiosyncratic treatment. The danger increased with the lack of co-ordination among the considerable numbers of visiting staff invited to teach, who might be little concerned with the contextual nature of the full programme, or who saw their own contributions as essentially disparate and personal inputs. Heenan, who from the beginning had a shrewd sense of this Achilles heel, had to be careful not to interfere unduly with the principal's freedom of choice in curriculum design, although it was on this score that later criticisms of the teaching at Corpus Christi was to concentrate. Heenan sensed, as he was later to make explicit, that there was little time, in a course of such limited length, for lectures 'not concerned with theology or teaching techniques'.[15]

As with any growing institution, a number of problems began to emerge in the first year of operation. The first related to buildings. The principal had been engaged in discussions with the diocesan architect concerning the adaptation of existing buildings for the new college but, by April, these had led to more substantial changes than first predicted. Richards told Heenan that the overall costs would be much higher than the £4000 originally anticipated. Moreover he declared: 'The lecture space and dining facilities which the convent hoped to provide for us, have been found for various reasons to be impossible. We have to provide our own.'[16]

There were also additional expenses concerned with washing and toilet facilities, and with furniture and equipment. In order to assimilate (and eventually subsume) the catechetical work of the CEC, as many as five temporary buildings might have to be erected. The extent of the provision needed, and the cost of the building operations, concerned the cardinal who counselled that 'it would be most unwise to instruct the architect to draw up elaborate plans before we know where the money is going to come from to pay for them'.[17] The college was essentially a diocesan enterprise, and it had only been possible to start in that way because the provision of little new capital had been envisaged. 'If extensive building is going to be necessary,' Heenan warned, 'the College must become national without delay.'[18] He would see Mother Loreto of the Sion nuns, to discover why the arrangement she made with him had now become impossible as it had been first envisaged.

Immediate financial panic was obviated a month later, however, by the diocese agreeing to underwrite necessary approved costs as an interest-free loan to the college, the debt to be assumed by the hierarchy (through the CEC), when the bishops accepted the college as a national, rather than a local, facility. Heenan intended that the latter would become effective in 1966, when a governing body would need to be in place, representative of the various interests.[19]

A second early problem related to the recruitment of students for the opening year in September. There was a modest response to advertisements. Fifty-four had been accepted, of which thirty-six were nuns and nine were priests. The remaining nine laypeople (or most of them) were dependent on obtaining appropriate grants from local education authorities. Support from the bishops was also problematical. By June only one diocesan priest, outside Westminster, had been sent by his bishop and he was from the Menevia diocese in Wales. By July, the numbers of acceptances had reached thirteen priests, eight laypeople and forty-three nuns. Fr Richards was contemplating putting a ceiling of fifty on the number of nuns to be accepted, 'lest it look too much like an entirely nuns' show'.[20] Again, fortune smiled! By the middle of July, the DES had approved Corpus Christi for secondment purposes, on salary, for teachers wishing to attend. This concession augured well for lay recruitment in the second and subsequent years.

A third difficulty arose from the cardinal himself having reflective thoughts. Writing to Richards on 27 May 1965, he intimated that one of the reasons the bishops had not sent more priests for the autumn term might be that there needed to be more experience in catechetics among the team. He suggested that Peter de Rosa should go to a catechetical centre abroad for a year's training, before joining the staff. Heenan could supply an appropriate substitution for him for a year.[21] Richards resisted this idea, arguing that 'his qualifications to teach catechetics are the same as mine', and adding that 'neither of us has received specialized training for the task, and we are expecting over the first few years to do as much learning as teaching at the new institute'.[22] He said, 'I personally would find it impossible to envisage the coming year without him to consult and to advise me, as he has done so ably up to the present. I have already put him in charge of the studies at the college, and continue to have absolute confidence in his capacity to make Corpus Christi a success.'[23]

With such a strong reaction to his proposal, the cardinal yielded, but he was still desirous, 'since we have no priests trained specifically for catechetics', to train a priest with an eye to joining the staff at the college later.[24] The response to this idea was that Corpus Christi itself would provide such training but, to avoid the charge of the blind leading the blind, Richards suggested 'someone like Fr John Perry' might be sent to Strasbourg (where there was a specialism in the teaching of adolescent boys), 'with a view to returning eventually to Corpus Christi'.[25] Not entirely mollified, Heenan remarked that he did not know Perry, but would ask his Vicar General about him. If practical catechetical training was not feasible for Fr de Rosa, Heenan was anxious to provide both Richards and de Rosa with some, albeit very limited, classroom experience to ensure their credibility with lay teachers.

Furthermore, he told Richards that he was 'most anxious that the new college will not give a purely theoretical course'. Fr de Rosa was to be asked to undertake a short spell in the classroom in the Cardinal Griffin school because 'it is important to know the human material with which the pupils of Corpus Christi will have to deal after their course'.[26] The cardinal also suggested that Richards himself should gain similar experience in a secondary modern school in a poor area, for it was important to know the needs of the Catholics of the labouring classes. In a Manning-like statement, Heenan added: 'We are losing our poor but we have not lost them yet. That is why I want you to know the problems from personal experience.'[27]

The debate about school experience and the interconnection with catechetics underlines once again the dangers of a precipitate start to a work of this kind, a situation for which the cardinal must shoulder the blame. It is understandable that Richards and de Rosa would have found little time at their disposal to accommodate Heenan's wishes when they were manifested at such a late stage. Heenan's worry was, nevertheless, a legitimate one, as Fr Richards admitted. 'I am sure Fr de Rosa will be as keen as I am,' he declared, 'to have first-hand experience of schoolwork, and we had already intended to join in the observation and practice classes as far as time allows. Not that we could ever hope to become experts in this field. Our work will normally be at a different level ...'[28] He was content to leave the pedagogical work in the hands of the nuns, Sr Aloysius and Sr Romain, who had specific expertise. Fr de Rosa, however, was amenable to Heenan's suggestion, admitting: 'I am sure that to have no knowledge of all the types of schools they [the students] will go into, will be a handicap to us in our relationships with them.'[29] He arranged to live at Commercial Road with Mgr Derek Worlock, while undertaking a short two-week initial assignment in school. There appears to have been little attempt to attract lecturers from university departments of education, or more input from colleges of education, to offset the worry about pedagogical expertise. It is rather surprising that Archbishop Beck of Liverpool, himself a former secondary school headmaster, did not insist upon the need for greater professional input.

The college, nevertheless, opened on time and the principal wrote to Cardinal Heenan, who was again in Rome, on 4 November:

> I thought you would like to know how your new baby is growing. Judging from the noise it makes, and the grey hairs it is beginning to give to the foster parents you have left in charge, it is lusty enough and in sound health! Not that there is nothing but shouting: an air of cheerful seriousness pervades the College, and an atmosphere of great brotherliness (not to mention sisterliness) which encourages us that the first month has gone well, and promises well for the months to come!

It was an upbeat report, although it contains also a hint of regret at inadequate interviewing processes in regard to a few students whose 'superiors have no doubt sent them here to be sorted out by us'.[30] Heenan was later to contend there were too many students who fell into this category, and not only in regard to the first intake.

Finances remained delicate but the annual income of £16,000, and the promise from Archbishop Beck of a continuing annual subvention of £3000 for a few years from the CEC to support its former catechetical work, would leave the college in a healthy state.[31] Nevertheless, to enhance the income of the whole venture, and especially the catechetical inheritance from the CEC, it had been decided to organize a number of extra-mural programmes. Peter de Rosa was soon running such a course for 200 within the college itself, and Sr Romain was embarking upon a similar venture for a like number in Camden Town. It was hoped that these short courses would provide 'a solid catechetical formation to (those) teachers who have asked for the extensions of the College's activities'.[32]

Fr de Rosa and Sr Aloysius were also preparing to initiate similar courses at Farnborough and Southampton, although they had not yet sought the approval of the newly appointed bishop of Portsmouth (since 21 December 1965), Mgr Derek Worlock. Bert Richards himself was already giving a course on scripture and theology in the hall of the French Church at Leicester Square, with Fr Peter Harris. Somewhat spectacularly, de Rosa was beginning to organize something even yet more systematic, 'a more comprehensive course of catechetics', which, in Richards' words, was 'for the whole of the London area in which we hope to cater for a maximum of 1000 teachers'. Such numbers

> will enable us to employ the very best experts in the various branches of catechetics, and give a solid grounding, perhaps over a course of two or three years, to the many teachers who are in need of such formation. The French Church at Leicester Square has agreed to put its hall at our disposal twice a week from next October for this purpose.[33]

The lusty infant had rapidly become ready for long trousers but, unfortunately, it was the rapid and somewhat ill-considered extra-mural programme, in which speculative theology was thought not to be a luxury, which was to provide the foundation for major complaints soon to arise. With hindsight, it is evident that too much was being undertaken too precipitately, before the college had the opportunity to establish academic and pedagogical credentials, and before many participants had acquired an appropriate knowledge-base upon which such an extramural programme could take root and become universally beneficial.

The following year, 1966, brought new problems for Corpus Christi. It was not only the year when Charles Davis left the priesthood, with an attendant blaze of publicity, but it was the year when responsibility for Corpus Christi was transferred from a local diocesan venture to one of national status, under the direction and control of the episcopacy, and with its own representative governing body. The transfer of responsibility could not have occurred at a worse time for the college, when sensitivities were heightened over growing diversity in theological debate among Catholics, and the desire of some theologians to break loose, as they saw it, from the constraints of the *magisterium*, which they deemed to be stifling their academic freedom. It was little wonder, given the nature of the institution and its popularizing approach, that it would receive a measure of scrutiny. Heenan had already informed de Rosa that the first academic year of the institution's work was bound to be essentially experimental, making it necessary to take stock of the entire venture by Easter of 1966.[34]

He also alerted Richards to the point that, as the college came under the oversight of the hierarchy, it would be necessary to involve the bishops in important consultations and decision-making.[35] Episcopal support, indeed, was crucial if good diocesan priests were to be seconded to the college for training in catechetics with a view, in some cases, to establishing local diocesan centres elsewhere in the country. Heenan acknowledged that, although the bulk of the financial responsibility for the welfare of the institution was likely to remain a Westminster affair, there were other considerations in which the bishops might be interested. Caution, however, at this time did not seem to be much-valued advice at Corpus Christi!

As the college ended the first term of work of its second-year intake of students, Heenan's postbag was becoming heavy, with correspondence from episcopal, clerical and lay sources, reeling from the shock of the publicity accompanying the departure from the priesthood of

Charles Davis who, while more directly associated now with Heythrop, had nevertheless been one of the listed guest lecturers at Corpus Christi. The effect of the Davis defection, a few days before Christmas, drew unwelcome attention to the college and the nature of its theology, a situation which, before two years were to pass, would be much aggravated by the vice-principal's leading the attack – with fifty-five others – on Pope Paul VI's encyclical of July 1968, *Humanae Vitae*.[36] Peter de Rosa's letter in that regard was addressed from Corpus Christi, and was a sequel to an earlier round robin of May 1968, organized from the college and addressed to the bishops, which aimed at securing a more rapid response to the requests of former priests who might wish to marry. Referring to the de Rosa letter to *The Times* on *Humanae Vitae*, a correspondent to Heenan remarked that it was 'all the more shocking in that it came from the catechetical centre, a centre of incalculable influence on future generations of Catholic teachers and children'.[37]

While there seemed to be an unfortunate tendency in the college to shoot itself in the foot in terms of national and, indeed, international issues, more sui generis complaints about the content of the teaching, at both the college itself and in the extra-mural catechetical programmes, began to manifest themselves halfway through the second year of the programme. At first, Heenan thought the college was entrapped in the general malaise of dissent that had begun to surface more voluably after the end of the Second Vatican Council in 1965. His relations with Bert Richards at this time indicate that Heenan was not concerned about the theological orthodoxy of teaching at Corpus Christi, at least not during 1966, but that he was worried at the presentation of the programmes' 'new theology', as he called it, to students not adequately prepared to assimilate it.

Some of his concerns seem trivial today, and were mainly matters of jargon and the terminology employed in lectures. In April 1966 he was telling the director that 'there is no need to talk about Christ-centred theology. If it is good theology, it is bound to be Christ-centred. Nor should we cease talking about the Faith. It is something more than the Christian message ...' He also commented, adversely, on the use of the form 'the Eucharistic Celebration' for the Mass, and warned that laypeople might increasingly reject new catechetical approaches that were held hostage to similar language.[38] These were, however, minor issues and Heenan was as aware as anyone else that new ideas are often thought to be false simply because they are new.

In early 1967 Heenan became more concerned about the teaching at Corpus Christi College in the light of the increasing number of complaints from those attending some of the main programmes of study. A cache of the complaints referred simply to the pedagogy being employed, the alleged poor quality of the teaching in some courses, and the obscurity of language often used. Complaints were particularly vocal in connection with the Leicester Square extra-mural programme. While not making an issue of the orthodoxy of the teaching, the cardinal began to question the wisdom of failing to relate subject matter and presentation to the qualifications and/or expertise of the audience involved, and of not making sufficient allowance for the level of theological awareness possessed by participants. All of this really constituted a pedagogical, rather than a specifically theological, worry. Heenan insisted matters could be improved by providing courses more germane to the theological grounding of participants. Similarly, there was need for greater and more penetrative selection processes for students to be admitted to the long residential programme. The same argument could be advanced in regard to the extra-mural courses that were currently open to all comers, regardless of ability to cope with the theological thought processes involved.

While there was no open disagreement between the cardinal and the principal or vice-principal of Corpus Christi, no discernable meeting of attitudes seemed to be taking place. Matters began to assume more serious proportions in February 1967, when the then Apostolic Delegate, Archbishop Hyginus Cardinale, approached Heenan about disquieting reports he had received 'from various sources', concerning 'some of the teaching imparted' at the college 'and certain aspects of the college's life'. The delegate asked the cardinal to furnish him 'with accurate and exhaustive information about the college' so that he could be in a position 'to give a true picture of its aims and activities to the Holy See',[39] which had also received complaints.

For his part, Fr Bert Richards asked the governing body of Corpus Christi to separate again the administrative work of the college and the Catechetical Centre, both for financial reasons and because, no doubt, he hoped to offset some of the criticism and complaints from students of the college itself. Before this request could be effectively dealt with, however, Heenan asked Archbishop Cardinale for time to prepare a full report, while admitting that he, too, had received complaints, referring especially to the lectures 'to several hundreds of teachers' at the Leicester Square course, which was planned to continue until 1970, and perhaps later. Bert Richards told Heenan frankly, in March 1967, that he also had received complaints from 'puzzled' teachers and he was to hold an open forum at Leicester Square that month, on two dates, to answer questions.

But 'if there really is going to be a theological renewal,' he warned Heenan, 'and not the mere retailing of theological opinions', there would be a consequence of 'an amount of difficulty in some minds'.[40] The college could vouch for the orthodoxy of the teaching at Leicester Square, Richards argued, but added, 'I suppose that with an audience of 1100, from whom we demand no qualifications or training, there are bound to be some who will misunderstand things.'[41] Heenan had himself addressed the students, at the opening of the previous year's course in Leicester Square, and was invited to do so again, both there and at Corpus Christi College itself at the end of each course.

Heenan informed Richards that he had to prepare a report on the college for the Holy See and that he would show it to Richards when completed before it was sent for transmission to Rome. Richards was requested to supply some of the factual details. The cardinal revealed his innermost feeling, however, to Archbishop Beck of Liverpool, saying that 'the teaching is probably orthodox but tactlessly delivered and, in any case, widely misunderstood'. He added, 'They simply will have to learn to be much more careful.'[42]

In all the correspondence between the cardinal and the college there is no measure of discourtesy on either side; it is a polite exchange and, when criticisms are raised, they are openly and clearly presented. If Heenan is at fault in any of this, it is in that he failed to take firmer action for reform at an early stage, before critical positions were reached or attitudes had polarized between critics and defenders of the institution.

The principal was concerned, early in 1968, at criticisms some priest students of Corpus Christi had made to the cardinal and, in

March of that year, Heenan sent him a selective digest of what he had received, preserving the anonymity of writers. Some of the more trenchant criticisms received from priest students of the college were again concerned with pedagogical, managerial and organizational issues, as distinct from theological points, although the latter were not entirely absent.[43] Concern was expressed that the lecturers and teaching supervisors were often not available for guidance, discussion or feedback, and some seemed little concerned with the life of the institution, which replicated the life of a seminary or training college rather than that of a university-type establishment. Some of the lectures were deemed to be elementary, poorly delivered or boring, one of the lecturers being accused of having 'a big chip on his shoulder which came out over and over again', another as being 'a bit facetious in lectures and rather morose and silent outside'. Some of the pedagogical lectures were considered a waste of time, badly organized and laboured, 'the teaching staff in general' being notable 'for never being in the house'. A priest considered that the theology lectures from visiting authorities were of a good, even very good, standard but much was lost because the rapid turnaround of visitors was not supported by an adequate tutorial system. The theology presented was considered 'progressive' and among the students this attitude 'was very much in evidence'.

The criticism went on: 'For some individuals, progressive and modern had become synonymous with good. This uncritical attitude led to a certain scorn for any traditional Church teaching, simply because it was traditional.'[44] One lecturer was reported as seeing little point in the dogmas of the Immaculate Conception or the Assumption and, 'during discussions episcopal and religious use of authority were often reviewed unfavourably'. Another priest student complained that Corpus Christi seemed more interested in theology than catechetics, yet students had gone there for the latter. A number of teachers who had gone there 'come away feeling that they had been put through a very rapid course of reorientation – I have even heard the word "brainwashing" used rather unkindly – in their doctrinal thinking, but they are still left without any guidance on how to put this new approach to children ...'.[45]

Equally direct criticisms were made relating to the Leicester Square extra-mural lectures. One religious wondered 'whether some of the lecturers, through lack of pastoral experience, are sufficiently aware of the harm that can be done by leaving a theologically unsophisticated audience with the wrong impressions'.[46] The writer had met teachers 'who are being disillusioned by some of the things said at the Leicester Square course' and 'who have completely lost heart in teaching religion'. One of the problems might be that 'a clear dividing line is not being drawn between doctrine and speculation' and the 'lack of prudence' in this was damaging. Another religious emphasized the same points, specifying especially the teaching of one lecturer at Corpus Christi who 'causes much anxiety in some by his iconoclastic remarks, dogmatic views and brusque manner in dealing with objections or caveats'.[47]

The catalogue of complaints was lengthy but, when examined carefully, the brunt of the dossier seems to justify Heenan's opinion, that immature pedagogical skills were at the root of the college's problems, rather than a positive attack on orthodoxy, an immaturity accompanied in the work of some lecturers by a satisfaction, perhaps, at being able to shock a captive and ill-prepared audience or make a memorable impression upon it.

Cardinal Heenan, of course, could not avoid some of the blame and, not being a professional theologian himself, he was somewhat in awe of those who claimed the legitimacy of theological debate without undue interference by the *magisterium*. The time was rapidly approaching, however, when he did come to question the orthodoxy of some of the teaching at Corpus Christi and particularly that of the participants in 1968 in the *Humanae Vitae* debate. Peter de Rosa's percipient approach to Heenan in January 1969 maintained the encyclical had split the Church into two camps that would persist for years to come and that it had, furthermore, 'retarded the beneficent influence of Vatican II'.[48] It was a view that did much to shape Heenan's thinking about the teaching at Corpus Christi. Indeed, de Rosa saw the papal teaching as holding up the progress of humanity. Later in the year, Heenan wrote to Fr Hubert Simes that because he had been chiefly responsible for Corpus Christi and its establishment, it was presenting 'a burden on my conscience to see that only the true faith is taught there'.[49] The tide had begun to turn. It is noticeable that Heenan became a more regular visitor to Corpus Christi and, from 1969, the growth of concern at the teaching in their national catechetical college became endemic among the hierarchy.

In March 1970, a complaint was raised from Heenan's old diocese of Leeds about de Rosa's contribution to a *Lift Up Your Hearts* programme on BBC radio, which appeared to express unorthodox views on the resurrection of Christ and also on the resurrection of the body generally. Heenan gently took up the points with the speaker and requested him to take the opportunity, when next talking at a school in the Leeds diocese, to affirm his orthodoxy in regard to Church doctrine. It was a minor incident but it is indicative of Heenan assuming a more interventionist role on issues of doctrinal vagueness, and becoming increasingly sensitive to complaints from the laity.

The director of Corpus Christi began to complain, in 1970, that the bishops were failing to support the college by not supplying it with clerical students; indeed by the autumn of 1970 not a single diocese in England and Wales (Westminster apart) had a priest studying at Corpus Christi. Anthony Bullen, of the Liverpool Catechetical Centre, himself not immune from complaints and later from an investigation by Rome, whom Richards consulted, sensibly advised Corpus Christi to concentrate upon attracting laypeople to the college, rather than clerics. Thirteen dioceses already had their own directors of catechetics and saw little point in allocating more men to the task.[50] This was undoubtedly one of the reasons for the lack of episcopal interest, but another important reason was the lack of clarity in regard to Corpus Christi's target group. Bullen thought the college was trying to be all things to all men. It should decide on a restricted target group, whether this was to be priests, to work in diocesan centres, laypeople whose job would lie in the field of adult education, or school teachers who were to become heads of religious education departments in secondary schools.[51] Wisely, Bullen saw mileage only in the last group, and not in the other two, which were areas likely to bring the college into most difficulty.

But perhaps it was already too late. Heenan informed Bullen in June 1970 that while Corpus Christi 'is certainly blamed unfairly for many things', he had no doubt 'that some priests have left Corpus Christi with less respect for the Pope and those in authority in the Church'. He added significantly, 'Nothing will eradicate from the minds of the bishops the fact that young Corpus Christi priests organized public opposition to Humanae Vitae.'[52] There was unrest among the governors of the college, as well as among the bishops and, indeed, threatened resignations from the former because of allegations of inadequate methods of consultation about the policy being pursued. Some of the governors wished to resign 'because they believe that Corpus Christi does actual harm to the Church'.[53] Closure of the college was not yet on the *tapis*, but there was clearly much to be adjusted before the next academic year.

One of those contemplating resignation from the governing body was Fr George Telford, the Southwark diocesan representative who was the director of the Catechetical Centre for that diocese. He told Heenan he was convinced 'that the root cause of present tensions lies in the theology which forms the basis of the catechesis promulgated by Corpus Christi College and its adherents ... Concern is now so widespread that it cannot be ascribed to alarmist rumours stirred up by a small, fundamentalist opposition.'[54] In his view, the problem was more serious than simply one of theological opinion, because 'so much of the "new" theology is in no way an organic development of Catholic tradition, but a contradiction of it, based on entirely novel principles drawn from phenomenology and existentialism which necessarily preclude an effective concept of a Magisterium'.[55] He pointed out that 'the adverse image of Corpus Christi which has been debated at every Governors' Meeting so far (to no apparent effect), is grounded in the hard facts of sad experience'.[56] To rely on a defence of 'misrepresentation' or of 'misquotation' failed to prognosticate an agenda for change or reform.

At the time, Telford was making his case and, with others such as Canon Leo McCartie of Birmingham (subsequently a bishop) and Rosemary Rendel (secretary of the Catholic Record Society), was contemplating resignation from the governors of Corpus Christi, unaware that Peter de Rosa was already on the point of resignation from the priesthood. The cardinal had been aware of de Rosa's inner struggle for two months but was anxious that the situation should not explode precipitately. Indeed, Bishop Pearson, the auxiliary Bishop of Lancaster, had been urging Heenan to show 'patience' in dealings with the college.[57]

At the governing body meeting, on 4 June 1970, Bert Richards expressed renewed concern that the college was not enjoying the full confidence of bishops and religious superiors. The bishops had almost unanimously declared their intentions of not sending any more priests, and some religious superiors had withdrawn accepted applicants before the year's study had begun. The year 1969–70 had two-thirds of its places filled, and it looked as if 1970–1 might have only half its total of students, with just some fifteen from England itself.[58] From the ensuing discussion, a good measure of mistrust of the theology taught at the college became evident; the de la Salle Brothers, for instance, preferring to send their young men abroad for studies or to the bachelor of divinity courses offered in secular universities within the UK. The crisis of confidence in Corpus Christi and its programmes of study had bitten deeply and was unlikely to be lessened by the ambiguous stance taken, in the view of a recent Health Management Institute of Ireland (HMI) analysis, that 'no definite theological standpoint is adopted at Corpus Christi'.[59] To stimulate the flagging interest, the cardinal proposed a two-day conference on catechetics, to be held in the college on 14–15 December 1971, attended by the bishops and diocesan directors of catechetics.[60] It was inevitable, Heenan foresaw, that the status of the college would have to revert to that of a local diocesan institution if episcopal indifference prevailed. The national governing body would have to be disbanded.

Peter de Rosa's departure from the priesthood in 1971, followed shortly afterwards by John Perry's, both on issues relative to *Humanae Vitae*, cemented the determination for radical change. The departures, of course, increased the difficulties facing Bert Richards. At this stage, Richards had no wish to abandon his priesthood, or his direction of the college, but Heenan, aware it would be extremely difficult to introduce new staff into the establishment with Richards in situ, began to cast around for other names. The point was made explicit by Bishop Gordon Wheeler, who thought it would not work to appoint a new vice-principal under present management. Fr Michael Keegan, whom Heenan had in mind, was Dean of Rotherham and a busy parish priest. He was only four years younger than Richards, and had pursued his priestly studies in Rome, following three years of military service. He was a trained teacher from Strawberry Hill College and had also undertaken a year's course in catechetics at Lumen Vitae. He had been on the academic staff at Trinity and All Saints College, Leeds, and was qualified and experienced to take over the direction of Corpus Christi should Bert Richards stand down. Keegan was not averse to taking up the task and Leeds Diocese was prepared to release him to undertake the work. He was also well known to Heenan from his own days as Bishop of Leeds.

In early August 1971 Cardinal Heenan's private secretary, Mgr Frederick Miles, was asked to discuss some of the problems of Corpus Christi with its director and, in particular, to ascertain if he was fully aware that Corpus Christi would have to change if it was to survive at all and inspire public confidence. Miles's report, while factual and helpful, was nonetheless clear that radical reform could not be effected without a change of principal. Richards was immediately concerned that Heenan did not want him to go ahead with inviting four particular guest lecturers for the 1971–2 session, whose involvement in *Humanae Vitae* debates would, in the cardinal's view, be counter-productive in effecting cultural change in the establishment. Richards was unwilling to deviate from the approach he had adopted as he did not think the staff, or such as were likely to remain, would support such change. He considered he was being asked to go back ten years in his thinking.

Crisis point was reached on 21 August 1971, when Richards wrote to the cardinal in the name of the college to protest at Heenan's objection to the four visiting speakers,[61] which he regarded as indirect censorship of the teaching programme, and an infringement of the college's academic freedom. He declared that 'it emerges fairly clearly that there is between yourself and us a divergence of understanding on the nature of religious education that it would be inappropriate for us to remain as staff in charge of your College'.[62] The letter was countersigned by Fr Peter Wetz, who had informed the Provincial of the White Fathers that he wished to be released from his congregation, as and when canonically possible; by two nuns, Sr Ruth Duckworth and Sr Rena Boyd; and by Fr Frank Somerville, SJ. The Jesuit Provincial, however, was to indicate that he was willing to provide a suitable replacement for Somerville.[63] In view of the fact that some sixty-five students (most of them from overseas) had been accepted for the 1971–2 academic session, the staff was prepared to serve out the appropriate academic year 'on the understanding that we continue to enjoy for that period the academic freedom we have enjoyed so far'. Resignations would thus take effect from July 1972. There was little time for discussion as Fr Richards was leaving the country shortly and would then be in Switzerland for three weeks.

Before responding to the ultimatum, Heenan sought the advice of his fellow metropolitan archbishops in England and Wales, as to whether or not he ought to accept the offer of a transitional year, in view of the commitments to students. He also asked the apostolic delegate for his opinion. There was a division of view. Archbishops Cowderoy of Southwark and Murphy of Cardiff did not find it acceptable to allow the college to continue under its current management. Cowderoy thought Richards was behaving as if he was running a theological university rather than a catechetical centre.[64] Murphy was worried because Corpus Christi was married to only one school of theology, an impression 'not minimized when a list of visiting lecturers is presented, all of whom would be associated with one school of theology and two of whom have openly opposed the authentic teaching of the *Magisterium*'.[65] Murphy also thought that Desmond Brennan and Sr Romaine, who did not sign the letter, could be kept in post.

The public announcement of the acceptance of the resignations, and the changes to the staff of Corpus Christi, took place on 21 December 1971 amid a blaze of publicity and comment. The statement of Heenan was sent to Fr Richards, before being made public, and the college produced a statement of its own, the accuracy of which was challenged by the archbishop. It was because of this that Heenan addressed the students of Corpus Christi on 11 January 1972. In this address he emphasized the issue was not one of academic freedom but of responsibility. 'A bishop has the right and, indeed, the duty,' he declared,

> to decide what is to be taught and who is to teach in a diocesan college of catechetics. The press understandably assumed when told of its worldwide reputation and eminent lecturers that Corpus Christi must be a university or institute of theological research. It is, of course, nothing of the sort. It is a college founded to teach Catholic theology to future catechists.[66]

His approach subscribed to the concept of the Church, simply stated by George Telford to Peter de Rosa as being that of 'a community of people who are committed to a defined faith'. In that definition could be sought the essence of the problems facing both the college and the bishops.

The meeting of twenty-eight bishops for the catechetical conference at Corpus Christi, shortly before Christmas, had shown up the difference in concepts about the nature of the Church. The atmosphere was tense. On the morning the conference was about to begin, Heenan received a letter from Fr Richards, giving details of arrangements he was making for teaching programmes in the academic year 1972–3, by which time Fr Michael Keegan would be in control. An Irish Jesuit, a Dutch priest and a religious brother from the USA were all involved. Heenan pointed out that new staff would be appointed, in consultation with the new principal, who was also attending the catechetical conference. The exchange ensured the conference began on a tense note and, indeed, a heated exchange between the cardinal and the staff took place on the second day. Although there could be no going back, what the future held was problematical. Much damage had been caused to the name and raison d'être of Corpus Christi, and the task facing Fr Keegan was the daunting and well-nigh impossible one of rebuilding confidence, with an undisputed commitment to theological orthodoxy. In this task he secured the services of Fr Hugh Lavery of Ushaw as his vice-principal.

The problem of Fr Bert Richards remained, and the matter of his suitable future employment. Bishop Alan Clark, at that time auxiliary Bishop of Northampton, wrote to Heenan in January 1972 that he had never agreed with Heenan that issues, other than the orthodoxy of the teaching at Corpus Christi, were the essential problems with the college. 'I have not changed my mind,' Clark wrote, following two days of debate with Bert Richards at the catechetical conference, 'that the staff of C.C. were erroneous in their conscientious convictions.' He did not think Richards, while always 'wide-open to trends of thought' had 'a solid theological appraisal of the Church and the presence of Christ in the Church'.[67] Bishop Anthony Emery wrote in similar vein,[68] as did the historian, Dom David Knowles, nauseated by what he described as the tone of the college's defence and its 'interminable propaganda'.[69]

It was in July 1972 that Heenan admitted the strength of Clark's views. The occasion consisted of reports on a number of lectures given in New Zealand to teachers of catechetics by Fr Bert Richards, after laying down his role at Corpus Christi. The themes were on the humanity of Christ, the divinity of Christ, the resurrection and miracles.[70] The apostolic delegate for New Zealand, Archbishop Raymond Ettledorf, alarmed at the furore being created there by the lectures, wrote to Cardinal Heenan about the orthodoxy of some of them, especially in regard to the resurrection. He sent Heenan tapes of the lectures, and wrote: 'Richards's existentialist interpretation led him to the conclusion that it did not matter whether Christ arose from the dead bodily.' Heenan responded that he, personally, could not entrust him with another teaching post after Corpus Christi.[71] Two months later Heenan wrote to Richards that he found it hard 'to accept that you still believe the same Creed as I do'. He doubted if he accepted 'the doctrine of the Blessed Trinity' or that he meant the same thing as other Catholics when he recited the words *et Homo factus est* in the Nicene Creed.[72]

Richards, after reconsideration, declined an invitation from Heenan to discuss his theological position, informally, with bishops Christopher Butler and Alan Clark, unless Nicholas Lash could also be present. Lash was Dean of St Edmund's House, Cambridge, where Richards was spending a year's sabbatical on leaving Corpus Christi. Lash was to seek laicization in 1975. In Heenan's view, what had been intended as a discussion leading to mutual understanding may thus have been turned into an inquisitorial confrontation. Heenan raised matters with Richards about his concept of the Trinity and the incarnation, and the virginity of Mary and the Assumption. The difficulties arose, Heenan considered, because, to paraphrase Richards's own words, he had become not so much a theologian as a popularizer.[73]

Heenan wanted Richards, now in his early fifties, to become a parish priest. He felt that, in a non-academic métier, he was unlikely to disturb the faith of his parishioners. Richards, however, was unwilling to go down this route, his desire being to continue working in third-level education. Against Heenan's advice, he applied for a lectureship at Heythrop College but he was not short-listed. He felt that this may have been because Heenan would have withdrawn his own clerical students from Heythrop if he thought they were to be taught by Richards. The

Rector of Heythrop, however, made it clear that the successful applicant was a highly qualified and experienced scholar. Similarly, Heenan was concerned that Richards seemed to be trying to secure appointments for himself, without taking into account the needs of the diocese. While he was unwilling to give Richards another sabbatical year in Cambridge, he was willing for him to be incardinated into another diocese, although he pointed out to him that this would be unlikely to lead to his teaching theology.

When Bert Richards resigned from the priesthood in June 1975, he specifically stated that he was announcing his resignation 'because it has been made progressively clearer to me over the past three years that as a priest I am not free to teach theology in any Roman Catholic establishment in this country'.[74] He had secured a teaching appointment at Keswick Hall College of Education, subsequently incorporated into the University of East Anglia.

It is somewhat ironic that it was left to Bishop Christopher Butler to write to the Congregation for the Doctrine of the Faith on 20 November 1975, three weeks after the demise of Cardinal Heenan, to expedite the dispensation from priestly obligations, including that of celibacy.[75]

NOTES

Grateful acknowledgment is made to the late Cardinal Basil Hume for permission to consult the appropriate Heenan papers and to Fr Ian Dickie, then archivist of the Westminster Diocesan Archives (WDA), for making the relevant records available. All references are to the Heenan Papers, Westminster Diocesan Archives (WDA), unless otherwise secified.

1. Maurice J. Kelleher to Heenan, 30 October 1964.
2. Brian Charles Foley, 'De Cura Animarum: a voice for the priesthood', in Alberic Stacpoole (ed.), *Vatican II By Those Who Were There* (London 1986), pp. 255–69.
3. Kelleher, *op. cit.*
4. Fr John McCoy to Heenan, 27 January 1965.
5. Heenan to McCoy, 28 January 1965.
6. David Konstant to Heenan, 2 March 1965.
7. Heenan to Konstant, 4 March 1965.
8. Heenan to Charles Davis, 27 June 1964.
9. Davis to Heenan, 21 March 1965 and 28 March 1965.

10. Bert Richards to Heenan, 15 February 1965.
11. Heenan to Bert Richards, 16 February 1965.
12. Archbishop's House, Westminster, press release of 11 March 1965.
13. Heenan, copy of letter to Peter de Rosa, 16 March 1965.
14. Draft prospectus of the London Institute of Religious Education (subsequently Corpus Christi College) sent by Hubert Richards to Cardinal Heenan, 10 April 1965.
15. Heenan's address to Corpus Christi students, 11 January 1972.
16. Bert Richards to Heenan, 20 April 1965.
17. Heenan to Bert Richards, 26 April 1965.
18. *Ibid.*
19. At the Low Week Meeting of the hierarchy in 1966, Cardinal Heenan and Archbishop Beck were given the task of drawing up a suitable list of governors for Corpus Christi. It was decided that each province of the Church in England and Wales should have one representative each, selected by the archbishop concerned, Heenan being chairman of the governors and Beck vice-chairman. The headmasters of Beaumont College and St Aloysius' Highgate, the President of the Grail, and two nuns (from Our Lady of Sion and Holy Child) were to be invited, as was Derek Lance, then head of a secondary modern school. Heenan named David Konstant as the nominee of Westminster, Beck selected Anthony Bullen for Liverpool, Leo McCartie (future Bishop of Northampton) was to be chosen by Birmingham, Canon Matthew Quilligan by Cardiff and Fr George Telford by the Southwark Archdiocese. Fr Richards was ex officio and he asked to bring Fr de Rosa with him. The latter request was granted by the first meeting. The meeting, intended for 15 July 1966, had to be postponed until the following February because of the illness of Archbishop Beck who had suffered a thrombosis.
20. Bert Richards to Heenan, 1 July and 4 August 1965.
21. Heenan to Bert Richards, 27 May 1965.
22. Bert Richards to Heenan, 28 May 1965.
23. *Ibid.*
24. Heenan to Bert Richards, 4 June 1965.
25. Bert Richards to Heenan, 9 June 1965.
26. Heenan to Bert Richards, 11 June 1965.
27. *Ibid.*
28. Bert Richards to Heenan, 13 June 1965.
29. De Rosa to Heenan, 24 June 1965.
30. Bert Richards to Heenan, 4 November 1965.
31. *Ibid.* Bert Richards to Heenan, 16 November 1965.
32. Bert Richards to Heenan, 4 November 1965.
33. *Ibid.*

34. Heenan to de Rosa, 21 June 1965.
35. Heenan to Bert Richards, 24 September 1965.
36. For the encyclical and a good synopsis of international reaction, see John Horgan (ed.), *Humanae Vitae and the Bishops* (Dublin 1972).
37. Letter to Heenan, 2 August 1968.
38. Heenan to Bert Richards, 27 April 1966.
39. Archbishop Hyginus Cardinale to Heenan, 13 February 1967.
40. Bert Richards to Heenan, 2 March 1967.
41. *Ibid.*
42. Heenan to Archbishop Beck, 15 March 1967.
43. Extracts from letters to Heenan, copied to Bert Richards, 2 March 1968.
44. *Ibid.*
45. *Ibid.*
46. *Ibid.*
47. *Ibid.*
48. De Rosa to Heenan, 18 January 1969.
49. Heenan to Fr Hubert Simes, 17 December 1969.
50. Anthony Bullen to Bert Richards, 5 June 1970.
51. *Ibid.*
52. Heenan to Bullen, 11 June 1970.
53. *Ibid.*
54. George Telford to Heenan, 9 June 1970.
55. *Ibid.*
56. *Ibid.*
57. Bishop Thomas Bernard Pearson to Heenan, 19 June 1970.
58. Minutes of the governing body meeting of Corpus Christi College, 4 June 1970.
59. Heenan to Bert Richards, 9 June 1971.
60. Heenan to Bert Richards, 24 April 1971.
61. Bert Richards to Heenan, 21 August 1971. The names were those of Gregory Baum, Enda McDonagh, Jack Dominian and John Marshall.
62. *Ibid.*
63. Bernard Hall, SJ, to Heenan, 2 September 1971.
64. Cowderoy to Heenan, 13 September 1971.
65. Murphy to Heenan, 27 August 1971.
66. Cardinal's address to students of Corpus Christi College, 11 January 1972.
67. Bishop Alan Clark to Heenan, 13 January 1972.
68. Bishop Anthony Emery to Heenan, 11 January 1972.
69. Dom David Knowles to Heenan, 23 January 1972.
70. Apostolic Delegate for New Zealand and the Pacific Ocean to Heenan, 28 August 1972.

71. Heenan to Archbishop Etteldorf, 2 September 1972.
72. Heenan to Bert Richards, 3 November 1972.
73. Heenan to Bert Richards, 22 February 1973.
74. Press release, 10 June 1975.
75. Bishop B.C. Butler to the Prefect for the Sacred Congregation of the Doctrine of the Faith, 20 November 1975. Butler was Vicar Capitular of the vacant See.

VINCENT ALAN McCLELLAND is Emeritus Professor at the Institute of Education in the University of Hull. He has published extensively on teacher education, English liberal education and Catholic education. For many years he was external examiner in the School of Education, TCD, and a friend of Val Rice.

International Trends in Denominational Schooling

DAN MURPHY

This paper aims to examine the major issues currently affecting policy and practice in denominational education, in a number of selected school systems throughout the world. The concept of denominational schooling is itself a highly complex one, but I am using the term, quite simply, to signify schools that are committed to the promotion of the value systems and beliefs of a particular religious denomination – Catholic, Protestant, Jewish, Islamic or whatever. I intend to concentrate largely on the tradition of schooling within the Judaeo-Christian heritage as this is the one most relevant to our concerns in this country. Within that context again, my comments will be focused mainly on schools within the Catholic and Protestant Christian traditions.

Initially I want to place the whole issue of denominational education in historical perspective, as it seems to me that this is essential for the proper contextualizing of the various issues on which I propose to comment. I would like therefore to refer very briefly to some historical issues that seem to me to have a bearing on current concerns in this entire field. At the outset, I want to point to the ancient character of denominational education, and to the interdependence of religion and education that has existed in the traditions of formal schooling from its earliest origins.

There is evidence, for example, that schools founded specifically for the promotion of religious belief existed in Babylon and Egypt from about 2500 BC. Schools had been founded for the training of Sumerian priests in Babylon during the reign of Hammurabi (1948–1904 BC) and Egyptian temple schools were known to have been active in Thebes, Heliopolis and Memphis by the time of the Fourth Dynasty (c.2500 BC). There is evidence that schools for the training of priests existed in Assyria from the seventh century BC. Buddhist doctrine was taught to Chinese scholars in India shortly after this, in the fifth century BC, and this led subsequently to the establishment of Buddhist schools in various parts of India and China.

From our particular perspective the most significant development was the emergence of Jewish education in the period immediately following the return of the exiles from Babylon, early in the sixth century BC. The first knowledge we have of a formal system of Jewish schooling comes from about 530 BC, when a scribe and teacher, Ezra, founded schools and colleges in Palestine for the teaching of the sacred books of Judaism, thus initiating a tradition that has continued unbroken amongst the Jewish people down to the present time. To this period also can be traced the establishment of study houses, which, together with the synagogues, have become the hallmark of Jewish life and culture ever since.

Side by side with Jewish education there developed Greek education in the fifth century BC and Roman in the third century BC, neither specifically religious in themselves, but both eventually being absorbed into the Jewish, and subsequently the Christian, traditions of schooling. From an early stage in the history of Christian education there existed a highly potent synthesis of Hebrew, Greek, Roman and Christian elements in its schooling traditions. From the Hebrew tradition, the Christians inherited much of their ethico-religious teaching, which, of course, they re-interpreted in light of the New Testament, and from the Graeco-Roman tradition they derived much of their cultural, and particularly their linguistic and literary, heritage.

That synthesis was in evidence in the work of the first Christian catechetical schools of the second century and was further developed in the monastic, cathedral, parish and chantry schools of later centuries. It was strongly in evidence, for example, in the Celtic monastic schools established in Ireland in the sixth century, whose scholastic traditions were extended in Merovingian Europe by the Columban monks later in the seventh century, and to Carolingian Europe by the *peregrine* in the ninth. That eclectic classical-Christian tradition was sustained by the monastic and mendicant orders in their schools throughout the medieval period and it survived the Reformation in the denominational schools established by the Catholic and Protestant churches in subsequent years.

The classical-Christian tradition of schooling exhibited certain characteristics that have remained constant through the ages and some of these are still relevant today. At its core was a conception of education as being necessarily both a sacred and a secular process, requiring the integration of both of these elements for a truly authentic philosophy of teaching and learning. The monastic schools, for example, taught a curriculum that combined formal religious studies, in the spheres of scripture and theology, with a range of classical disciplines, the Greek and Latin languages and their literatures, as well as various aesthetic and practical activities. The Christian school, therefore, had a dual motivation from its outset. It was educational both in the purely evangelical sense in which it sought to disseminate the teachings of Christianity and in the liberal-classical sense in which it sought to develop the whole range of individual potentialities – spiritual, moral, intellectual, aesthetic and physical – through the secular classical curriculum.

Moreover, the two objectives were not discrete or separate: one was derived logically from the other. The obligation of the Christian school to disseminate Christian teaching was seen to carry a corresponding obligation to develop individual potentiality, whether linguistic, mathematical, scientific or aesthetic, and the promotion of all this through the secular curriculum was seen as being just as central to the realization of the Christian educational ideals as the formal instruction in scriptural teachings.

It is essential to insist on this dual process as the defining characteristic of Christian education. It indicates a paradox that is central to the whole process; it is essentially formative – doctrinally and morally – while also being liberal or liberating in the original classical sense of an education whose ultimate goal is the promotion of individual freedom.

The process got a huge impetus from the liberal body of Christian educational theory that emerged in the sixteenth century, beginning with the work of Erasmus and reaching full flowering with the writings of Comenius in the seventeenth century. It embraced a variety of denominational perspectives, including the Catholic as promoted by Loyola and the Jesuits, the Puritan by Comenius, the Lutheran by Pestalozzi, the Pietist by Oberlin, and many others.

This tradition was the informing philosophy of most of the schools of Europe until the nineteenth century. It was the basic philosophy of the early church-run elementary schools of France, Germany, Scandinavia, the Austro-Hungarian Empire and Great Britain. It provided the basic rationale for the secondary academies in all these countries – the *collèges royaux* and the *lycées* in France, the *Gymnasien* in Prussia and Austria, the *folkeskolen* in Scandinavia, and the grammar schools of England. It remained the dominant influence in schooling until early in the nineteenth century when the combined forces of enlightenment humanism and rationalism, together with the emergence of State-sponsored schooling, brought about the gradual secularization of education and led to new, and frequently conflicting, relationships between Church and State, and school and community, leading in turn to a far greater range of schools – public and private, denominational, multi-denominational and secular – and to radical changes in curriculum policies and in the status of religious education in schools.

From all this emerged new conceptions of how the ideals of Christian education, whether in its Catholic or Protestant forms, were to be promoted. In some instances they were provided through schools controlled by the churches, with some measure of State support; in others through the State system of schools itself, in others again, through schools provided entirely from private sources. Several different models emerged for the furtherance of Christian education and I propose to focus on a number of these that seem to me to illustrate with particular clarity the wide range of modes in which Christian education is currently provided. I want to look, firstly, to the entirely private systems of Catholic education that emerged in the USA and Australia; secondly, to the State-controlled Protestant and Catholic schools that emerged in Germany and Scandinavia; and thirdly, to the church-controlled system of Catholic schools that emerged in France. In each instance I want to explore the nature of Church–State relations and various other issues affecting the provision of denominational education, from all of which I hope to draw conclusions relevant to the ongoing role of denominational schools in a pluralist society.

The whole question of the relationship of sacred and secular education became a highly divisive issue between Catholic and Protestant churches in the USA in the middle of the nineteenth century. Catholics generally saw the promotion of Christian education as the central and all-embracing responsibility of the school, working in conjunction with church and home, while the main Protestant churches (by no means all) saw it as one that should be discharged primarily by church and home, each taking a major responsibility for religious formation, with the school providing secular instruction, together with minimal religious education through a commonly taught scripture-based programme.

Up to the 1840s, most American schools had in fact been run by the churches or by various voluntary organizations. Catholic schools were run by the parishes or by the different religious orders invited to the US by Bishop John Carroll in the late 1790s and early 1800s. The Episcopalian, Presbyterian, Congregationalist and Methodist churches were all involved in the provision of schools and, very significantly, in the promotion of Sunday school education in their churches. The emergence of the common school movement in the 1840s, with its common programme of scripture study for children of all denominations was, however, broadly acceptable to the Protestant churches. Their strong Sunday school traditions could compensate for the loss of denominational instruction, but it was viewed with deep apprehension by the Catholic Church.

This whole issue became the main focus of debate at the Baltimore conferences of the Catholic hierarchy in the 1880s, the reports of which make fascinating reading on the Catholic conception of the role of the school. The critical issue for the Catholic bishops was the provision of religious education for Catholic children in accordance with their own traditions, and the effective linking of this with all other school activities. Several of the bishops, most notably Cardinal James Gibbons and Archbishop John Ireland, were concerned at the ghettoization that could result from a separate Catholic school system, to say nothing of the awesome financial implications of providing schools entirely from Church resources for the growing Catholic population, its numbers hugely augmented by the millions of new immigrants then arriving in the country, most of them from Ireland. The compromise proposed by Archbishop Ireland – that the Church itself would provide religious education in the schools outside normal school hours – was rejected by the State authorities, including the courts, and the move towards the creation of a separate school system thenceforward proved inevitable.

A vast programme for the provision of Catholic education, at primary, secondary and tertiary levels, followed the Baltimore conferences. Catholic parochial schools increased from 2246 to 5852 between 1880 and 1920 and had further increased to 9274 by 1960, by which time there were 3.6 million children in the schools – all of this being achieved without any form of State support. By then there were also over 1500 Catholic high schools catering for 500,000 students. Currently the enrolment figures stand at 2.5 million, the reduction resulting mainly from a declining birthrate, although it is significant that, for a variety of reasons, only about half the Catholic population has supported Catholic schools throughout most of the period in which they have been provided.

Side by side with the separate school system there also exists a thriving tertiary system – with twenty-eight colleges and universities provided by the Jesuits alone – to provide third-level education with a strong Catholic ethos for those who wish to avail of it. Research on Catholic schools in the US has repeatedly confirmed the high quality of the education offered in these schools. Whether the system can continue to survive in current financial conditions is a matter of speculation – it depended heavily on the sacrifices of religious teaching orders in the past and their numbers have now been greatly depleted – but there is evidence that considerable uncertainty hangs over their future unless the US authorities follow the example of other countries around the world who consider they have a democratic responsibility to allocate State resources to all schools providing an education in accordance with public norms of accountability – as American Catholic schools most certainly do.

One such country is Australia, whose denominational schools have much in common with the USA, most of them having been established originally by Irish immigrants in the nineteenth century. Despite attempts by the educational authorities in the 1830s to introduce a common schooling system in the six Australian colonies – modelled interestingly on the Stanley proposals for a national school system in Ireland in the same period – education there remained under the control of the Anglican, Catholic, Presbyterian, Congregationalist and Methodist churches until the third quarter of the century. Each of the denominations controlled a number of schools in which a curriculum was provided in accordance with their individual traditions. Gradually, however, they came to accept the inevitability of a common State-controlled system of schools, starting in south Australia in the 1850s and culminating in the establishment of a State system in western Australia by 1880, all of which left the Catholic Church in the country in a similar situation to that of the USA.

All of the colonial school authorities had long been determined to end the expensive and inefficient dual system whereby State schools co-existed with denominational schools, but were eventually able to do so only when the proposal became acceptable to the Protestant churches. By the 1860s, the Congregationalists had declared they would support a State system, and the Wesleyan and Presbyterian churches similarly agreed to support the proposals, so long as they were guaranteed the right to provide religious education through their Sunday schools. A Presbyterian General Assembly declared in 1869 that it 'approved of a national in preference to a denominational system' and by the 1870s large numbers of their schools had been closed. The Anglican Church, which had vehemently opposed the proposals for a Stanley-type system of national education in the 1830s, was divided on the issue but its schools declined in number in the 1860s and 1870s until eventually their members reluctantly embraced the State system also.

The dismantling of the dual system was vehemently opposed by the Catholic Church whose numbers at that time constituted one-third of the entire population, the vast majority of them Irish immigrants. Again they insisted on the need to have religious education in accordance with Catholic tradition in their schools and stressed the importance of integrating ethico-religious and secular instruction. The whole issue was debated intensively at conferences of the Australian hierarchy and eventually they decided to create a voluntary system of schools, financed entirely from church resources, as in the USA. The schools survived on voluntary funding until the 1960s, largely through the sacrifices of the religious orders. Inspectors' reports through the years have confirmed the high standards that have been maintained in Catholic elementary and secondary schools, some of the latter, especially those under the control of the Jesuits and the Christian Brothers, being amongst the most prestigious in the country.

Longitudinal research since the 1960s, particularly the work of Marcellin Flynn, further attests to the high standards maintained in the Catholic schools, despite the huge obstacles they faced in providing education without State support. Their position changed dramatically, however, in the early 1960s when Premier Robert Menzies, following intervention from his close friend, Archbishop Daniel Mannix, provided grants for Catholic schools and these have been systematically improved by successive administrations since that time. By 1990 there were about 600,000 children in Catholic schools in the country, representing approximately 20 per cent of the school population and most of their costs, both capital and recurrent, are now covered by the State.

I should emphasize the fact that this is the *general* pattern of denominational education in the USA and Australia. It is important to point out that not all Protestant communities supported the move towards common schools in either country – there are still significant numbers of Protestant schools of various denominations in both – nor indeed did all Catholics support their own denominational schools, either in the USA or Australia. Currently, about half the Catholic population in the USA send their children to State schools and a smaller proportion do so in Australia. Correspondingly, Catholic schools in both countries have always enrolled a minority of non-Catholic pupils – currently in the order of 12 per cent in the US and 20 per cent in Australia.

Quite a different pattern of Protestant education is observable in several parts of Europe, particularly in Germany and Scandinavia, where there are large Protestant majorities in their populations. Full provision for denominational education, both Protestant and Catholic, is currently made by the State itself in Germany. Determined to heal the centuries-old divisions between Catholics and Protestants in the country since the Reformation, the State authorities, in the immediate postwar era, designed a system of schools whose objective was the promotion of the two main Christian traditions.

Officially all State-funded schools in the country are Christian; in practice most are denominational or multi-denominational. Only about 5 per cent of German schools are classified as private and few of these were founded for ideological reasons, most being special schools, such as those founded by the Steiner Society, or schools founded for children with special educational needs. Article 7 of the West German Constitution guaranteed that 'religious instruction would be part of the ordinary curriculum' and stipulated that 'such instruction be given in accordance with the tenets of the religious communities'. This provision is now being extended to the five new *Bundesländer* from East Germany that were brought into the Federation in 1991.

All State schools – *Gründschulen, Gymnasien, Hauptschulen, Realschulen* and *Gesamptschulen* – are required therefore to provide religious instruction on a denominational basis. Children, however, have the right to refuse to take religious instruction; in the case of children under fourteen that right is exercised by their parents, after that age by the children themselves. It is interesting that the obligation on schools to provide religious education is based both on religious and cultural considerations. As well as emphasizing the need to provide for the religious needs of the Catholic and Protestant denominations, the regulations point to the cultural importance of Christianity as part of the German national heritage and justify its status in the official curriculum on the same grounds as literature, art, music, history and other strands in their cultural inheritance. The syllabuses for religious education are approved by the relevant church authorities in all cases, as are the teachers appointed to provide it. The licence to teach religion – the *missio canonica* for Catholics and the *vocacio* for Protestants – is conferred in all cases by church authorities. In the Northern *Bündeslander*, where the population is predominantly Protestant, most schools are effectively Protestant schools; in areas with a high Catholic population, such as Bavaria and the Rhineland, most are effectively Catholic. Catholic schools, in many instances, have emblems and symbols of religion on display, such as crucifixes and statues, and liturgical ceremonies are held frequently as part of their normal routine. Schools with children from mixed religious denominations divide them into different groups for religious education.

A similar pattern of denominational education has emerged in the three education systems of Scandinavia, although, unlike the German model, all three are predominantly Protestant, with very limited provision for the education of cultural minorities. This can be illustrated by the contemporary system in Norway where there has been a continuous tradition of Protestant schools since the Reformation Statutes of 1539 decreed that church revenues should be used to found a school in every town, in which children were to be taught to read and write and to be given a thorough grounding in the scriptures. Parents were encouraged to teach young children at home until they commenced formal schooling at the age of seven and church deacons were required to provide religious instructions once a week in their churches for all the children of their parishes. It was not until the 1700s, largely through the influence of the Pietist movement, which insisted that confirmation be made compulsory for all children, that these ideals were eventually realized in Norway. With its highly homogeneous population, over 90 per cent of which is Lutheran, its schools have continued to promote the values and ideals of the Lutheran faith. A reform process initiated in the 1950s has created a totally comprehensive system of education in the country, but the provision of religious education remains compulsory at all levels and is still taught in accordance with Lutheran tradition. This is justified, as in Germany, on the basis of both religious and cultural considerations.

A programme of moral education is provided for those not willing to follow the official course of religious studies and there is some provision for the education for minorities, but the overwhelming majority of Norwegian schools have a strong Protestant ethos. This is illustrated in the recently issued documentation for the introduction of new curricula in Norwegian primary and secondary schools, which has an explicitly-declared Christian philosophy. 'Education shall be based on fundamental Christian and humanistic values', the main policy document begins. It continues: 'The Christian faith and tradition constitute a deep current in our history ... it has imprinted itself on the norms, world view, concepts and art of the people.' The prescription of religious education at all levels of schooling, from the pre-school to the upper secondary, together with the homogeneous cultural background of most of the children in the schools, effectively means that the comprehensive system in Norway is a denominational one, committed to the promotion of the values of the Lutheran tradition.

There are major problems inherent, however, in the denominational policies on schooling currently existing in both Norway and Germany. In both countries, minorities – Asian Catholics and Muslims in Norway, Turkish Muslims in Germany – are becoming increasingly aggrieved at the failure of the national systems to accommodate their cultural traditions. The problems exists on a far greater scale in Germany by virtue of the greater numbers involved and I will refer briefly to some recent developments there to clarify current thinking on the issue.

The first problem has been the accommodation of non-believers in the Christian schools. There has been strong resistance to the introduction of religious education in the schools of the new *Bundesländer* in the East, where schools had been thoroughly secularized in the years of communist rule and teachers competent to teach religion are scarce. The dual programme of religious and ethical education currently taught in the Western *Bundesländer* has been implemented, with considerable difficulty, in four of the Eastern *Bundesländer* but in the fifth, Brandenburg, religion has been absorbed into a 'life orientation and ethics programme' (LER) in which the religious content has been diluted. The churches, particularly the dominant Lutheran Church, in Brandenburg, are deeply unhappy with this programme and are insisting that the LER be accompanied by a full optional programme in religious education in all schools. This is currently being implemented but only with the greatest difficulty because of teacher shortages and the indifference of much of the populace to religious education.

The problem of cultural exclusion is more acutely felt by the several millions of Turkish immigrants who have settled as guest workers in Germany since the economic boom of the 1960s, and whose children attend State schools in large numbers because of the limited availability of Islamic schools. Recent research by Dana Simel on the problems of Islamic children in Bavarian schools has indicated widespread feelings of exclusion by these children in the overwhelmingly Catholic school system of the province. Regulations for the Bavarian *Volkschülen* state that schools 'are Christian schools in which the children will be instructed and raised according to the principles of the Christian confession'. It continues that 'the school supports the guardians in the religious upbringing of their children' and that 'school prayer, school worship and school devotions are outgrowths of this support'. Christian education is not limited to the religion lesson: Christian values are expected to pervade the general curriculum and the entire atmosphere of the school.

Simel's survey shows that only minimal provision is made in the schools of Bavaria for the religious needs of Islamic children and it is generally left to the parents and a small number of Koranic tuition centres, where after-school instruction is provided by voluntary organizations, to make amends for this.

Interviews with school principals revealed widespread fears that if instruction in the Islamic faith were provided in State schools it would have a strong fundamentalist character and would constitute a barrier to good relations between Christian and Muslim children. There is a widely held view, however, that understanding of other religions should be promoted in all schools, religious prejudice being seen as deriving mainly from ignorance of other faiths. Reforms currently in progress on religious education in various German *Bundesländer* do indicate a determination to promote greater levels of social concern, and a more sympathetic understanding of other religious traditions through the school programmes.

Significant progress in this direction has already been made in the official religious education courses in Norway. In addition to providing instruction in accordance with the confessional traditions of the Lutheran faith, the religious education programme gives substantial attention to the traditions of other religions as well. The whole problem does indicate the difficulty of providing adequately for minorities in a pluralistic society where the State school system is wholly organized on denominational lines.

In complete contrast to the situation currently obtaining in Germany and Scandinavia, State education in France is officially secular and denominational education is provided on a private basis entirely, although with substantial State support since 1959. Conflicts relating to church schools have a long ancestry in France, beginning with the Decree on the Secularization of Education in the Revolutionary Constitution of 1791, later to be reversed by Napoleon Bonaparte who restored to the Church the right to teach both in the *écoles primaires* and the newly founded *lycées*, in the Concordat of 1801. Religious and moral education were given a central role in the curricula both of the parochial schools and the *lycées* under the new and subsequent regimes. The position of the churches was strengthened further by the Falloux Law of 1850 and the conditions then created remained more or less in force, until the Ferry Reforms of 1870 led to the creation of a national system of education, in which the teaching of religion was prohibited in all State-funded schools. The law of 1902, which imposed even greater restrictions on the work of the religious teaching orders, such as the De La Salle Brothers, further widened the rift between Church and State. Apart from some minor concessions to the churches in the years of the Vichy regime, and some further small concessions (mainly allowing scholarships to be tenable in private schools) in 1951, there was no State support for religious education until the de Gaulle administration of the late 1950s.

In 1959 de Gaulle's education minister, Michel Debré, introduced the 'contract by association', by virtue of which church-run schools were eligible for State grants, on condition that they taught the official curriculum, that religious instruction was given outside school hours, and that their teaching appointments were subject to sanction by State authorities. He also introduced the 'simple contract' according to which schools received a proportion of their maintenance costs, together with teachers' salaries, without having to seek State sanction for teaching appointments. Schools were free to charge fees to pay for their capital expenditure and to cover the shortfall between recurrent expenditure and State subventions. By the 1970s one-seventh of all French children (numbering 1.7 million) were attending State-funded private schools, about 95 per cent of which were under the control of the Catholic

Church. Their position had been improved by the Pompidou administration, which extended the benefits of the 'contract by association' to schools formerly under the simple contract arrangement in 1970, thus greatly strengthening their autonomy while also improving their financial circumstances.

All this changed dramatically with the election of the socialist candidate, Francois Mitterrand, to the presidency in 1981. In the election campaign Mitterrand promised to create a 'unified and secular system of education', clearly intimating a policy of nationalizing private schools. After the election Mitterrand considerably diluted his election promises, but his minister for education still put forward proposals that would have greatly increased State control over church schools. These involved significant controls by local authorities over the funding of private schools and the full integration of teachers in private schools into the national teaching service. The storm of protest that ensued – demonstrations attracted crowds of one million in Paris and over 800,000 in Bordeaux – left the government in no doubt that the majority of the electorate, despite voting socialist in 1981, still wanted private schools to retain their autonomy.

A survey showed that 71 per cent of parents supported the private sector's right to retain its independence and to its continued subsidization by the State. By then there were 11,000 private schools, over 95 per cent of them Catholic, staffed by 15,000 teachers and serving the needs of two million children. The government capitulated and a modified arrangement was negotiated with the private sector, virtually guaranteeing their rights to run their schools with minimal State interference. A number of practical measures were introduced, giving local authorities the right to be consulted on teaching appointments and introducing some limited budgetary controls, but nothing like the high level of State intervention and the introduction of civil servant status for all teachers, envisaged by Mitterrand and his ministers. In July 1984 *Le Monde* reported that the government had been 'ulcerated' by the experience and concluded that France had 'witnessed a far-reaching movement in society which went far beyond the row over schools'.

Ultimately, the justification for denominational education derives from fundamental rights of conscience, and the rights of parents to have their children educated in accordance with their own religious convictions, and these rights, when claimed by substantial numbers in any society, must be guaranteed in the name of democracy. This principle was tested fully in the events I have described. In recent years a French minister for education, François Bayrou, sought to further improve the financing of private schools, by giving them the same access to local-authority funding as State schools, but this has been resisted successfully by various interests within the education system. It does nevertheless illustrate the changed climate of public policy on denominational education that has resulted from the events of the early 1980s. There remains, however, a major issue currently of great concern in the private sector in France. Because of their reliance on private funding for all of their capital and some of their recurrent expenditure, Catholic schools have usually charged substantial fees, particularly in the second-level sector. This has resulted in a high degree of social elitism, many of the schools being prestigious and much sought after by socially ambitious parents.

Surveys in the 1980s suggested that much of the support for private schools was motivated by considerations such as these rather than concern for religious freedom. A leading figure in contemporary Catholic education there, Fr Max Cloupet, has recently spoken of the problem of social exclusion in the private sector and sees the need for Catholic schools to extend their activities in the future into the more disadvantaged sectors of French society. That concern is one that is held by many in denominational education at the moment and reaches far beyond the conditions existing in Catholic education in France.

All five systems I have described will serve to illuminate different aspects of the same theme. The evidence of contemporary practice in each of these systems, together with the large body of research that can be drawn on for an evaluation of the work of the schools in each instance, point to three main issues, each of which bears directly on the role of denominational schools in a pluralist society. The first, quite simply, concerns the contribution of denominational schools to the common good of society as a whole or, to put it more plainly, the value of their work when judged purely in terms of education-related criteria. In the current climate of school effectiveness, much research has been focused on the work of denominational schools, most of it with highly favourable results in terms of their academic excellence, efficient management of educational resources, attention to individual needs, sound disciplinary procedures, provision of pastoral and counselling services, liaison between home and school, the career advancement of their pupils, and other such considerations. Given the fact that denominational schools are part of the State systems of education in Germany and Scandinavia, the quality of the education they provide is clearly monitored through the official agencies of evaluation in those countries and is considered generally effective in terms of their national norms.

The research of Coleman, Hoffer and Kilgore, Greeley and Rossi, Bryk and Convey – to mention only the most notable – in the USA, and of Praetz, Parrington, Carpenter and Western, Fahy and Flynn in Australia, have all provided abundant and compelling evidence of the effectiveness of Catholic schools in those two countries. In many instances this evidence has been provided longitudinally over periods as long as thirty years. Similar findings have been reported on Catholic schools in France, most notably during the controversies of the early 1980s. I will not dwell on this issue at further length; I will simply confine myself to affirming the overwhelming evidence that current research provides on the worth of denominational schooling, in the various cases I have explored, when judged by the norms of basic educational accountability.

A second issue prominent in much of the research is the danger of social elitism in denominational schools. There are two main reasons for this. Firstly, as has been demonstrated from experience in France, denominational schools are frequently fee-paying, often needing this income to compensate for inadequate State funding, and this can exclude those from disadvantaged sectors of society who are unable to meet the costs involved. Secondly, denominational schools are frequently victims of their own success: their standards of academic excellence and their disciplined ethos frequently making entry to them highly competitive, and forcing them to operate selective admission policies to cope with the numbers seeking places. There is evidence, however, that plans are currently in progress in France to extend the Catholic school system into areas of poverty and deprivation. 'Our aim,' Fr Cloupet has said, 'is plurality not greater autonomy.' Research in Great Britain similarly suggests that the Church's mission to the poor is greatly endangered by the dominance of market forces (school leagues tables etc.) in British education and suggests that many schools, catering for deprived communities, are unable to survive in conditions where inequitable norms of scholastic performance are imposed.

Research evidence from the USA and Australia, however, indicates a very impressive record in catering for deprived minorities in Catholic schools. A study, for example, conducted in 1989, showed that black and Hispanic students, large numbers then disadvantaged, constituted 23 per cent of enrolments in US elementary schools and 22 per cent of those in its secondary schools. The study showed that these students generally displayed higher levels of academic attainment than their counterparts in public schools, their success being attributed to a number of factors – high academic expectations in the Catholic schools, strong community support and attention to individual needs.

An especially significant development in this context was a recommendation by John Chubb of the Brookings Institute, in a report that was critical of State-sponsored compensatory educational programmes, that church-run schools be used as models for the kind of institution most appropriate for serving the needs of at-risk pupils in the USA. He suggested school ethos as the decisive factor in alleviating disadvantage and saw this as being most effectively exemplified in schools under private control. It is ironic that schools, such as those in the US, that are dependent entirely on voluntary funding, should have so impressive a record in the provision for deprived minorities, although many commentators have pointed to the fact that they were founded originally for poor immigrants in the mid-nineteenth century and have long experience in providing education for the poorer sectors of their society. The findings of American studies on this issue are strongly parallelled in several Australian studies, most significantly in the longitudinal studies conducted by Flynn at the Australian Catholic University since the 1960s.

There is finally the question of how far denominational schools promote religious tolerance and multi-cultural consciousness amongst their pupils, an essential requirement in an age of pluralist democracy and one deeply bound up with the authenticity of their own Christian ideals. The great danger is that schools committed to a denominational ideal will promote religious exclusivity, or even divisiveness; equally, it has to be recognized that the strength of these schools comes from their denominational distinctiveness, their integration of all school activities around the goal of ethico-religious formation, and, most of all, their strong and caring community ethos. Research from the USA suggests that pupils in Catholic schools are less prejudiced in religious matters than those who attend public schools and similar findings are reported from Australian research. A leading Australian researcher points, however, to the growing ethnic and cultural diversity of Australian society, together with the relentless growth of secularist humanism there, and concludes that Australian Catholic schools in the future will have to redefine their aims to ensure that they are sufficiently encouraging intellectual openness and understanding of other cultural traditions.

If widely supported then much can be achieved in this sphere, through enlightened programmes in religious education. Simel, in her work on German schools, stresses the need to go beyond the goal of religious tolerance – an ideal perceived by many as having largely negative connotations – to genuine understanding of other traditions, both religious and non-religious, and she sees this as being achieved mainly through religious education. Such a process enables denominational schools to maintain their own religious identity while relating it to the conditions of social, cultural and religious pluralism in which they exist. Many writers on religious education have echoed this call for the promotion of greater interfaith understanding, but equally there is profound concern in many quarters that denominational schools, whether Catholic or Protestant, must not be absorbed into a multi-faith pluralism that will diminish and weaken their cultural distinctiveness, rendering them less effectual as schools, to say nothing of the effective promotion of their ethical and religious ideals.

DAN MURPHY was senior lecturer in the School of Education and a Fellow of TCD. His works include *Martin Buber's Philosophy of Education* (1988), *Tolstoy and Education* (1992) and *Comenius: A Critical Reassessment of his Life and Work* (1995). He was a long-time colleague of Val Rice, and died in 1998.

A History of Guidance and Counselling in Ireland: American and European Influences

MICHAEL O'ROURKE

> But I cannot deny my past to which myself is wed,
> The woven figure cannot undo its thread.
> Though yet her name keeps ringing like a bell
> In an underwater belfry.
> —Louis MacNeice

It was during the early 1900s that modern guidance and counselling in the United States had its first origins, when the progressivist education movement was at its zenith. John Dewey, in *Democracy and Education*, had suggested that pupils and teachers should plan together, that the child's personal and social environment should be enhanced, and that the developmental needs of each child should be nurtured and fostered.[1] Following Dewey's publication of *Democracy and Education*, the progressive education movement advocated that the school should cater for a variety of abilities and aptitudes, in a more positive and encouraging classroom environment. Such an educational philosophy of a holistic view of development with a caring, pastoral schooling environment, appealed greatly to many teachers, and established the first foundation stones of the guidance and counselling movement. Indeed, the ideas of Rousseau, Pestalozzi, Froebel, Jacques Maritain, Paul Tillich, Paulo Freire and John Dewey greatly influenced the early pioneers of modern education.[2] These intellectual giants extolled a view of a more pupil-centred education, which would cater for the academic, personal, spiritual and vocational needs of pupils. School counsellors were easily attracted to this new evolving philosophy of education.[3]

Vocational guidance movement and the influence of Frank Parsons

Near the end of a long career as a social reformer, Frank Parsons established a Vocations Bureau in Boston, in 1908, the purpose of which was to provide vocational guidance for out-of-school youths. Parsons believed that individuals must have dependable information about professions, and about themselves, in order to make good occupational choices.[4] He also considered that 'the role of the vocational counsellor was to make such information available and to help individuals comprehend and utilise it'.[5] By 1913, the National Vocational Guidance Association was organized and, in 1915, the first guidance journal, *Vocational Guidance*, was published. A new helping profession with the title of 'guidance and counselling' had been launched.

Mental health movement

There were several parallel movements, in the early part of the twentieth century, which ushered in what would become known as the mental health movement.[6] However, it was a publication in 1908, *A Mind That Found Itself*, which brought about major reforms in the treatment of mental illness, and would later encourage the introduction of health education programmes in schools. The author, Clifford Bears, was a former mental patient, and he focused the attention of an increasingly humanitarian public on the plight of the mentally ill. He states:

> A pen rather than a lance has been my weapon of offence and defence; for with its point I have felt sure that I should one day prick the civic conscience into a compassionate activity, and thus bring into a neglected field

earnest men and women who should act as champions for those afflicted thousands least able to fight for themselves.[7]

Sigmund Freud's psychoanalytic ideas were becoming significant in the treatment of mental health problems and in mental health studies. William James, Adolf Meyer and other psychologists were instrumental in launching the mental hygiene movement, to educate the public about psychiatric illness and its treatment. School guidance counsellors were now at the forefront of implementing health education programmes in elementary and second-level schools.

Psychometric testing

The introduction and development of standardized psychometric tests was to have a major impact on the growth of the guidance movement. In 1905 the French psychologist, Alfred Binet, and his colleague, Theodore Simon, developed a scale to measure mental ability, in order to help the school system in Paris to classify students for educational instruction.

> Binet's scale popularised the idea of using psychometrics to solve practical problems and was also the forerunner of modern day intelligence testing ... Psychometrics offered school guidance not only the tools for assessment but also corresponding respectability because the tools seemed so precise and scientific. Psychometrics emphasized objectivity, individual differences, prediction, classification and placement.[8]

During World War One, the armed forces developed the alpha test, the beta test and other psychometric techniques, which were used in high schools. The success of the military use of tests popularized the idea of using group tests in education.

Space exploration

The guidance movement received a further impetus from the launch of the first Russian satellite, Sputnik 1. Americans were alarmed by this major scientific accomplishment, as they perceived a Russian dominance in science and technology. Politicians responded by introducing the National Defence Education Act of 1958. This NDEA law provided federal funds for training guidance counsellors and for the enhancement of school counselling programmes. There was now a perceived desire to identify academically trained students, and guide them into strategic careers in science and engineering. Fears of Russian educational superiority, after the launch of Sputnik 1, represented the lift-off of the American school guidance and counselling movement. Within six years of the introduction of the NDEA, the number of full-time, high-school guidance counsellors had increased from 12,000 to 30,000 (one for every 510 students).

Developments in counselling psychology

The idea of psychoanalysis held a special attraction for Americans, but for it to become assimilated into the culture required an Americanization of Freud's thinking. John McLeod suggests:

> There emerged in the 1950s a series of writers who reinterpreted Freud in terms of their own cultural values. Foremost among these were Carl Rogers, Eric Berne, Albert Ellis, Aaron Beck and Abraham Maslow. Many of the European analysts who went to the US, such as Erikson and Fromm, were also prominent in reframing psychoanalysis from a wider social and cultural perspective, thus making it more acceptable to an American clientele.[9]

The ideas of psychoanalysis resonated with American society because the American Dream insisted that all people could better themselves, and emphasized the pursuit of personal happiness of the individual as a legitimate aim in life. Indeed, counselling and psychotherapy offered a fundamental radical method of self-improvement. American society demonstrated a much greater degree of social mobility.[10] McLeod considered that 'People were likely to live, work and marry outside their original neighbourhood, town, social class or ethnic group. There were therefore many individuals who had problems in forming satisfactory relationships, or having a secure sense of personal identity.'[11] There was now a greater need for vocational guidance and personal counselling. Numerous visits, by Sigmund Freud, C.J. Jung and Alfred Adler, to the United States gave a powerful impetus to the new science of counselling psychology.

Person-centred therapy and Carl Rogers

With the emergence of a school guidance profession, between the 1930s and the 1950s, the key emphasis was on vocational guidance. Early guidance counsellors had the following responsibilities: vocational guidance, psychometric testing, subject choice and class selection, administrative responsibilities, attendance and follow-up, consultation with teachers and parents. However, from the 1950s onwards, Carl Rogers and his model of person-centred therapy was having an impact on education and counselling. Rogers' view of the client as an equal, and his positive view of the individual's potential, harmonized more with an American way of life that was positive in outlook than did the more pessimistic, deterministic Freudian psychoanalysis. Rogers even suggested that the pupil or client assumed responsibility for solving his or her problems in this radical client-centred and non-directive approach – a revolutionary departure from the directive, counsellor-centred model of an earlier era in American history. Directive and non-directive approaches each had proponents, but the new emphasis represented merely a psychological shift, from a 'tradition-centred' society to a more open 'inner-directed' way of life. 'If I keep from imposing upon people they become themselves' was a favourite Rogerian comment. This person-centred approach to life and decision-making was very much in harmony with this psychological shift of a changing America, in terms of social and cultural mobility.

In the school guidance and counselling movement, the impact of Carl Rogers resulted in

> the overnight replacement of testing by counselling as the key guidance function. In turn, counselling would rise to such eminence in the next few years that it would compete and contend with guidance in regard to the use of the counsellor's time and the overall purpose of counselling and guidance. What began as an adjunct tool of guidance would now raise a challenge for ascendancy in its own right.[12]

Rogerian person-centred therapy and counselling influenced and dominated the field of counselling, both in schools and clinics, throughout the 1960s and 1970s. It was welcomed as an alternative model to the directive, patriarchal, authoritarian approaches in schools.

However, there were criticisms of this model, and many educationalists called for a more proactive approach – the emphasis on the therapeutic relationship was recognized as valuable but not sufficient for all occasions. J.M. Whittner called for a more preventionist, interventionist and developmental approach to school guidance and counselling. He states: 'Very little attention was being given to the co-equal emphasis on prevention and on environmental intervention techniques so desperately needed in schools. Little attention was being given to counsellor education programmes on the consulting and the co-ordinating roles needed by effective developmental school counsellors.'[13] Whittner's advocacy for a more proactive developmental guidance approach came at a time when others were voicing similar views. It was a momentum that would bring significant change to an emerging model of guidance and counselling in the period from the 1970s to the present.

Developmental guidance: prevention to diagnosis to intervention

Gilbert Wrenn, in his highly acclaimed 1962 book, *The Counsellor in a Changing World*, chided guidance counsellors for having allowed themselves to become too narrowly focused on one-to-one counselling and the needs of the few. He recommended a more expansive approach, and encouraged school counsellors to develop appropriate school guidance curricula and proactive programming.[14] James Conant, in *The American High School Today* (1959), argued that all high-school students should have access to a school counsellor.[15] Likewise, Don Dinkmeyer, a distinguished Adlerian psychologist and educationalist, advocated a more developmental approach to guidance and counselling. This approach was very much in line with Adlerian principles in individual educational psychology.

The American School Counsellor Association (ASCA) attempted to respond to the challenges through *School Counselling 2000* and suggested a more integrationist approach:

> School counsellors should work directly with students, teachers, community members, and employers collaboratively in order to develop policies and programmes that address the challenging problems that have been

widely identified ... This more integrationist approach will find a balance between designing and delivering programmes in a curricular fashion that will enhance personal, social and educational problems. To do so, counsellors will work with teachers to offer programmes cooperatively and counsel students as effectively as possible individually and in groups but over a limited number of sessions. Consulting, coordinating and managing skills are needed in order to bring it together successfully.[16]

This more balanced approach, combining careful intervention and prevention, promised a greater degree of success than either approach alone. This particular model of a comprehensive, developmental approach to school counselling has been receiving considerable support from within and from outside the profession over the past decade. The current US guidance and counselling model, 2002, encompasses:

Personal counselling interventions.
Curriculum guidance programming.
Vocational guidance, assessment, testing.
Information systems, acquiring, storing, disseminating information.
Referral and co-ordination.
Consultation with students, parents, teachers.
Accountability, evaluation and audit.
Transition enhancement, managing transitions from home to school, school to school and from school to work.
Preventionist and interventionist counselling.

The approach of the American guidance and counselling model, in the early decades of the twentieth century, was based more on a Rogerian, person-centred focus, with an emphasis on one-to-one counselling. However, criticisms of this approach resulted in a more developmental proactive style of guidance and counselling, which would achieve greater results for a greater number of pupils. Prevention and intervention were highlighted, with the guidance counsellor cast in the role of consultant to parents, teachers, pupils and outside agencies. This more balanced approach seems appropriate for meeting the current and future developmental needs of a more diverse student population.

Indeed, a succinct description of this more balanced philosophy is presented in the following school's guidance programme from Wake County, North Carolina, which states:

> Schools are a microcosm of society reflecting a culture characterised by diversity, complexity, and changing values in the home, school, and community. Today's society affects our students in ways that can impact achievement ... Our school system supports a developmental, balanced approach to school guidance and counselling. Classroom guidance, small group and individual counselling, parent involvement, and other activities continue to be the focus of the plan. In addition, current needs may dictate that school counsellors respond in new roles such as staff developer, or case manager. School counsellors will assess the needs of the school, will create and implement a balanced guidance programme that address those needs, and will continuously evaluate the outcomes.[17]

European guidance dimensions

In many European countries, the emphasis is very much on educational and career guidance. This tradition resulted from an unease with the adaptation of a US individual counsellor model, which was first voiced by ministers of education at a European Community Meeting in 1976. Guidance provision was formally identified as a major need in secondary schools in 1976, and over the years two main models emerged for European secondary schools.

The first is that guidance may be carried out by mainstream teachers, who combine their guidance work with normal subject teaching, and may or may not have had some specialist training.[17] This approach is often based on a 'home room' or 'tutor group' arrangement, in which a teacher is responsible for the welfare and educational guidance of a particular group of pupils, for the whole school year and, sometimes, throughout their school career. Normally, these home-room tutors represent the school's first-line guidance system.[18] Austria, Denmark, Norway and Finland are examples of countries using this approach. It should be noted that only in Finland is specialist training compulsory before a teacher is allowed to offer educational and career guidance in school.

The second model is to have specialist counsellors, often with a psychological background, based in schools. Normally they do not teach, except in those schools or systems in which educational and career guidance is part of the compulsory curriculum, but they may organize workshops and programmes relating to various aspects of personal development, including educational guidance and preparation for the world of work.[19]

In many European countries, responsibility for career guidance is divided between the ministry of education and the ministry of labour, or employment agencies, both public and private. The concept of a school-based guidance counsellor is alien to the French; there are approximately 4500 counsellors, who work in 518 Centres for Information and Guidance (CIOs) throughout France. Counsellors are generally trained psychologists, who specialize in guidance psychology. They guard their independence fiercely, and divide their time between working in their offices and visiting two or three schools. Guidance counsellors act as technical advisers to the principal and staff, and also work as counsellors for pupils.

In Britain, the school guidance and counselling service was not to blossom, as had been expected by the counsellors of the early and mid-1970s. This was due to changes inside and outside the school, within the theory and practice of counselling itself, and to the economic and political shifts that took place during that period.[21] Within the schools, there was a movement away from specialist counselling, to a system where more and more teachers were valuing and using counselling skills.[22] The European Community Action Programme of 1985 advised that guidance and counselling should not be a separate activity, but an integral part of the curriculum.[23] There also followed a shift in emphasis from personal counselling to educational and vocational counselling.[24] In their recommendations, the Committee of Enquiry into Discipline in Schools, set up in 1988 under the chairmanship of Lord Elton, urged every school 'to develop a "whole school behaviour policy" involving, and supported by, everyone directly involved with the school itself'.[25] According to Richard Hooper and Peter Lang, the main reasons for this shift were the decrease in full-time counsellor posts, and the closing of a number of full-time counselling courses, due to lack of public funding.[26]

Outside the school, there were heated public debates regarding the aims and methods of education. The rise of Thatcherism in the 1980s saw the re-emergence of 'simplistic views about the preferability of traditional methods, of hard work and high standards, and of "tough-minded" attitudes to the problems and needs of young people. In these circumstances, the growing conflict between counselling and establishment values might seem inevitable.'[27] Importance was attached to the education of students with skills suited to the perceived needs of industry.[28] An effect of the economic recession of the 1980s was severe cutbacks on what were considered to be non-essential services within education, such as remedial education, guidance and counselling.

By 1985, less than 10 per cent of schools in England and Wales employed a counsellor.[29] Of the 351 counsellors who had been working in the English and Welsh school system in 1977, only 90 remained in 1987.[30] By 1993 school counsellors seemed to have come and gone.[31] What is often referred to as counselling in the 1990s may instead be 'crisis conversations, general advice-giving, career interviews, informal pupil-teacher discussions or discipline-linked interviews'.[32] Fewer and fewer British schools are now employing counsellors, and although teachers are increasingly committed to the idea of counselling, they sometimes do not have the time to offer more than informal counselling during lunch hour.[33]

Training programmes

The qualifications of guidance counsellors vary a great deal from country to country, and within countries too. In Finland, guidance staff are highly qualified by international standards. Student counsellors are normally experienced and fully trained teachers who are selected for a full-time year of specialist training. Indeed, this writer is of the view that the Finnish model of school counsellor is very similar to the Irish model and represents one of the most advanced guidance and counselling systems in Europe. Furthermore, it is cross-curricular and integrationist with the involvement of other teachers and community services.

A more coherent European model needed

A European Commission report in 1994, *Educational and Vocational Guidance in the European Community*, identified nine different activities for careers education. These included:

> Information; subject options; careers and courses; job vacancies.
> Assessment and diagnostic judgments.
> Advice, suggestion, guidance.
> Personal counselling.
> Work experience, work shadowing.
> Placement, job entry.
> Advocacy and negotiating directly with institutions.
> Feedback, from employers and individuals on courses.
> Follow-up.

Despite the ideals outlined in this report, the key characteristic of most European guidance systems is a plethora of delivery mechanisms.

The OECD report of 1996, *Mapping the Future: Young People and Career Guidance*, could be written for more recent times. It stated:

> The key characteristic of most national guidance systems is incoherence, gaps and unnecessary overlap – or even a lack of any real system at all. More effective planning and liaison are without doubt part of the solution, but this can be difficult in some countries because of the different cultures of educational institutions and those working in the labour market.[34]

The report considers that this incoherency in guidance systems results in a weak professional identity, which perhaps explains why recognition of the importance of educational and career guidance has been so long in coming.[35] Similarly, career counsellors are not well integrated with the counselling psychotherapy profession, which prefers to focus on therapeutic issues and intense one-to-one counselling.[35] 'So career guidance too often finds itself in the wilderness, seen neither as a bona fide educational activity, nor as "real" counselling and lacking status in either field'.[37]

Indeed, it is interesting to note that similar observations are made by Richard Sweet, in the 2004 OECD report, *Career Guidance and Public Policy: Bridging the Gap*.[38] He states:

Many of the problems that emerged during the review are general themes. These include poor co-ordination of services across portfolios and weak instruments for steering services, including lack of adequate evidence; poor monitoring of inputs and outcomes and weak accountability mechanisms; relatively old fashioned delivery methods and training and qualification arrangements that are ill-adapted to support more innovative delivery systems; large gaps in provision (for example limited career education in schools and weaknesses in career information).[39]

Professor Ronald Sultana, of the University of Malta, makes observations very similar to Richard Sweet's. He calls for a more coherent system of guidance services, and he had this to say of the OECD report of 2004:

> In particular, the research data indicates that while career guidance increasingly features on the agenda of many European governments, with goals for services being reframed in the light of lifelong learning policies, there are a number of serious weaknesses that need attending to. Access, for instance, tends to be largely limited to students and the unemployed. The focus is all too often on immediate decisions, failing to take into account lifelong learning and career development. Training for service providers tends to be limited and inappropriate, given the range of client needs that has to be catered for. There is often a lack of cross-sectoral collaboration between different ministries, and with stakeholders. The evidence base is too weak to provide policy makers with useful data on outcomes, costs and benefits. Most significantly, few European countries have developed a coherent system of guidance services that caters for the needs of the citizen in a holistic manner, and which targets career-related concerns across the life cycle. With career guidance taking increasingly varied and disparate forms, there is a need within countries for stronger mechanisms to articulate a vision and develop a strategy for delivering services more effectively.[40]

The OECD report of 2004 is an outstanding study and review of guidance services, which covers twenty-nine European countries, and it represents one of the most extensive datasets ever collected on guidance across Europe. It provides essential information that will help policy-makers and practitioners to benchmark their own systems in relation to those of others for years to come.

Guidance and counselling in Ireland: a retrospective, 1960–2000

Investment in Education, the OECD report of 1966, argued that a career-guidance service was needed in all secondary schools in Ireland and stated: 'We believe that the establishment of adequate career guidance is necessary in all branches of the education system.'[41] The report was followed by the momentous decision to introduce free secondary-school education in September 1967. The subsequent influx of 18,000 extra pupils, from different backgrounds, added a new momentum to the guidance and counselling movement in Ireland, and represented a decisive factor in the emergence of the guidance and counselling profession. Further momentous developments in the period 1965–7 occurred with the establishment of comprehensive and community schools; regional technical colleges were established; a psychological service was introduced by the Department of Education and Science; and the City of Dublin Vocational Education Committee expanded its vocational guidance service for schools under its authority by appointing a psychologist to run its service.

A huge volume of educational articles on the subject of guidance and counselling resulted from this new awareness of its importance. Desmond Swan, Educational Psychology Department, UCD, introduced an article on the subject in the May 1968 issue of *The Secondary Teacher* as follows:

> When there was but one road around Ireland, the choice of routes could have presented no great difficulty to the traveller – he either went right or left. Things have changed since then ... it makes no sense to set out on a journey without a guide or, at least, a sufficient knowledge of the route and reliable estimate of our chances of ever reaching our destination.[42]

Donald Akenson's apt comments best articulated the great social, educational and economic changes that Ireland was undergoing in the 1960s and 1970s. Akenson observed that: 'Undeniably, early in the 1960s, the Republic's politicians discovered education. Almost overnight schools were changed from legislative orphans to a topic of continual public interest and debate. The most important innovations came in the financing of schools, the introduction of free post-primary education and the creation of new forms of post-primary institutions.'[43]

A major international conference on counselling and vocational guidance was held at The Hague in 1970. Its co-ordinator, Professor E.F. O'Doherty, Department of Psychology, UCD, spoke of the need for counselling services, to address what he called 'the cultural conflict' between young and old.[44] O'Doherty was of the view that the cultural conflict was the result of a changing value system by which the new generation lived. He considered: 'The transitory values of the adult generation have their roots in nineteenth-century thinking, and have consisted in idolising things such as security, respectability, conformity, possessions, whereas the values of the younger generation seem much more to enhance ideas of liberty, exploration, insecurity, non-conformity, solidarity with one another, and honesty.'[45] O'Doherty's socio-psychological analysis of cultural change in the Ireland of the late 1970s and early 1970s represented a resounding endorsement of the felt need for counselling services alongside vocational guidance.

The training of guidance counsellors

Perhaps the most significant event, in the development of guidance services in Irish schools, was the introduction of the first full-time, one-year postgraduate course in guidance and counselling at UCD. The secondary teachers' journal, Astir, published a series of articles by Professor Desmond Swan on guidance and career choice in education. Swan captured the essence of the skills of the guidance counsellor, which remain timeless in providing a succinct role definition. He stated:

> The guidance counsellor's role demands a high degree of skill in dealing face-to-face with young people; a thorough knowledge of the psychology of adolescence in particular ... experience in interviewing young people is also indispensable; the dynamics of this situation are indeed subtle; so subtle that the amateur is likely to miss the whole point and not to realize it. When to intervene, when to remain silent, what to watch for that may be of significance: nothing less than the whole structure of the developing personality is involved, the bravado, the repressions, the unperceived self-deceptions, which we all use.[46]

Professor Swan argued the case for 'the maturely qualified counsellor' who would be supported by an appropriate system of 'class teachers' and 'careers teachers'. An essential element was the ability of the counsellor to respond to individual human difference. In 1968, the Institute of Guidance Counsellors (IGC) was established, by early graduates of the UCD course and the concept of 'career guidance and counselling' was increasingly promoted.[47]

Further courses of full-time postgraduate training were established in the 1970s. The Catholic bishops initiated a full-time course at the Mater Dei Institute in Dublin in 1972, and it was recognized by the Department of Education. The course was directed by a Carmelite priest and provided schools with more than a hundred guidance counsellors, 1972–6, when the absence of government grant-in-aid forced its cessation.[48] TCD offered a guidance and counselling psychology specialization from 1977, with a master's qualification. The MEd degree in guidance and counselling has been training guidance counsellors from 1977 to the present time. As a consequence of these postgraduate training programmes, by 1979 guidance counsellors were employed in about 50 per cent of Irish secondary schools. University College Cork introduced its one-year full-time course in 1981, with a major emphasis on counselling in the second-level schools.

It is interesting to note that a major boost to the training of guidance counsellors in Ireland emanated from a report published in December 1977 by the Irish Institute of Training Managers (IITM), and the Institute of Personnel Management (IPM). This report from the private sector was, indeed, timely and far-seeing. Dr Eileen Doyle states:

> Perhaps because the report was the work of the private employer sector the members were conscious of the grave problems facing so many young people in the transition from school to adult and working life. Periods of work experience were therefore recommended and employers were challenged to collaborate generously in such provision. The wisdom of designing school curricula in such a way that students would experience close links between 'general education and vocational training' was stressed. What was needed was a system of 'continuing educational and vocational guidance involving the participation of parents, teachers and community' and a more enlightened approach to the initial and continuing training of teachers.[49]

Dr Doyle considers that the report was far ahead of its time, in distinguishing between 'guidance' and 'counselling' and in promoting equal educational opportunities for girls and for students and adults with disability of any kind.[50] 'At the time there were approximately 831,000 young people in the education system and the working party estimated that an additional 600 guidance counsellors were needed to ensure that 150,000 boys and 142,000 girls were served. The IITM was the first group to advocate the appointment of a second counsellor for schools of 500 students.'[51]

Under siege in the eighties

During the 1970s, psychometric tests, such as the differential aptitude tests (DATs), were standardized for the Irish population, and both intelligence tests and aptitude tests were administered extensively. Psychometric testing became a very useful tool in the armoury of the newly emerging professional. Indeed, the role of the guidance counsellor continued to expand to include 'any area of responsibility which is not immediately claimed by others of the school staff'.[52] Such responsibilities included liaison with parents, arranging visits to industries, dealing with behavioural difficulties and co-ordinating the schools pastoral care service. In a major speech in 1979 Turlough O'Connor, senior psychologist in the Department of Education and Science, called for a team approach to pupil guidance and suggested that the 'guidance counsellor must come out of the closet' and become a member of a team of teachers involved in various aspects of the guidance programme. The American one-to-one counselling model was now under scrutiny and O'Connor was calling for a more integrationist, preventionist, and developmental approach.

However, it was in the 1980s that the guidance and counselling service came under closer scrutiny and a 1981 series of articles by *Irish Times* journalist Christina Murphy no doubt helped to bring the guidance counsellor out of the shadows, and into relatively high visibility as a professional person in his or her own right. Murphy wrote:

> I have to say that guidance teachers do manage to convey to me, an outsider, an aura of separateness, of wanting to distance themselves from other teachers and of being somewhat too conscious of emphasising their

special status. I feel there is a tendency for subject teachers, and school management, to be somewhat wary of the role of the guidance teacher, and that any suggestion of elitism or separateness can only serve to flame this suspicion.[53]

In the early years of the guidance service, the Department of Education and Science was prepared to allow every school with 250 pupils to release a teacher to follow a course to become the guidance counsellor. However, with the worsening economy of the 1980s, the provision of guidance counsellors was greatly affected by the decision of Gemma Hussey, the minister for education in the 1983 coalition government, who instructed that only schools with more than 500 pupils would be entitled to an ex-quota guidance counsellor.[54] This was a catastrophic decision for the newly developing service, and the reduced resources were increasingly given to vocational guidance, with little time for personal and social problems. Smaller schools were greatly impacted and by 1987 there was only three, out of twenty-four, vocational schools that had a guidance counsellor on an ex-quota basis. With the economy beginning to improve in the late 1980s, the Department of Education (DES) appointed a committee to report on school guidance. This 1987 report provided incontrovertible quantitive evidence of the state of provision and its declining status.

From the late 1980s, the school guidance committee of the Department of Education and the Institute of Guidance Counsellors worked together to improve the provision of guidance to students in schools. In 1995 the new minister for education established the National Centre for Guidance in Education (NCGE), to assist the DES, educational institutions and guidance counsellors to develop the service as a support agency. The government budget of 1995 gave commitments to appoint extra psychologists, guidance counsellors and special-education teachers.

Encouraging times

In more recent years, a number of key developments have given new hope and strong support for a more expansive role for the school guidance and counselling service. The 1995 white paper on education, *Charting Our Education Future*, has given strong support for this trend, emphasizing 'a need for more emphasis on educational guidance and greater integration of the work of psychologists and teachers'.[55] Almost two years later, the 1997 report entitled *Principals' Perspectives of the Guidance Service in Post-primary Schools* was very complimentary of guidance counsellors in Irish second-level schools, but highlighted the main weakness of the current guidance system, which was its inability to respond to the increasing range of social and personal problems of the students.[56] To remedy this problem, principals called for a greater emphasis on counselling-skills training, earlier intervention within the school life of the child, systematic liaison with education, health and social services as well as a ratio of one guidance counsellor to 250 students.[57] The principals argued that a good case could be made for improved intervention, counselling and referral in order to deal with problems at an early stage thus saving money in the long term.[58]

Other encouraging developments in recent years include the establishment of more postgraduate training courses. In 1996 University College Maynooth (NUIM), announced the establishment of a one-year full-time higher national diploma in guidance and counselling and, in 1997, the University of Limerick offered the first two-year modular course in guidance and counselling. In 1998, this course was made available in two outreach centres, in conjunction with the Education Centre, Carrick-on-Shannon, and through the West Dublin Education Centre. Both outreach programmes were in response to teacher demand. The importance of this wider provision cannot be overstated, as it enables all teachers to qualify who wish to be considered for guidance and counselling appointments. All of the above courses are recognized fully by the DES.

Furthermore, in 2001, the DES introduced the first in-career development programme for the guidance counsellors of Ireland. This new MSc degree in educational guidance and counselling is provided by the Education Department, TCD, and is organized on a part-time modular basis over two years. Core modules include advanced counselling theory; micro-counselling skills; advanced counselling practicum; interculturalism and intercultural counselling; psychometrics in vocational guidance and administration; vocational guidance theory and practice; lifelong learning and lifespan developmental psychology; adult guidance; family systems therapy; grief and bereavement counselling; spirituality and counselling; research methodology and statistics.

Current and future provision in guidance and counselling

Of all the challenges to the professional identity of the guidance counsellor, keeping up to date with vocational guidance, psychometrics, counselling theory and practice, interculturalism and intercultural counselling, spirituality and counselling, information and communications technology must surely be a major challenge in 'cognisance of the signs of the times'. Trainers, at university level, are challenged to provide the most rigorous and advanced training possible. They pass the responsibility for keeping the torch of knowledge lit on to their students. Their students, in turn, being versatile and creative, make themselves valuable to their pupils and their pupils' parents by keeping the flame of self-renewal burning brightly in times of unprecedented change.

The activities and responsibilities that the modern guidance counsellor must address, in the Ireland of the twenty-first century, have recently been delineated in the publication of *Planning the School Guidance Programme* by the NCGE in 2004.[59] Guidance activities to assist students make choices include:

> Counselling – helping students to explore their thoughts and feelings, and the choices open to them; giving care and support to students learning to cope with the many aspects of growing up.
>
> Assessment – helping students to obtain a better self-understanding through the use of psychometric tests and other inventories.
>
> Information – providing students with objective and factual data on education and training opportunities, occupations, labour market information, entitlements etc.
>
> Advice – making suggestions based on the advisor's own knowledge and experience.
>
> Educational development programmes – facilitating the transfer of knowledge and skills relating to studying, examination performance, choices of subjects and levels.

Personal and social development programmes – facilitating the transfer of knowledge and skills relating to a student's personal and social development, self-awareness, decision-making and planning.

Referral – this includes two types of activity.
i) Referral of an individual student by the guidance counsellor to other Professionals outside of the school, e.g. The National Educational Psychological Service (NEPS);
ii) Referral of an individual student to the guidance counsellor by teachers, Board of Management, School Management and Parents.

Guidance activities to help students make transitions include:

Careers education/career transition programmes – enabling students to make transitions to further and higher education, training and employment.

Placement – work experience, work shadowing, and preparing students for employment.

Follow-up – following up former students regarding progression routes and destinations.

Other guidance activities to support the achievement of the aims of the school guidance programme include:

Consultation with parents, school staff and students.

Feedback – giving feedback to the board of management, school management and staff on the needs of individual students, groups and the school as an organization, and how the school guidance programme has supported students' choices and transitions.

Networking – establishing links with employers, relevant agencies and institutions to enhance guidance work with students.

Promoting change – assisting curriculum development in the school.

Managing, organizing and co-ordinating guidance activities into a coherent programme.

The NCGE programme document further states:

The school guidance programme is the specific set of learning experiences which a school provides in response to the guidance needs of its students. There are a number of principles that underpin the school guidance programme.[60]

The school guidance programme should:

Be accessible.
Recognize that guidance is a specialist area within education.
Recognize that guidance is a whole school concern.
Be impartial.
Be student-centred.
Be transparent.
Be balanced.
Be inclusive.
Be responsive.
Respect confidentiality in counselling and assessment activities.
Empower participants to take responsibility for their own development.
Promote equal opportunities.
Deploy and make full use of available resources.
Be reviewed on an ongoing basis.

Conclusion

Educational changes in Ireland have developed from economic, social and political influences within Ireland, and from trends and developments in Europe and the United States, which impact on local thinking. 'The Irish guidance and counselling service tends to be a compromise between the American model, which emphasizes personal counselling, and the European model, which has a narrower focus on the concept of career guidance,' states the 1993 report, *Counselling the Adolescent in a Changing Ireland*.[61] This compromise in the Irish system is well illustrated in the varying time devoted by different practitioners to the four tasks of career guidance, personal counselling, teaching and other activities.

The report includes a breakdown of the average percentage of time devoted weekly to each activity, based on a sample of 312 responses:[62]

Career guidance: 40 per cent
Personal counselling: 21 per cent
Classroom teaching: 28 per cent
Other activities: 8 per cent

The report considers: 'The picture that emerges is straightforward enough: career guidance is a task that must get done in every school; outside of that some personal counselling gets done if guidance counsellors do not have a sizeable teaching workload; where they do have a teaching workload very little counselling takes place.'[63]

Little has changed over the past decade. Indeed, management, students and parents expect that a good school will have a good careers' programme in operation; personal counselling, and having time for this important dimension, is seen as the icing on the cake! In any event, it is impossible to separate both roles. Students come to a counsellor to talk about subject choice, career choice, and university or technological institutes; inevitably, it emerges that the original problem was not the real one, and that there are other worries and concerns that require a therapeutic intervention. The role of career guidance and personal counselling cannot be separated, and the counselling dimension is a very important component, not alone in guidance but in teaching as well. Indeed, this writer is of the view that the roles of the good teacher and counsellor are synonymous and interchangeable. The ideal teacher is one who embodies the unity of both functions. Teaching and counselling are concerned with similar tasks. Nurturing relational capacities, empowering and building a positive assets search are key concerns in the daily duties of both teacher and counsellor. The distinguished Jewish philosopher, Martin Buber, emphasized that the teaching and counselling functions should indeed be integrated.[64] He finds it significant that he frequently treated the roles of teacher and therapist as interchangeable; several commentators have remarked on the closeness of these roles in his thinking on education and his ideal teacher was one who would personally exemplify that unity.[65]

Thus, whether as teacher, careers teacher or counsellor, the relationship in education is one of pure dialogue, and the key ingredients in that relationship must embody empathy, trust, acceptance, confirmation, respect and a caring concern for the well-being of each pupil. Teaching and counselling must be primarily based upon a psychology of optimism and hope. The distinguished psychiatrist, Irvin Yalom, reminds us that 'making the world a better place for others is surely a powerful source of meaning'.[66]

Whatever changes come in the role and function of the guidance counsellor, it is clear that what is being asked, whether of a personal counsellor or of a guidance teacher, is something of a real vocation. Anne Fletcher, in *Guidance in Scotland*, best summarizes the significance of that important role:

> Guidance I believe has the greatest scope within itself to bridge the gap between school and society; it may also bridge gaps within school, gaps between declared aims and pursued aims; between guidance staff and non-guidance staff; between subject-centred and pupil-centred approaches; between rules and procedures designed for the institution and those designed for people, so guidance might evolve both as an agent for change and as an agent for reconciliation. Whatever the programme formats and activities, counselling and guidance in schools will continue to require a great deal of guiding, listening and conforming, a considerable amount of counselling, and an abundance of caring ... and if you care, you will perpetuate the grandest tradition of the counselling profession, you will be relevant, and you will understand the uniqueness of your clients and their environments.[67]

NOTES

1. John Dewey, *Democracy and Education* (London 1916), p. 50.
2. Robert Gibson and Robert Higgins, *Techniques of Guidance: An Approach to Pupil Analysis* (Chicago 1966), p. 4.
3. Alfred Adler, *Superiority and Social Interest*, eds, Heinz Ansbacher and Rowena Ansbacher (London 1965), p. 321.
4. Stanley Baker, *School Counselling for the Twenty-First Century* (New Jersey 1996), p. 5.
5. Ibid.
6. Ibid.
7. Clifford Beers, *A Mind That Found Itself* (New York 1908), p. 78.
8. Baker, *School Counselling*, pp. 4–5.
9. John McLeod, *An Introduction To Counselling* (Milton Keynes 1998), p. 19.
10. Ibid.
11. Ibid.
12. R.F. Aubrey, 'Historical development of guidance and counselling and implications for the future', *Personnel & Guidance Journal* (February 1977), 292.
13. J.W. Whittner, *Managing Your School Counselling Programme* (Minneapolis 1993), p. 3.

14. Gilbert Wrenn, *The Counsellor in a Changing World* (Washington DC 1962), p. 46.
15. James Conant, *The American High School Today* (New York 1959), p. 72.
16. Baker, *School Counselling*, pp. 12–13.
17. *Ibid.* p. 2.
18. OECD report, *Mapping the Future: Young People and Career Guidance* (Paris 1996), p. 20.
19. *Ibid.*
20. *Ibid.* p. 21.
21. Patrick Hughes, 'Guidance and counselling in schools', *British Journal of Guidance and Counselling*, 13, 1 (January 1985), 13.
22. Judith Maybe and Bernice Sorensen, *Counselling for Young People* (Buckingham 1995), p. 10.
23. *Ibid.*
24. *Ibid.*
25. Jenny Mosley, *Turn Your School Around* (Wisbech 1993).
26. R. Hooper and P. Lang, 'Counselling revisited' in *Pastoral Care*, 6, 2 (1988), 28.
27. Hughes, 'Guidance and counselling', 10.
28. Maybe and Sorensen, *Counselling for Young People*, p. 11.
29. Hughes, 'Guidance and counselling', 18.
30. Maybe and Sorensen, *Counselling for Young People*, p. 10.
31. Keith Bovair and Colleen McLaughlin, *Counselling in Schools: A Reader* (London 1993), p. 15.
32. Maybe and Sorensen, *Counselling for Young People*, p. 13.
33. *Ibid.* p. 48.
34. OECD report, *Mapping the Future*, p. 19.
35. *Ibid.* p. 23.
36. *Ibid.*
37. *Ibid.*
38. OECD report, *Career Guidance and Public Policy: Bridging the Gap* (Paris 2004), p. 46.
39. *Ibid.*
40. Professor Ronald Sultano, 'Lifelong guidance: harmonising policy and practice' (unpublished proceedings of a conference on Lifelong Guidance held in Dublin, 30 April 2004).
41. OECD report, *Investment in Education* (Paris 1966), p. 128.
42. Desmond Swan, 'Education and after: a short guide to guidance in education and career choice', *The Secondary Teacher* (May 1969), 6.
43. Donald Akenson, *The Irish Education Experiment* (Dublin 1970), p. 54.
44. National Advisory Council on Education, *Report on Guidance and Counselling in School* (Dublin 1975), p. 11.

45. Ibid.
46. Eileen Doyle, 'Career guidance and counselling: historical perspective', *Institute of Guidance Counsellors Journal*, 25 (Spring 2001), 7–8.
47. Ibid.
48. Ibid.
49. Ibid.
50. Ibid.
51. Ibid.
52. Victor J. Drapala, *Guidance and Counselling Around the World* (Washington DC 1979), p. 118.
53. Christina Murphy, 'Guidance and counselling', *The Irish Times* (14 February 1981).
54. Department of Education, Circular 31/83 (Dublin 1983).
55. White Paper on Education, *Charting Our Education Future* (Dublin 1995), p. 96.
56. National Centre for Guidance in Education, *Principals' Perspectives of the Guidance Service in Post-Primary Schools: Summary Report* (Dublin 1997), p. 16.
57. Ibid. p. 22.
58. Ibid. p. 17.
59. National Centre for Guidance in Education, *Planning the School Guidance Programme* (Dublin 2004), p. 12.
60. Ibid. p. 13.
61. Liam Ryan, *Counselling the Adolescent in a Changing Dublin: National Survey of Second-level Schools in Ireland* (Dublin 1993), p. 63.
62. Ibid.
63. Ibid.
64. Daniel Murphy, *Martin Buber's Philosophy of Education* (Dublin 1988), p. 100.
65. Maurice Friedman, *Martin Buber: The Life of Dialogue* (London 2002), p. 21.
66. Irvin Yalom, *The Gift of Therapy* (London 2001), p. 37.
67. Anne Fletcher, *Guidance in Schools: The Development and Practice of Guidance and Counselling in Scottish Secondary Schools* (Aberdeen 1980), p. 70.

MICHAEL O'ROURKE is course co-ordinator of the MEd degree in educational guidance and counselling. His forthcoming publication is *Multiculturalism as Illuminated in Modern Irish Literature*. He was a student and long-time colleague of Val Rice.

From Psychotherapy to Pedagogy: A Holistic Journey Towards Self-Autonomy

MICHAEL O'SHEA

Introduction

While the author proposes that each individual is essentially unique and self-governing, individuals may feel impeded in their efforts to live as free, self-directing beings. Life situations, multiple options, external factors and psychological barriers may result in resistence to progress. The author proposes to explore the value of psychotherapy in identifying those issues that impede one's capacity to live a satisfying and more fully functional life. Furthermore, through the psychotherapeutic process an individual may identify those self-defeating contributory factors, which almost debilitate his/her efforts to free himself/herself from some pre-determined role or identity. This author is of the view that, within the therapeutic process, an individual may establish some desired life changes he/she might like to effect. A blueprint, or envisaged life plan, may emanate from such a journey of self-exploration. Submissions made by theorists, such as Sigmund Freud, Carl Jung, Carl Rogers, Viktor Frankl and Petruska Clarkson are included in this treatise.

Throughout this discussion, the author relies on his personal experience as an educationalist, working with adult learners who are engaged in the process of making significant life changes. Many of those who have identified a more fulfilling lifestyle may participate in educational programmes as a means of realizing their life's dream. In other words, by engaging with educational providers, an individual might locate the correct means by which he/she can move from his/her current situation to one that is more satisfying and appealing. The author examines a number of pedagogical approaches that serve to provide avenues to progression and, subsequently, to self-direction. Principally, the author focuses attention on adult-educational methodologies as a means of effecting that blueprint, which has emerged from some form of self-exploratory process such as psychotherapy. Special consideration will be given to progressive educationalists, including Paulo Freire, Jack Mezirow and John Dewey.

Psychotherapy: a personal journey towards self-discovery

Anthony Bateman *et al.* have observed that, as a dynamic process, psychotherapy is very much concerned with allowing the client to identify his/her inner world.[1] Rather than be considered a means to 'symptomatic relief', Bateman *et al.* have noted that psychotherapy helps the client to understand himself/herself.[2] They have addressed the issue of defence mechanisms, which help one to 'suppress, deny or disown' all those life experiences, memories and issues that one may judge to be unacceptable or painful.[3] Very often this material, which is directed away from conscious living, impacts upon one's 'motivational drives'.[4] Freud also stressed that the purpose of psychoanalysis for the client was to bring unconscious material into the conscious.[5] Freud was of the view that this goal is achieved by the lifting of repressions, and by the removal of 'preconditions for the formation of symptoms'.[6] Sandler *et al.* have stressed that, when understood in a Freudian context, human behaviour is often the product of a 'repetitive compulsion', i.e. a tendency to repeat earlier patterns of behaviour.[7] Since the therapeutic process is designed to help the client to acquire more control over his/her own life, Freud was adamant that every effort should be made, on the part of the therapist, to encourage the client to abandon any activity which 'leads to satisfaction in itself'.[8] In other words, the process of psychotherapy itself has been developed with a view to liberating the client from self-defeatist mannerisms, which impede his/her desire to move forward. Furthermore, based on hypotheses already discussed, a client may be restricted by extrinsic factors, which may reduce that essential sense of self-autonomy a client may have over his/her own life.

In *The Undiscovered Self*, Carl Jung suggested that, as one gains a greater knowledge of oneself, one may also shed 'some light on the powers slumbering in the psyche'.[9] In other words, it is only after one embarks on a journey of self-exploration that one may discover capacities and potential, which may previously have gone unnoticed. This 'shadow' side of oneself is not necessarily always inferior or negative, but may include abilities awaiting manifestation.[10] In a separate publication, Jung has advised that continuous adapting to one's environmental conditions is conducive to one's process towards 'individuation'.[11] Individuation is defined by Jung as 'the process by which a person becomes a psychological "individual", that is a separate, indivisible unity or "whole" '.[12] In this same publication, Jung further describes the journey towards individuation as 'self-realization' and 'coming to selfhood'.[13] Commenting on Jung's hypothesis, Robin Robertson has suggested that the quest for individuation is a lifelong process.[14] Robertson has considered individuation as the individual's unique destiny.[15] According to him, individuation is a destiny, which is shaped by the individual himself/herself, a form of 'inner healing and growth'.[16] Consequently, Robertson has acknowledged that individuation is fundamental to the human developmental process and is, therefore, instinctual.[17] Consequently, one may add that the human condition is destined for self-actualization and autonomy.

Indeed, from a humanistic perspective, Bateman *et al.* have suggested that 'humanistic psychology' refers specifically to 'human potential'.[18] Humanistic psychology emphasizes human capacities, and the innate human quest for self-actualization, which is conducted within a safe and inviting environment. According to Carl Rogers, one of the principle foundation stones upon which humanistic psychology is constructed is that the individual 'has within himself/herself the capacity and the tendency, latent if not evident, to move forward toward maturity'.[19] This essential principle Rogers entitled 'the mainspring of life'.[20] What this hypothesis amounts to, whether the individual knows it or not, is that he/she is the author of his/her own destiny. In this respect, the individual client should not be pushed in one direction or another, as part of any therapeutic process. Instead, he/she should be allowed the personal space to explore choices and avenues, which may lead to self-actualization. Emphasis is placed on a therapeutic relationship of trust, communication and understanding, between clinician and client. Indeed, this author is of the view that trusting the client's ability to direct the course of his/her own life is paramount to the psychotherapeutic process.

Petruska Clarkson has emphasized the point that one expected outcome of psychotherapy is that a client may be able to steer himself/herself away from a pre-determined life script, with a view to writing his/her own life narrative.[21] In other words, following effective psychotherapy encounters, the client may be able to liberate himself/herself from external influences and, instead, shape the course his/her life is about to take. Accordingly, as the client begins to visualize alternative life choices, he/she may begin to construct a mental blueprint of a more self-fulfilling existence. This author considers that this mental blueprint provides the foundation stone upon which real progression is achieved, in an organized and meaningful manner.

Against a backdrop of an unpredictable and often unsympathetic world, existential psychotherapist Viktor Frankl has suggested that an individual maintains some level of control over his/her own life, regardless of social or environmental situation. Frankl was of the view that one is master of one's own will and should, therefore, not relinquish that control to life circumstances or to another individual.[22] Frankl continued his discourse by stating that to relinquish one's freedom of will is tantamount to placing one's fate in the hands of another. This practice, when left unchecked, results in a lack of self-worth, the belief that one is inferior, a feeling of degradation and a loss of personal dignity. In short, to hand over control of one's freedom of will suggests that one hands over one's individuality. Frankl's own personal experiences of the concentration camps suggest that an individual can preserve independence of mind, even in the most horrific of situations.[23] Frankl told the story of those unique individuals who found the strength to exercise great acts of love and compassion, despite the fact they were living in an environment clouded by atrocious criminal acts against humanity.

Frankl has noted that 'humanity not only *is* but first decides what he/she is'.[24] He maintained that an individual does not simply exist, but always has a choice as to what his/her existence will constitute. He suggested that the individual is capable of changing his/her world, or even engaging himself/herself, in a process of self-empowerment. Frankl was an adherent to policies that sought to allow the individual to be responsible for self-determination. This author is of the view that Frankl's attitude represents the goal of any psychotherapy programme. Frankl observed that human freedom is not to be defined as 'freedom from' but 'freedom to', that is, the freedom to be the person one chooses to be in any given situation.[25] To be free, therefore, is to be free to plan one's own destiny, in contrast to allowing the past, or present, to completely dictate the terms of one's life. The main thrust of this whole discussion is that pedagogy is one avenue that may be taken in one's quest for freedom.

David H. Malan has argued that, with some individuals, past experiences and influences may obstruct their attempts to progress.[26] According to Malan, some consequences from such obstructions or controls, which may be extrinsic or intrinsic to the individual, include frustration and disappointment that may, in turn, result in anger.[27] Malan has suggested that one of the main tasks of psychotherapy is to enable the client to address his/her life issues, which impede upon his/her wish to pursue alternative life options.[27] One can only conclude from this that the psychotherapeutic process may engender a greater sense of self-awareness and self-determination within the client. In support of this reasoning, Rogers has argued that: 'The individual has within himself/herself the capacity and the tendency, latent if not evident, to move forward toward maturity. In a suitable psychological climate this tendency is released, and becomes actual rather than potential.'[29]

This author is of the view that two issues arise in this hypothesis. To begin, the tendency to move toward maturity, as discussed by Rogers, is possibly what inspires the client to access psychotherapy in the first place. In other words, the frustration that results from the feeling of being caught in a rut may provoke one to consider other options. The second issue, which arises from this statement of Rogers, is that, through the psychotherapeutic process, the client may progress from imagining a blueprint for future living, to living the dream. Janet Tolan has noted that, as the client progresses through his/her own personal therapeutic programme, he/she moves from viewing the world in terms of problems, to one where he/she wants to be.[30] In this discourse, Tolan addressed the fact that to *be* is to be open to new experiences.[31] The move from 'potential' to 'actual' may mark a period of significant transition for the individual. Furthermore, Tolan has advised that, once a person has achieved this state of awareness, and commitment to personal change, he/she begins to assume responsibility for his/her own life direction.[32] No longer is one founding current and future choices on past influences and experiences. Indeed, Rogers has stressed that: 'Whether one calls it a growth tendency, a drive towards self-actualization, or a forward-moving directional tendency, it is the mainspring of life, and is, in the last analysis, the tendency upon which all psychotherapy depends.'[33] This author is of the view that, while the vision of new potential arises through the psychotherapeutic process, the manifestation of this potential is achieved through constructive pedagogy.

The role of education in the quest for self-autonomy: education as re-education

Those who have embarked on the educational trail come from all backgrounds and have various life experiences. Based on his own experience, while working with adults who have decided to return to education, this author is of the view that most come lacking in confidence. In fact, individual self-esteem may have been eroded by life experience itself, or by past education encounters. Transition, particularly any significant life change, is often difficult to confront and effect. Nevertheless, some find the courage, possibly through a counselling/psychotherapy programme, to step into the world of lifelong learning. The questions that arise from this debate, however, centre on how an individual, or group of individuals, can progress from a seemingly debilitating environment to a state of self-autonomy. For instance, how can an individual, or group of individuals, move from a position of dependence to independence? To refer back to Frankl's original hypothesis, the question to be addressed is, how can a person move from a position of apparent despair to one of personal fulfilment? This author considers the considerable effort applied to pursuing such a transition since, effectually, the move is one from passivity to one where the individual begins to assume personal responsibility for his/her life choices. The author proposes that quality educational provision largely equips individuals to make those necessary, and often unforeseen, but significant, changes in life.

One interesting concept that has emanated from corrective educational circles is that of re-education. Many clients have, in the past, experienced disillusionment within the more formal educational structure. Indeed, the author considers re-education a pedagogical methodology, whereby clients may be provided with a more constructive, self-enriching and formal education. However, this process of re-education involves more than the mere transmission of knowledge. August Aichorn has considered that much human behaviour manifests itself in some form of neurosis.[34] According to Aichorn, as with Freud, the process of re-education necessitates bringing unconscious material to the conscious. This particular approach may impact upon those entrapped by feelings of despair or self-worthlessness, as discussed by Frankl.

It may be argued, therefore, that apposite education structures may enable a client to move, beyond a sense of meaninglessness and self-worthlessness, to a position where he/she may feel fulfilled and fully functional, within the social realm. Hence, in their interactions with clients, educators need to be very skilled, in order to create a safe environment so that clients, who may already be engaged in a process of reform, may explore some personal issues. According to Aichorn, some clients may need to learn to 'postpone and renounce satisfaction and to divert primitive instinctual urges into socially acceptable channels'.[35]

The old traditional methods of instruction may fail in this endeavour. Indeed, concerning the education of offenders specifically, the Council of Europe has noted that teaching methodologies, curriculum adaptation to suit the needs of the individual client, and self-motivation are not easily found within the more conventional teaching environments.[36] Hence alternative educational methodologies are invoked, in order to present a pertinent pedagogical strategy. In other words, in the case of vulnerable or isolated clients, re-education becomes a means whereby clients may be 'resocialized' and thus become normal socially functional beings. From this statement, one may establish a direct association between the intended goal of the psychotherapeutic process, and that of educational provision. This process of resocialization may be particularly applicable to those who feel isolated or vulnerable.

The author suggests that pedagogical modules addressing personal development, life skills, social skills, and the development of self-confidence and self-worth, may all intertwine, to become part of a holistic curriculum that may be applied in such circumstances. From this hypothesis, one may also attempt to establish a direct link between education and psychotherapy, as a complementary holistic technique, which may be used with those engaged in a quest for self-emancipation. In addition, within this same process, a client may learn to accept the existing social conventions.

Gisli H. Gudjonsson has observed that impaired intellectual and social functioning may result from acquired or developmental factors. In either event, victims of such impairments are often psychologically vulnerable. While intellectual impairments are measurable by way of standardized assessment, social-functioning deficiencies are harder to assess. Social function is related to an individual's capacity to look after his/her everyday needs, and adapt to changing situations. According to Gudjonsson, social functioning is 'usually measured by direct observation and/or by information gathered by informants'.[37] Nevertheless, Aichorn has also suggested that a client may be socialized through experience and training.[38] When one considers the therapeutic value of education, one begins to advocate the role of education as providing tangible avenues of progression.

For example, this author has worked with clients who are in the process of recovery from addiction. Once the clients have successfully negotiated various treatment programmes, and support/counselling processes, education becomes a significant contributor to the client's overall rehabilitation. It should be noted, nonetheless, that 'corrective education' is not necessarily perceived as an attempt to fix some anomaly within the individual. Rather, corrective educational structures and policies are specifically designed, with the intention of aiding the client to adopt a more positive vision about himself/herself and about what he/she has to offer.

Many of the pedagogical practices and resources, invoked within corrective educational structures, may be applied to other groups. Certainly, many of the principles inherent in the re-education process, if extended, could benefit a more diverse population. The author suggests that the ethos, ingrained in corrective educational structures, may be effective in motivating the client, who may dream of achieving more in life but may feel that further education is beyond his/her reach. For instance, the individual who feels he/she is restricted in his/her choice of careers, due to the socio-economic situation may, conversely, be encouraged to compete against the general population as an equal, and with confidence. Those who long to reach a state of self-autonomy may be motivated to lose the shackles of oppression and dependence. Furthermore, a person may consider himself/herself adequately self-assured to re-enter the job market after many years. By accentuating the positive, a client may come to appreciate his/her own intrinsic giftedness, and may subsequently exploit those natural abilities. In short, educational provisions need not simply be restricted to helping a client become academically proficient.

The influence of Paulo Freire

Following on from this discussion, South American educationalist Paulo Freire has acknowledged that positive 'transition' in life begins with the dream of something better.[39] He, in turn, invented the term 'conscientization' to describe a revolutionary process whereby individuals become aware of their plight. From this defining moment, the role of educators was to enable students to act constructively to improve their life situations. For Freire, conscientization involved the deepening of one's awareness of the reality of the situation within which one exists.[40] In the light of this hypothesis, the gradual process of conscientization entails a progressive movement, from maintaining a naïve consciousness to a more critical awareness.[41]

A conscientized person will obtain the ability to distinguish myth and fallacy from social reality.[42] Conscientization evolves, therefore, through addressing real issues, which offer an alternative to the blind acceptance of psychological manipulations or ideological propaganda.[43] In fact, a distinction is made between conscientization and 'critical consciousness'. It has been argued that the development of a critical consciousness can be the product of a 'banking' system of education. The process of conscientization, however, 'involves identifying contradictions in experience through dialogue and becoming a "subject" with other oppressed subjects – that is, becoming part of the process of changing the world'.[44]

The process of conscientization is considered more than just the identification of dehumanizing structures, existing within society. It also involves a 'radical denunciation of dehumanising structures accompanied by the proclamation of a new reality to be created by humanity'.[45] It may be concluded that conscientization, as developed within a progressive pedagogical environment, seeks to cultivate the critical dimension of the student.[46] It has been noted that attempts made to develop conscientization in isolation will be ineffective.[47] In reality, the process aims, essentially, at nurturing a communion between individuals who share a common vision of a society in transition.[48] Armed with new critical awareness, there emerges within the individual a new world vision. This new world vision may also be described as a more desired scenario. Indeed, a conscientization process that favours human domination can only be described as inauthentic.[49]

From a counselling/psychotherapeutic perspective, Fritz Perls *et al.* observed that human beings appear to possess an innate tendency to bring to completion all dimensions of the self.[50] Perls *et al.* continued this discourse by indicating that the human condition does not rest easy with unfinished business.[51] Interestingly, Freire also noted that once acknowledged, individuals embarked on a quest to resolve their own sense of 'unfinishedness'.[52] This position, upheld by Freire, certainly adds weight to this author's original hypothesis, that the psychotherapy/counselling process can actually progress into the pedagogical sphere. In other words, education may be considered the next stage, once the dream of an alternative future has been constructed. Freire was of the view, nonetheless, that a dream should not be confused with an escape into a fantasy world. Instead, a dream is considered one of the initial phases in the struggle for self-autonomy. Such a dream is founded upon the realistic hope that one need not always be restricted or enslaved by one's current life situation. Freire invoked the term 'critical optimism' to define the concept of hope within this particular context.[53] Where Frankl noted that the absence of hope resulted in despair, Freire was adamant that hope is a prerequisite, not only for personal change, but also for social transformation. The only alternative to hope is total surrender, which is made manifest, in the most extreme cases, through acts of deliberate self-abuse and suicide.

Freire has also noted, however, that hope must be grounded in concrete activity. Otherwise, dreams remain within one's imagination. However, while pursuing the quest for self-autonomy one cannot simply embark on a trail that lacks planning and reflection. Freire has observed that only through appropriate educational provision can one truly explore viable alternatives to one's current life situation. To adopt a Freirean terminology, the traditional 'banking' method of teaching, where the clients are simply expected to absorb any knowledge imparted by the teacher, may not be adequate. This particular pedagogical approach may only serve to undo what progress the client has made through his/her psychotherapy or counselling programme. Instead, educational structures may serve to develop the person in a more holistic manner, thus empowering the individual to adjust and overcome life's changing circumstances.[54]

In contrast to this more traditional teaching method, Freire has invoked the term 'problematizing' to describe a process whereby one is afforded the opportunity to explore the essence of an oppressive régime.[55] This particular pedagogical technique, when applied, would allow each individual to examine his/her reality as a totality that, in some way, might enlighten him/her as to his/her existential situation. Ironically, Freire has suggested that many individuals are enslaved by concepts they do not fully understand. Individual creative potential becomes impaired and lacks self-governing experience.[56] Particular teaching methodologies are subsequently constructed to facilitate individuals in the search for self-determination.

In support of Freire, Franke and Dewey

Reinforcing this theory is Herman Franke, who has suggested that emancipation occurs only when an individual breaks free from the control of others, and recognizes the concept of human rights.[57] The individual, who is already engaged in the reform process, may still be living in the same environment that contributed to those feelings of inferiority, helplessness or despair in the first place, and that resulted in the individual attending psychotherapy/counselling. Since lack of educational achievement, and some forms of helplessness, are linked to social disadvantage, not everyone can readily relocate to another district or a more socially friendly environment. The role of the teacher within such an educational structure must, therefore, remain non-authoritarian. The problem with an autocratic pedagogical strategy is that such a model could very easily replicate the controlling or debilitating environment, which resulted in the client lacking in confidence or feeling outside the education system. This author is of the view that educational methodologies should, instead, complement the psychotherapy/counselling process, in facilitating the client in developing his/her decision-making skills, in order to shape his/her own future. Accordingly, wrote John Dewey, the teacher assumes the role of 'leader of group activities'.[58]

The alternative to this more progressive educational approach is to replace one oppressive régime with another. Within a more democratic pedagogical practice, each client may be afforded freedom to choose the courses that he/she may wish to pursue, in so far that this procedure is possible. Indeed, in the case of adults, the client himself/herself may be the best judge of what he/she should learn, based on his/her personal interests and life experiences. Following participation in a programme of counselling/psychotherapy, the client himself/herself may be in the best position to determine his/her own life choices. Furthermore, tutors often vary teaching methodologies in order to accommodate the needs and life goals of individual clients. Educators conducting such programmes frequently allow for flexible structures, concerning subject matter and teaching styles.

MICHAEL O'SHEA

Freire's notion of effective pedagogical methodologies

It has become evident that if educational structures are to be effective they must address concrete life issues, as opposed to theoretical abstractions. Freire has outlined a process of codification defined as 'the representation of typical existential situations of the group with which one is working'.[59] This codification process involves surveying specific social problems, with a view to exploring some possible alternatives. In another publication, Freire has described codification as a mediation 'between the concrete and theoretical contexts of reality'.[60] Codification is further described as a process whereby clients and teachers, together, construct a series of objectives for potential realization. It is also one that clients participate in, in conjunction with literacy programmes.[61] It may be concluded, therefore, that only by re-evaluating one's social position can one eventually effect sufficient change. The author suggests that, taken in this context, education becomes a commitment to a cause.

Accordingly, the educator becomes a facilitator in the development of a greater critical awareness within clients. The aim of the exercise is to allow clients critically to analyse their social conditions, in an objective manner. Certainly, educational content should address the immediate needs of individual clients. Education, as an instrument of liberation, fails when it simply passes on pieces of general information, which may not be contextually applicable to clients' social conditions. The role of the educator, therefore, is to 'propose problems about these codified existential situations in order to help the learners arrive at a more and more critical view of their reality'.[62] Consequently, an educational curriculum that lacks contextual reality may be criticized for not preparing clients for concrete interventionist actions. The author suggests, therefore, that educational programmes must be relevant to individuals' life experiences. According to Maureen Killeavy *et al.*, in educational terms, relevance relates to 'matters of a socio-cultural nature, both in the context of global issues such as human rights and the problems of developing countries, as well as matters of local, community and personal concern'.[63]

The author considers that one's life vision is open to subjective variation and interpretation. Subsequently, the author questions the effectiveness of applying standardized textbooks, together with standardized syllabi, to all individuals who have a complexity of life situations. In other words, the author proposes that specialized syllabi should be constructed, invoking specialized texts, in order that individual needs should be addressed. Freire invoked the term 'extension' to describe an educational structure, which attempts to address concrete social issues, within the ordinary school curriculum.[64] As an educational construct, this concept of extension promotes individual participation in social transformation.

However, Freire was critical of this method of education, in that it provides subject material and techniques that may contravene the very essence of self-determination. Indeed, the process itself negates the concept of education as self-exploration. The author interprets this scenario as a pedagogical structure, which provides incongruent solutions to local problems. Rather than facilitating the development of critical reflection, education as extension simply replaces one form of knowledge with another. It constitutes a form of transference and cannot, therefore, be classified as authentic critical education. There also exists a fear that extension could result in an individual misinterpreting his/her personal social conditions. Freire has argued that any form of knowledge that leads to social transformation is essentially 'sensuous'. Consequently, it is imperative that educators should encourage clients to engage in a process of problematizing of their own existential situations.

In order to contextualize education even further, Freire recommended two types of textbooks. Firstly, there are textbooks that address current social issues, but which have been written by outsiders. Secondly, there are also in existence textbooks written by the oppressed themselves. These are of particular value, since they have been authored by individuals who have lived the experiences. This pedagogical practice, if applied, could result in clients already participating in personal-modification programmes, reading textbooks written by other individuals who have already grown through the educative process. Addicts, trying to free themselves from a substance dependency, may find it helpful to explore the experiences of those who have already succeeded in this endeavour.

Nevertheless, Freire has recommended that both textbook types should be afforded equal value, in order that clients should acquire an objective and subjective interpretation of existing phenomena.

Conclusion

From the outset, it has been intended to establish a link between psychotherapy/counselling services and educational provision. This author is of the view that both psychotherapy/counselling and educational programmes can be offered, in unison as part of a holistic rehabilitation provision, and that psychotherapy/counselling processes provide the client with possibilities for personal advancement. The deep journey of inner self-exploration, essential to any psychotherapy/counselling process, is designed to allow the client to become self-autonomous and a fully functional social being. The quest for self-emancipation and personal fulfilment is innate to the human condition, as submissions made by Freud, Jung, Rogers, Frankl and Clarkson have demonstrated. Furthermore, if the psychotherapy/counselling process allows the client to consider alternatives to his/her current life situation, then a blueprint for change may ensue.

Freire adopted the term 'conscientization' to describe the process of the student's growing self-understanding. This author is of the view that conscientization begins within the counselling/psychotherapeutic process, and is subsequently manifested through effective pedagogy. Ironically, similar language is shared between educationalists and those involved in counselling/psychotherapy. For example, the term 'unfinished' is invoked by both Perls and Freire to describe a state of personal incompleteness. Accordingly, the main thrust of the second part of this paper is rooted in the supposition that constructive pedagogical approaches will assist the client in turning a new life vision into a reality. Indeed, hypotheses presented by renowned educationalists, such as Freire, Mezirow and Dewey, which have already been included in this discussion, reinforce the point. Freire addressed the fact that unless one actively pursues a life's dream, that dream remains in the imagination. In short, one's own blueprint for a more fulfilling life may be a little more attainable, through a process of constructive dialogical pedagogy.

NOTES

1. Alan Bateman et al., *Introduction to Psychotherapy: An Outline of Psychodynamic Principles and Practice*, 3rd edn (Hove and New York 2002), p. 2.
2. Ibid.
3. Ibid. p. 3.
4. Ibid. p. 4.
5. Sigmund Freud, *The Standard Edition of the Complete Psychological Works of Sigmund Freud*, vol. xvii, *An Infantile Neurosis and Other Works* (London 1981), pp. 159–68.
6. Sigmund Freud, *Introductory Lectures on Psychoanalysis* (London and New York 1991), p. 486.
7. Joseph Sandler et al., *The Patient and the Analyst* (London 1992), p. 41.
8. Freud, *Standard Edition*, p. 163.
9. Carl Gustav Jung, *The Undiscovered Self* (London and New York 2002), p. 75.
10. Ibid.
11. Carl Gustav Jung, *On The Nature of the Psyche* (London and New York 2001), p. 46.
12. Carl Gustav Jung, *The Essential Jung: Selected Writings* (London 1998), p. 418.
13. Ibid.
14. Robin Robertston, *Introducing Jungian Psychology* (Dublin 1992), p. 7.
15. Ibid.
16. Ibid. p. 44.
17. Ibid. p. 7.
18. Bateman et al., *Introduction to Psychotherapy*, pp. 172–3.
19. Carl R. Rogers, *On Becoming a Person: A Therapist's View of Psychotherapy* (London 2002), p. 35.
20. Ibid.
21. Petruska Clarkson, *On Psychotherapy* (New Jersey and London 1994), p. 44.
22. Viktor E. Frankl, *Man's Search for Ultimate Meaning* (New York 2000), p. 15.
23. Viktor E. Frankl, *Man's Search for Meaning* (London and New York 1984), p. 68.
24. Viktor E. Frankl, *The Doctor and the Soul*, trans. Richard and Clara Winston (New York 1986), p. 21.
25. Ibid. p. 52.
26. David H. Malan, *Individual Psychotherapy and the Science of Psychodynamics*, 2nd edn (London and New York 2001), pp. 10–11.
27. Ibid. p. 11.

28. *Ibid.* p. 16.
29. Rogers, *On Becoming a Person*, p. 35.
30. Janet Tolan, *Skills in Person-Centred Counselling and Psychotherapy* (London and New Delhi 2006), p. 114.
31. *Ibid.*
32. *Ibid.* p. 115.
33. Rogers, *On Becoming a Person*, p. 35.
34. August Aichorn, *Wayward Youth* (London 1936), p. 9.
35. *Ibid.* p. 7.
36. Council of Europe, *Standard Minimum Rules for the Treatment of Prisoners* (Strasbourg 1973).
37. Gisli H. Gudjonsson, *The Psychology of Interrogations and Confessions* (Chichester 2003), p. 320.
38. Aichorn, *Wayward Youth*, p. 7.
39. Paulo Freire, *Pedagogy of Hope: Reliving Pedagogy of the Oppressed* (New York 1999), p. 8.
40. Paulo Freire, *Pedagogy of the Oppressed*, trans. Myra Bergman Ramos (Middlesex 1986), p. 81.
41. Paulo Freire, *Education for Critical Consciousness* (London 1974), p. 19.
42. Paulo Freire, *Cultural Action* (Massachusetts 1988), p. 48.
43. Freire, *Critical Consciousness*, p. 48.
44. Tom Heaney, 'Issues in Freirean Pedagogy', available at http://www3.nl.edu/academics/cas/ace/resources/Documents/FreireIssues.cfm.
45. Freire, *Politics of Education*, trans. Donaldo Macedo (New York, Westport, Connecticut, and London 1985), p. 85.
46. Freire, *Cultural Action*, p. 30.
47. *Ibid.* p. 46.
48. *Ibid.*
49. See Freire, *Cultural Action*, p. 85. and Freire, *The Politics of Education*, p. 75.
50. Frederick Perls *et al.*, *Gestalt Therapy: Excitement and Growth in the Human Personality* (London 2003), p. 203.
51. *Ibid.*
52. Paulo Freire, *Pedagogy of Freedom: Ethics, Democracy and Civic Courage* (New York and Oxford 1998), p. 56.
53. Paulo Freire, *Pedagogy of the Heart*, trans. Donaldo Macedo and Alexandre Oliveira (New York 1998), p. 58.
54. Freire, *Pedagogy of the Oppressed*, p. 118.
55. Freire, *Cultural Action for Freedom*, p. 21.
56. Freire, *Critical Consciousnes*, p. 20.
57. Herman Franke, *The Emancipation of Prisoners: A Socio-Historical*

Analysis of the Dutch Prison Experience (Edinburgh 1995), p. 6.
58. John Dewey, *Experience and Education* (London and New York 1963), p. 59.
59. Freire, *Critical Consciousness*, p. 51.
60. Freire, *The Politics of Education*, p. 5.
61. *Ibid.*
62. Freire, *The Politics of Education*, p. 55.
63. Maureen Killeavy *et al.*, 'Making curriculum relevant to the lives of second-level clients: teachers' classroom practice', *Journal of the Educational Studies Association of Ireland*, 22, 1 (2003), 109.
64. Freire, *Critical Consciousness*, p. 51.

MICHAEL O'SHEA is the adult education officer with Meath Vocational Education Committee and part-time lecturer on the masters in education programme in guidance and counselling in the School of Education, TCD. He studied under Val Rice and completed a PhD in guidance and counselling in the School of Education in 2004.

The Status of Mathematical Knowledge and its Implications for Mathematics Education

ELIZABETH OLDHAM

Introduction and context

René Thom famously asserted that all mathematics pedagogy rests on a philosophy of mathematics.[1] This paper examines different philosophies of mathematics and then discusses the likely implications of each for mathematics teaching. The subject is topical, at the time of writing, because mathematics education in Ireland is undergoing reform, and successful implementation of the intended reforms may require teachers to adopt pedagogical approaches, foreign to their own espoused philosophies of mathematics. There are important implications for pre-service teacher education, and for teachers' continuing professional development.

The paper has been developed from work done under Professor Val Rice's supervision, when I was reading for the higher diploma in education in TCD, 1969–70. In order to indicate its importance to me personally, and hence to explain my gratitude to Professor Rice for helping me to undertake it, a short personal history is relevant.

I read for a degree in mathematics in TCD from 1961 to 1965. Students at the time – at least my immediate circle and acquaintances in College! – typically could put forward reasons for their choice of college course: reasons based on the intrinsic worth of the subject, rather than on its potential for offering employment and financial gain. Courses such as medicine or sociology might be perceived as being of obvious value to humankind; choosing mathematics at the time (in interesting contrast to the value now put on it as a contributor to the 'knowledge society') required more defence. My own reason was that it was 'as near as one could get to absolute truth'. This was, perhaps, a more mature version of a teenage liking for certainty, which had pointed me towards specialization in mathematics in the first place, and was expressed, for example, as follows: 'In history, people may disagree as to whether or not King John was not a good man; in mathematics, at least 2 + 2 = 4.'

As a graduate student at the University of London, I took a course in mathematical logic and the foundations of mathematics from Dr G.T. Kneebone of Bedford College – and it is not too much to say that this changed my (mathematical) life. I was fascinated to learn of the crisis that beset the foundations of mathematics around 1900, and of the various attempts to ground the subject in such a way as to establish the certainty that had so attracted me. I was even more fascinated, first, when I realized that these attempts had failed, and again when I encountered the alternative view of a *fallible* mathematics, presented by Imre Lakatos to a seminar at the London School of Economics. I had chosen mathematics because I thought it dealt with absolute truth; I fell more deeply in love with the subject when I discovered that it did not.

At this stage of my life, I was beginning to read philosophy. I was also following up interests in rationales for mathematics in the school curriculum. It was against this background that I returned to Trinity to take the higher diploma and prepare myself for a career as a teacher. In a most enjoyable year, Professor Rice's course on the philosophy of education was a highlight, for which the previous few years had prepared me well. A second highlight was the writing of a research paper or minor thesis, then part of the diploma programme, which offered a chance for students to engage in academic writing in education. For someone from a mathematical background, it was a first opportunity to engage in academic writing of any sort and, to me, it was a revelation. In the context of examining the work of Israel Scheffler, I was able to record much of what I had learnt about the foundations of mathematics and to examine the implications for education.[2] The experience was wonderful; it was, perhaps, the key incident that ultimately pointed me towards a career in academe. As indicated above, the work was done under Professor Rice's supervision, and – as I realized later – was an endeavour after his own heart, echoing some of his own great interests. At the time, we talked about possible publication. With hindsight, it would have been ideal to write a paper together; however, the culture of the period, in arts and education, was so averse to appending a supervisor's name to students' papers (even if the supervisor had contributed greatly to their formulation) that the possibility was never explored. Now, perhaps, it is appropriate that some of the work can be used in this volume, as a tribute to the man who gave me the opportunity to undertake it.

The paper addressed the work of Israel Scheffler, with regard to mathematical knowledge, and to do so it outlined the contemporary understanding of philosophies of mathematics. The central parts of the paper dealt with Scheffler's work, related and applied to the different philosophies of mathematics. The final section, on mathematics education, was built around my (then) tentative hypothesis that a teacher's espoused philosophy of mathematics would affect how he or she taught the subject. In what follows here, the outline of philosophies of mathematics is given more or less in full. Excerpts are drawn from the description and application of Scheffler's work, in order to provide a background to later research on the philosophy of mathematics, and mathematics education. The final section is replaced by a brief account of that research, in which the themes that I addressed in my innocence as a graduate student have emerged as important threads, and implications for implementing curriculum reforms are then considered. In the conclusion, the discussion is applied to the recent initiative in Irish mathematics education, 'Project Maths'. The updated paper is thus intended not only to pay tribute to Professor Rice, but also to provide an overview of some issues that should be considered in Irish mathematics education at a time at which – for the first occasion since the 1960s – its nature is undergoing a major critique.[3]

Philosophies of mathematics

BACKGROUND

This section describes the basic philosophies of mathematics, which emerged in the century from 1870 to 1970: logicism, formalism, intuitionism, and (most recently) empiricism. All these arose in one way or another as an answer to the 'critical movement' that, around the turn of the century, cast doubts upon the validity of much existing mathematics.[4] Logicism was developed in an attempt to show that all mathematics is ultimately reducible to logic (and is 'true'). Formalism aimed to establish the validity of mathematics by showing that it is non-contradictory. The goal of intuitionism is both more ambitious and more limited: to rewrite as much as possible of mathematics, in a form that satisfied particularly strict canons of rigour. None of these three philosophies has been entirely satisfactory from a mathematical point of view, and empiricism attempts to answer their failure.

An account – inevitably rather simplified – is given of the main features of each school of thought. Since this paper considers the work of Israel Scheffler with respect to mathematics, and since Scheffler explicitly discusses the ideas of Poincaré, whom on the authority of Kleene[5] and Kneebone[6] is identified as a forerunner of the intuitionistic school, intuitionism is considered first.

INTUITIONISM

'As an explicit philosophy,' Kneebone points out, 'intuitionism has been developed chiefly by L.E.J. Brouwer (1881–1966) and his Amsterdam school; but its general tenets have been shared by many working mathematicians ...'.[7] Such people believe that mathematicians must start from objects given in intuition: the natural numbers are the most fundamental examples. (Kronecker, another forerunner of intuitionism, in the course of an after-dinner speech, made his famous remark: 'God made the integers; all else is the work of man.'[8]) Moreover, they must reason *constructively* about these objects. Every entity in an intuitionist theory, if not actually given in intuition, can be produced in principle by a finite construction, and every proof is such that its component statements are intuitively obvious, or follow from previous ones, in a constructive way. In his avowedly propagandist essay on constructivism, Errett Bishop seems to write in a rather different theological spirit from Kronecker (although in the same one, mathematically) when he says: 'When a man proves a positive integer to exist, he should show how to find it. If God has mathematics of his own that needs to be done, let him do it himself.'[9]

Thus to an intuitionist, the statement 'Q is true' means 'A constructive proof of the statement Q, starting from intuitively clear concepts, has been given.' Indeed, the argument can be taken further: what is intuitively clear, to one person, may not be to another, and the intuitionist must really cast the statement in the form 'I have seen (or heard or read or thought up) a constructive proof of Q.' This is rendered here as 'I have a proof of Q.' Similarly, 'Q is false' means 'I have a refutation of Q.'

It follows that there is room for a class of 'don't know' statements, between the true and the false ones, and intuitionists do, indeed, grant the existence of such a class. A 'don't know' statement may become true or false tomorrow, if someone offers a proof or a refutation; until such time, it must be counted as neither true nor false. An immediate consequence is that the *Tertium non datur* 'Q or not Q' does not hold in intuitionistic mathematics. This rules out the following reductio ad absurdum argument, so often used in classical (that is, traditional) proofs of a statement Q:

Suppose Q is false.
If so, a contradiction follows:
therefore, Q is not false.
Therefore, Q is true.

For the intuitionist, the non-constructive last line of the argument is invalid. The failure to produce a refutation of Q does not itself produce a proof of Q. A similar argument shows that to an intuitionist 'not (not Q)' and 'Q' do not mean the same thing. Altogether, then, intuitionistic standards of proof are exceptionally rigorous, although they do allow for a slight personal element.

For a more extended discussion of intuitionism, the reader is referred to the writings of Heyting.[10] It suffices here to state the intuitionistic claim that 'mathematics is identical with the exact part of our thinking',[11] and to note its consequence (illustrated above), that an intuitionist cannot accept the whole of classical mathematics. Also, one of the surprising aspects of intuitionism is that it sees logic as nothing more than a particular branch of mathematics.

LOGICISM

Entirely the opposite view is basic to the next school of thought to be discussed: logicism, as its name suggest, takes its whole stand upon logic. The archetypal logicist was Bertrand Russell (1872–1970). He firmly believed that all mathematics was reducible to logic, and in his great classic *Principia Mathematica*, written with A.N. Whitehead,[12] he aimed to deduce all pure mathematics from certain logical truths. (This was, indeed, only the first stage of a programme to deduce all absolute truth from basic logical axioms.) To Russell, mathematics is an edifice of propositions of the form P→Q (P implies Q), theoretically already in existence. This does not mean that all of them are known; they are not. But they are 'there', fixed and immutable, and open to discovery rather than invention.[13]

The *Principia* is written as a formal deductive system, in which theorems are deduced from the basic 'true' axioms by 'truth-preserving' inference-rules, and specific mathematical terms are introduced by definition. The system is thus intended to be objective and absolute. The intuitionist situation, in which a sequence of statements could legitimately form a proof in the eyes of one person, but not of another, is an invalid one from the logicist point of view.

FORMALISM

The third main branch of mathematical philosophy is linked with the name of David Hilbert (1862–1943). As its name suggests, formalism is to do with formalized theories, but it treats them differently from the way in which Russell treats his formal system in *Principia Mathematica*. Far from being absolute truth, a formalist's theories are basically meaningless.

A formalist's axiomatic system must satisfy the following four requirements. Certain basic (or 'primitive') symbols are required; rules must be specified, determining *admissible* ways in which these symbols may be joined together to form 'formulae'; a number of these formulae must be designated as 'axioms' or 'initial formulae'; and finally 'rules of inference' are required, to indicate that, given a formula (or some formulae), one may pass to another formula related to the given one(s) in a certain way. Then, if one starts from the axioms and plays the game according to the inference rules, one generates certain formulae. These are called 'derived formulae' of the system.

In such a system there must be a special symbol, say '¬', which is designated as 'negation'. If, for any formula Q, both Q and ¬Q can be derived, the system is said to be *inconsistent*. Otherwise it is *consistent*. Any consistent formal system is (a part of) mathematics.[14]

That is the 'real' formalist view – but it can be said that there are probably few 'real' formalists.[15] In general, such a formal system is interesting for mathematicians, only if it can be interpreted as a mathematical theory. That is to say, meanings are assigned to the basic symbols: for example, the negation sign always given the meaning 'not', while some other symbols may be interpreted as numbers. Formulae are defined in such a way that they 'make sense' under the assignment of meanings to their component symbols (for example, if read as sentences in the English language, they are grammatical). Logical or mathematical postulates are chosen for the axioms, and truth-preserving forms for the rules of inference. Consistency now means freedom from contradiction: it is impossible to derive 'Q' and also 'not Q'. Clearly if this could be done the system would be, in a certain way, invalid. Thus consistency is one possible guarantee of significance.

So far, then, a formal system, using an initially meaningless object language, has been described. Arguments *about* the system as a whole – for example, proofs of its consistency – are to be carried out in a meaningful metalanguage. These arguments must conform to standards even more stringent than the intuitionistic one, and the reasoning required in this context is referred to as 'finitary'.

The basic idea is as follows. Classical mathematics does involve non-finitary reasoning. But if a mathematical theory is formalized, it becomes clearly enough defined for people to reason *about* it, as well as *in* it. In particular, they can hope to show, by finitary reasoning, that the theory is consistent. This is the famous 'Hilbert programme', which aims to justify the non-finitary portions of mathematics by showing that they never lead to contradictions. As late as 1927, Hilbert himself was prepared to say, 'I believe that I can attain this goal completely.'[16]

OBJECTIONS TO LOGICISM AND FORMALISM: THE MOVES TOWARDS 'MODERN MATHEMATICS' AND EMPIRICISM

The aim of formalism, then, was to justify classical mathematics, by proving that the non-finitary parts of it do not lead to contradictions: 'the game of mathematics is safe'. The aim of logicism was, likewise, to justify mathematics, but by deriving it from a few objective truths: 'mathematics is absolute truth'. As indicated above, both these schools of thought arose in the attempt to save classical mathematics from the criticism that assailed its validity, during the late-nineteenth and the early part of the twentieth century.

However, both attempts failed. Russell found that to produce a system that (apparently) supports all mathematics, he had to include an axiom that was far from being an obvious objective truth. The downfall of the Hilbert programme came with the discovery that a Hilbertian formal system, interpretable even only as arithmetic (much less the whole of mathematics), cannot be proved consistent by the finitary methods envisaged, a breakthrough enshrined in an important paper by Kurt Gödel.[17] Meanwhile, Brouwer, and his school – likewise inspired by the critical movement, but believing that the attempt to save classical mathematics should be given up – were pursuing the heroic task of rewriting as much of the subject as they could, according to their own standards of rigour. But most working mathematicians (as distinct from philosophers) are not prepared to make this kind of sacrifice, and so must look for some other basis for the subject. The result, anyway, is a very unnatural mathematics. Errett Bishop wrote: 'In Brouwer's case there seems to have been a nagging suspicion that unless he personally intervened to prevent it the continuum would turn out to be discrete ... [This remedy] makes mathematics so bizarre that it becomes unpalatable to mathematicians, and foredooms the whole of Brouwer's program.'[18]

One response was that of the syndicate of mathematicians, known collectively by the name of Frenchman Nicolas Bourbaki: a group that, according to Kneebone, had 'a clear right to speak for mathematicians of a more recent generation',[19] and the work of which produced the so-called 'modern mathematics', which affected many school curricula from the 1960s.[20] The Bourbakiste view of mathematics is as 'the study of structures, or systematic patterns of relations, each particular structure being characterized by a suitable set of axioms',[21] with its manipulation being based on a system of predicate calculus. Thus far, it is in the formalist tradition, but the Bourbakistes do not attempt to justify their working by consistency proofs. For them, mathematics is a valid activity in its own right; its philosophy is not really their concern. They sum up their attitude in the following passage:

> We believe that mathematics is destined to survive, and that the essential parts of this majestic evidence will never collapse as a result of the sudden appearance of a contradiction; but we cannot pretend that this opinion rests on anything more than experience. Some will say that this is small comfort; but already for two thousand five hundred years mathematicians have been correcting their errors to the consequent enrichment and not impoverishment of their science; and this gives them the right to face the future with serenity.[22]

The Bourbakistes wrote as mathematicians. A more philosophical (and more radical) view is expressed by Imre Lakatos, who said: 'Kalmár gave a paper proposing that mathematics is an empirical science: its origins are empirical, its methods scientific, and its justification cannot exceed the justification of science ... Tarski sums up by saying that now everyone agrees that mathematics is empirical, but how can we formulate it properly?'[23]

According to Lakatos, formalism in particular is *not* the answer to Tarski's question. For one thing, the absence of meaning, in strict formalist theories, is foreign to his way of thinking; he takes his stand firmly on the idea that it is legitimate to talk of truth in mathematics – or, at least, in certain branches of it, such as arithmetic and set theory. However, he points out that formalism's unquestioning acceptance of the validity of *metamathematics* is at variance with its requirement that consistency proofs should be given for *mathematics*. If consistency proofs are to be given at all, then should not the metatheory itself be justified by a met-metatheory, and so on, thus giving us an infinite regress?

Lakatos prefers to accept that mathematics is fallible, and to alter the approach to it accordingly. In his paper, 'Proofs and refutations',[24] he says: '[The paper's] modest aim is to elaborate the point that informal, quasi-empirical mathematics does not grow through a monotonous increase in the number of indubitably established theorems, but through the incessant improvement of guesses by speculation and criticism.' Both as regards these guesses, and in his manner of dealing with infinite regress, he acknowledges his debt to Popper:

> Popperian *critical fallibilism* takes infinite regress in proofs and definitions seriously, does not have illusions about 'stopping' them, accepts the sceptic criticism of any infallible truth-injection ... A 'Popperian theory' can only be conjectural. We never *know*, we only guess. We can, however, turn our guesses into criticisable ones, and criticise and improve them ... The new central question, *How do you improve your guesses?* will give enough work for philosophers for centuries; and how to live, act, fight, die when one is left with guesses only, will give more than enough work for future political philosophers and educationalists.
>
> The indefatigable sceptic however will ask again: 'How do you *know* that you improve your guesses?' But now the answer is easy: I guess. There is nothing wrong with infinite regress in guesses.[25]

Perhaps, to be consistent, he should have closed the second paragraph quoted above with the remark, 'At least, I guess not.'

This section has described the four main philosophies of mathematics, as recognized around 1970, as well as outlining the approach of the Bourbakiste group of mathematicians that gave the world modern mathematics. In the following section, the status of mathematical knowledge for each of the four philosophies is considered, using the work of Israel Scheffler.

Mathematical knowledge and the writings of Israel Scheffler

SCHEFFLER'S PHILOSOPHICAL APPROACHES TO MATHEMATICAL KNOWLEDGE

In the introduction to his book, *Conditions of Knowledge*,[26] Israel Scheffler outlined three broad philosophical approaches to knowledge, the rationalistic, the empiricistic, and the pragmatic. In each case, he referred to the views on mathematics held by adherents of these schools of thought. For the rationalist, 'Mathematical truths are general and necessary, and may be established by deductive chains linking them with self-evident basic truths. Demonstration forges the chains, intuition forges the basic truths. Intuition, moreover, guarantees each link in the chain of demonstration.'[27] In what he calls the empiricistic philosophy, mathematics 'may be understood to represent either "internal" logical relationships among concepts, or very abstract, although still empirical, generalizations based on experience'.[28] Pragmatism, on the other hand, 'sees mathematics as an apparatus useful for elaborating the impact of hypothetical ideas, for showing their connections with practical consequences and exhibiting their mutual relationships'.[29]

It can be seen that the three broad philosophical approaches to knowledge do not correspond exactly to the categories identified above, from the point of view of the world of mathematics. The 'rationalistic' view of mathematics appears to be a mixture of the logicist and intuitionist. However, it seems to presuppose the simultaneous success of the logicist and intuitionist programmes, whereas the point was made above that neither is entirely satisfactory. For the second school, the empiricistic, care must be taken not to confuse Scheffler's terminology with that used elsewhere in this paper. Of the two possible empiricistic views of mathematics that he distinguishes, the first tends to remove the subject to the realms of formalism, and only the second is akin to empiricism. By an entertaining quirk, the pragmatic view comes closest in formulation to formalism, with its acceptance of the meaningless element, and its concern for mutual relations. This view is derived partly from the relevant passage in *The Anatomy of Inquiry*,[30] as well as from *Conditions of Knowledge*.[31] However, in other ways the spirit of the two philosophies could hardly be more different.

Scheffler's own understanding of mathematical knowledge seems to be akin to the view that he himself calls 'rationalistic'[32] – an amalgam of the logicist and intuitionist. This conclusion is based on three factors: his actual description of this outlook (which seems to be written with a ring of conviction); his major reference books (such as those of Quine, who is in the logicist tradition, while having some affinity with intuitionism)[33] and his frequent references to mathematics in *Conditions of Knowledge*. These deal with adequate evidence for mathematical knowledge; in order to discuss them, it is necessary first to consider how he defines propositional knowledge.

Scheffler's definition of propositional knowledge ('X knows that Q', where Q is a proposition) is considered at length in *Conditions of Knowledge*. The definition in its first form[34] runs:

X knows that Q
if and only if
(1) X believes that Q
(2) X has adequate evidence that Q
(3) Q.

Scheffler later replaces condition (2) by the modified form:[35]

(2') X has the right to be sure that Q

due to A.J. Ayer.[36] This is done, primarily, to deal with the case when the concept of evidence is not applicable. In mathematics, however, the concept of evidence (in one form or another) is meaningful; so for this paper the definition is retained in its original form.

CONDITIONS OF KNOWLEDGE FOR MATHEMATICAL PROOF

In *Conditions of Knowledge*[37] Scheffler provided a detailed investigation of the evidence condition (2) in connection with mathematical proof. A key issue is the nature of adequate evidence. Scheffler makes valid points about the fact that having the evidence potentially available, and having the statement of what we want to prove, does not mean having the proof. (In formalist terms, this fact is an instance of the general result that any system powerful enough to express much mathematics is undecidable: there is no mechanical way of checking if an arbitrary given formula is derivable.[38]) In this context, the following formulation can be considered:

(2) X recognizing that he or she has a proof of Q.

This is intended to mean that X really does have a proof, and that X thinks it is a proof for the right reasons. Thus, the following definition of mathematical knowledge is tentatively adopted:

X knows that Q
if and only if
(1) X believes that Q
(2*) X recognizing that he or she has a proof of Q
(3) Q.

For each philosophy, this definition can be critiqued in accordance with the tenets of that philosophy, and with regard to truth and proof; on the one hand to see if the definition is adequate, and on the other to eliminate any redundancy. It is argued here that for the three traditional philosophies, similar formulations are possible, in each case requiring only a suitable form of the evidence condition (2*), on the grounds that this encompasses conditions (1) and (3). However, it is also argued that such a reduction is not possible in the case of empiricism.[39]

With regard to intuitionism, the proof would not meet the criteria unless X recognized it as being a proof; the element of recognition is redundant, and the evidence condition can be stated as (2I): X has an intuitionistic proof that Q. The subjective element in intuitionism implies that 'X has a proof of Q' means the same as 'Q', so (2I) is equivalent to (3); moreover, having a proof involves believing it, so (2I) implies (1). Hence, the knowledge definition can be given as:

X has intuitionistic knowledge that Q
if and only if
(2I) X has an intuitionistic proof that Q.

In the case of logicism, having a proof does not necessarily entail recognizing that it is a proof, so a fuller evidence condition (2L) is required: X recognizing that he or she has a logicist proof that Q. Such a proof guarantees Q in the logicist scheme of things (although the reverse implication is not true, Q could be true, but no proof might yet have been discovered); it also compels belief. For logicism, therefore, the knowledge definition takes the form:

THE STATUS OF MATHEMATICAL KNOWLEDGE

X has logicist knowledge that Q
if and only if
(2L) X recognizing that he or she has a logicist proof that Q.

Formalism deals not with truth but with derivability in a particular system, say A: 'truth' applies to statements in the metatheory (arguments about A rather within A). Taking account of both derivations and metatheoretical arguments, the evidence condition for formalism can be rendered as (2F): X recognizing that he or she has a formalist proof that Q is derivable in A. Arguments similar to those for logicism show that (2F) implies – but is not implied by – (3) and also implies (1). The formalist version of the definition therefore becomes:

X has formalist knowledge that Q is derivable in A
if and only if
(2F) X recognizing that he or she has a formalist proof that Q is derivable in A.

For empiricist knowledge, arguments do not have the same compelling force and mathematics loses its uniquely absolutist status. In this case, the statement '(2*): X recognizing that he or she has a proof of Q' is too strong. Scheffler's original formulation is appropriate, with 'adequate evidence' probably referring to an apparently correct proof (but one that cannot provide certainty). In the absence of certainty, (2) does not imply (3). Moreover, the additional factor of belief is necessary, so (2) does not imply (1). Thus, the three conditions are independent:

X has empiricist knowledge that Q
if and only if
(1) X believes that Q
(2) X has adequate evidence that Q
(3) Q.

A *radical* empiricist might assert that 'knowledge' and 'truth' are not meaningful concepts. However, in this case the topic falls outside the scope of Scheffler's work, and can be omitted.

MATHEMATICAL KNOWLEDGE, PROOF AND UNDERSTANDING

Scheffler's discussion of the kind of evidence needed to satisfy the evidence condition can be investigated further. His context was that of 'a boy' learning mathematics: nowadays, presumably, he would not have limited his analysis to students of one sex! In particular, he examined Poincaré's claim that in order to be convinced by a proof, most people need not only to check the argument on a line-by-line basis, but also to appreciate the general strategy behind the argument – hence, to 'see the end from afar'. While in sympathy with the claim, Scheffler was somewhat less demanding than Poincaré in his requirements.

The argument in the previous subsection indicates that, for proofs or derivations according to logicist and formalist criteria, there is no such requirement. Line-by-line checking – establishing that each statement in the proof either is an obvious truth (logicism), or an axiom (formalism), or has been correctly established on the basis of earlier statements – is sufficient to guarantee the proof, or derivation, of the final statement. For intuitionism, perhaps, some sense of the overall strategy is necessary for recognizing a proof; Scheffler's interest in such a strategy being clear to the student is a pointer to the intuitionist element in his view of mathematics.

However, whatever about the necessity of appreciating the overall strategy, the desirability of doing so is not an issue. For the person learning mathematics, the endeavour is much more meaningful when the strategies, as well as the results, make sense. Hence, it is in accordance with the spirit of Scheffler's work that the discussion turns to implications for mathematics education.

Implications for mathematics education

The paper up to this point reflects work written up, under Professor Rice's supervision, in 1970. In its concern with the philosophies of mathematics considered in the preceding hundred years, and, in particular, with the debate about whether the foundations of the subject could be made secure, the analysis has not dated appreciably.[40] However, developments in the 1980s saw discussion of philosophies of mathematics emerge in a different context: that of mathematics education. Such discussion focused more on the beliefs about or conceptions of mathematics held by *users* of the subject, in particular, by teachers. Moreover, my own tentative thesis, with regard to mathematics education – that a teacher's espoused philosophy of mathematics would affect how he or she taught the subject – was addressed both theoretically and empirically by many writers.[41]

By the 1990s, when the work of Lakatos, and others of like mind, had become more widely known, it had become usual to classify views of mathematics broadly as 'absolutist' or 'fallibilist'.[42] On the one hand, logicism, formalism, and even intuitionism, in seeking to safeguard mathematics as a body of knowledge, are essentially absolutist. Also absolutist is the view of mathematics as a bag of tricks – useful but unsupported by meaning or reason – that serves to produce correct answers to exercises or problems. This view, which unfortunately may be rather prominent among the non-mathematical public, and even among non-specialist teachers of mathematics,[43] is perhaps a degenerate form of what Scheffler called pragmatism. The label 'mechanistic', drawn from a currently prominent approach to mathematics education, is used here.[44] On the other hand, approaches such as those of Lakatos, with more focus on continuing activity and uncertainty – on process rather than product – epitomize fallibilism. People who view mathematics essentially as an activity concerned with the solution or attempted solution of problems, and not as a body of knowledge, belong to a fallibilist, rather than an absolutist, tradition.

Just as modern mathematics affected many school curricula, especially in the 1960s, so the problem-solving approach has been influential in the formulation of curricula from the 1990s.[45] Moreover, just as modern mathematics curricula, when taught by teachers who were unaware of (or perhaps out of sympathy with) its philosophical roots, tended to degenerate into mechanistic curricula (rules without reasons),[46] so it might be argued that curricula, based on problem-solving approaches, are unlikely to be implemented successfully by teachers whose own views of mathematics – tacit or explicit – are firmly absolutist. Such a conclusion would be bad news for the mathematics curricula that are focused on a problem-solving approach.

However, a more nuanced argument is required. There has been a tendency in the literature to make a simplistic association between, on the one hand, teachers' absolutist views and transmission approaches to classroom practice, with students learning by rote, and on the other, teachers' fallibilist views and constructivist approaches to classroom practice, with students developing understanding.[47] Admittedly, in some cases, the associations may be strong. Teachers holding fallibilist views are likely to emphasize problem-solving activities that allow students to construct their knowledge, and to make sense of what they learn. Teachers holding mechanistic views are likely to encourage rote learning by their students, because they (the teachers) either do not have, or do not value, genuine understanding; they may well employ apparently efficient transmission approaches to teaching. However, in the case of those espousing other absolutist views, the simplistic analysis is inappropriate. Logicist, formalist and intuitionist conceptions of mathematics involve considerations of truth and meaning, albeit in somewhat differing forms; they are essentially about understanding. (A possible exception could be made with regard to extreme formalism, but, as pointed out above, there are few extreme formalists.) Teachers espousing such conceptions may well believe that a constructivist approach is suited, for example, to developing an understanding of theorems that present absolute truths (logicism); or to seeing the relationships that allow mathematics to be viewed as the study of structures (influenced by formalism); or – perhaps most naturally – to building up insights that determine knowledge (intuitionism).

Relevant considerations here are the source of authority with regard to mathematics as perceived by the students, and the type of evidence that is offered to them. Teachers with fallibilist conceptions of mathematics might work within the social constructivist paradigm that sits very comfortably with such views, establishing communities of learners who create and validate their own understanding of the subject. Teachers with absolutist conceptions might not work in such a way, but, with regard to their likely approaches, the holders of mechanist views can be distinguished from the others. For students learning from mechanist teachers, the authority is that of the teacher who tells them 'the rule'; the concept of evidence is irrelevant. For other absolutists, the authority is, and the evidence is provided by, the internal logic of mathematics itself. An archetypal example is that of the approach to solving equations. A mechanist might say: 'Take it over and change the sign.' The students may wonder: 'Take *what* over, and change the sign to *what*, and *why*?' Answers to the first two questions are likely to be specific to the equation being considered, and the answer to the third is: 'Because that's the rule.' The other absolutists would emphasize the reason: 'An equation relates two expressions that are equal. Whatever is done to one side must also be done to the other, in order to maintain equality.' In this case, the answer makes intrinsic sense, and, moreover, can be generalized to all future work on equations.

The argument can now be summarized, with regard to the implications for curriculum implementation: '[Changing] instructional practices in mathematics classrooms can not only be a matter of new curricula or of providing materials, but also a matter of challenging traditional personal philosophies of teachers. That is why philosophical reflections become more and more part of teacher education programs.'[48]

If it is assumed that constructivist classroom practices sit comfortably *only* with fallibilist views of mathematics, then the teacher education (or re-education) programme, needed for implementation of a curriculum that emphasizes constructive approaches, is formidable. It has to allow for critique of, and change in, perhaps deeply held beliefs about both the subject and the pedagogy. However, if constructivist practices are viewed as good ways of achieving meaningful learning of a more traditional version of mathematics, and if that more traditional view is taken to be acceptable, then – at least for teachers with logicist, formalist or intuitionist views – the chief focus can be put on pedagogy. For teachers with mechanist views, however, initial teacher education, and professional development programmes, would have to address both beliefs and pedagogy.

Conclusion

This paper has used the work of Israel Scheffler and other writers to illuminate different philosophies of mathematics, and to highlight the implications of each for mathematics education. It remains to consider the applications of the arguments to current mathematics education in Ireland.

After an interesting period in which public debate about second-level mathematics education in Ireland moved from preoccupation with content and assessment, to consideration of teaching and learning, a novel approach in the Irish context was adopted in order to address the perceived issues. 'Project Maths' was initiated in twenty-four schools, on a pilot basis, in autumn 2008; a revised curriculum is being phased in, and is intended to be implemented nationwide by 2015.[49] While the literature on the project refers chiefly to emphasis on problem-solving and applications, presentations to groups of teachers and others have focused, especially, on teaching and learning for understanding.

The themes raised in this paper are likely to be crucial in determining whether or not Project Maths achieves its aims. The support for, and involvement of, teachers, especially in the pilot schools, is much greater than for previous curriculum changes; an encouraging aspect is that some attention is being paid to beliefs about mathematics. It would be exciting if a body of teachers came to espouse fallibilist views, and hence introduced (or gave greater emphasis than at present to) social constructivist practices in their classes, and allowed learners to understand their mathematics, and also validate their own learning. However, it would be satisfying enough if teachers espousing absolutist views emphasized (or increased their emphasis on) learning for understanding, and, in the course of their teaching appealed, at least, to the authority of mathematics itself. Many do so already, but there is evidence that many do not.[50] In any case, there is a major task ahead for teacher education, in addressing teachers' understanding of mathematical knowledge, and its implications for the successful implementation of meaningful learning in mathematics.

The original version of this paper, written under the supervision of Professor Rice in 1970, ended by posing a question that can be asked in extended form here: to what extent should the philosophy, or philosophies, underlying a course in mathematics, be made explicit, not only to the teachers, but also to the students? One thought-provoking answer is given by Prediger, Viggiani-Bicudo and Ernest, and is offered here in conclusion: 'The idea of making explicit the implicit philosophies is not restricted to teacher education or professional discussions of reform curricula. Instead, it should also be transported into the classrooms itself. Perhaps only if students can reflect on central questions in philosophy of mathematics themselves, they will develop a well-balanced and reflective knowledge of mathematics.'[51]

NOTES

1. R. Thom, 'Modern Mathematics: Does it Exist?' in A.G. Howson (ed.), *Developments in Mathematical Education: Proceedings of the Second International Congress on Mathematical Education* (Cambridge 1973), pp. 194–209.
2. E.E. Oldham, 'Mathematical knowledge and education: a study based on the work of Israel Scheffler' (unpublished higher diploma in education minor thesis, TCD 1970).
3. The thinking in the sections of this paper, on philosophies of mathematics and on the work of Israel Sheffler, is put forward as it was in 1970. However, the prose has been edited somewhat, to conform to a style of writing that is found in philosophy and education, rather than in mathematics (which tends to use the first person plural, e.g. 'We shall now ...', 'Let us examine ...' – an approach that did not appeal to Professor Rice!), and to reflect the passage of time, which rendered some comments anachronistic.
4. For a good account of the critical movement, see G.T. Kneebone, *Mathematical Logic and the Foundations of Mathematics* (London 1963), pp. 133–55.
5. S.C. Kleene, *Introduction to Metamathematics* (Amsterdam 1952), p. 46.
6. Kneebone, *Mathematical Logic*, p. 244.
7. *Ibid.*
8. *Ibid.* p. 249.
9. E. Bishop, *Foundations of Constructive Analysis* (New York 1967), p. 2.
10. See in particular A. Heyting, *Intuitionism: An Introduction* (Amsterdam 1966), pp. 1–12.
11. This remark by Heyting is quoted (translated from the German) in Kleene, *Introduction to Metamathematics*, p. 51.
12. A.N. Whitehead and B. Russell, *Principia Mathematica* (Cambridge 1910–1913).
13. Kneebone, *Mathematical Logic*, pp. 156–8 and pp. 312–19; G.T. Kneebone (unpublished lectures, Bedford College, University of London 1965–6).
14. Again arguments are synthesized, chiefly from Kneebone, *Mathematical*

Logic, pp. 40–208, *passim*, and from notes taken in Kneebone, unpublished lectures; almost any book on formal logic would provide a source here.
15. Imre Lakatos attributes to H.B. Curry an 'extreme' formalist position, which really does recognize any consistent formal system as being mathematics; he points out that even Curry is interested in applications, usefulness, and so forth (notes taken from I. Lakatos, Unpublished seminar presentation, London School of Economics, University of London, 10 November 1966).
16. D. Hilbert, *From Frege to Gödel: A Source Book in Mathematical Logic 1879–1931*, ed., J. van Heijenoort (Massachusetts 1967), p. 464.
17. K. Gödel, 'Über formal unentscheidbare Sätze der Principia Mathematica und verwändter Systeme 1', *Monatshefte für Mathematik und Physik*, 38 (1931), 173–98.
18. Bishop, *Foundations of Constructive Analysis*, p. 6.
19. Kneebone, *Mathematical Logic*, p. 326. Again, Kneebone's book (especially p. 118 and pp. 325–30), together with his lecture notes, is a major source of information. It should be noted that Kneebone writes as if Bourbaki is an individual, rather than a syndicate or group. [Since the original version of this paper was written, Bourbakiste modern mathematics has become less influential.]
20. See for example F. van der Blij, S. Hilding and A.I. Weinzweig, 'A synthesis of national reports on changes in curricula' in H. G. Steiner (ed.), *Comparative Studies of Mathematics Curricula: Change and Stability 1960–1980*, Materialen und Studien Band 19 (Bielefeld 1980), pp. 37–54.1; A.G. Howson, C. Keitel and J. Kilpatrick, *Curriculum Development in Mathematics* (Cambridge 1981). [Obviously, these were not part of the original paper; the comments on the impact of modern mathematics are added with hindsight.]
21. Kneebone, *Mathematical Logic*, p. 326.
22. N. Bourbaki, *Elements of Mathematics: Theory of Sets* (Paris 1968), p. 13.
23. Imre Lakatos, unpublished seminar presentation, University of London, 10 November 1966.
24. Imre Lakatos, 'Proofs and refutations', *British Journal for the Philosophy of Science*, 14 (1963–4), 6. He uses the term 'quasi-empirical' (also rendered 'empiricist'), because mathematics does not necessarily deal with the spatio-temporal, as does a truly empirical scientific theory.
25. Imre Lakatos, 'Infinite regress and foundations of mathematics', *Aristotelian Society*, xxxv (1962), 165. Unfortunately, elsewhere in this paper Lakatos uses the word 'empiricist' rather differently from the way he uses it in his later work, and here it does not describe his own views.
26. I. Scheffler, *Conditions of Knowledge* (Illinois 1965).

27. *Ibid.* p. 2.
28. *Ibid.* p. 4.
29. *Ibid.*
30. I. Scheffler, *The Anatomy of Inquiry: Philosophical Studies in the Theory of Science* (New York 1967), pp. 182–7.
31. Scheffler, *Conditions of Knowledge*, p. 68.
32. *Ibid.* p. 2.
33. Kneebone, *Mathematical Logic*, pp. 190 and 396. Professor Rice, in a personal communication to the author (1970), reinforced the likelihood of such influence.
34. Scheffler, *Conditions of Knowledge*, p. 21.
35. *Ibid.* pp. 58–65.
36. A.J. Ayer, *The Problem of Knowledge* (Harmondsworth 1956), pp. 31–5.
37. Scheffler, *Conditions of Knowledge*, pp. 68–72.
38. This follows from the work of A. Church, 'An unsolvable problem of elementary number theory', *American Journal of Mathematics*, 58 (1936), 345–63; and J.B. Rosser, 'Extensions of theorems of Gödel and Church', *Journal of Symbolic Logic*, 1 (1936), 87–91.
39. Fuller arguments were presented in the original paper (Oldham, 'Mathematical knowledge', 1970).
40. A similar analysis is made in John Dossey, 'The Nature of Mathematics: Its Role and Influence' in D.A. Grouws (ed.), *Handbook of Research on Mathematics Teaching and Learning* (New York 1992), pp. 39–48.
41. Key references include T.J. Cooney, 'A beginning teacher's view of problem solving', *Journal for Research in Mathematics Education*, 16 (5) (1985), 324–336; Dossey, 'The nature of mathematics'; P. Ernest, 'The philosophy of mathematics and mathematics education', *International Journal for Mathematical Education in Science and Technology*, 16 (5) (1985), 603–612; A.G. Thompson, 'Teachers' Beliefs and Conceptions: A Synthesis of the Research' in Grouws, *Handbook*, pp. 127–46; and S. Lerman, 'Problem solving or knowledge centered: the influence of philosophy on mathematics teaching' in *International Journal of Mathematical Education in Science and Technology*, 14 (1) (1983), 59–66, cited in Thompson, 'Teachers' Beliefs'. The work of Paul Ernest in the philosophy of mathematics education is particularly notable.
42. Thompson, 'Teachers' Beliefs', pp. 127–46.
43. J. Sowder, 'The Mathematical Education and Development of Teachers' in F.K. Lester (ed.), *Second Handbook of Research on Mathematics Teaching and Learning* (Charlotte, North Carolina 2007), pp. 157–224. The large body of work on teacher knowledge and beliefs, except as related above to philosophies of mathematics, is outside the scope of this paper.
44. The approach is that of 'realistic mathematics education'; see, for example,

J. de Lange, 'Real problems with real world mathematics' in C. Alsina *et al.* (eds), *Proceedings of the Eighth International Congress on Mathematical Education, Sevilla 14–21 July 1996* (Seville 1996).

45. See for example W.H. Cockcroft, *Mathematics Counts: Report of the committee of inquiry into the teaching of mathematics in schools under the chairmanship of Dr W.H. Cockcroft* [The Cockcroft Report] (London 1982); NCTM, *Curriculum and Evaluation Standards for School Mathematics* (Reston, Virginia 1989); NCTM, *Principles and Standards for School Mathematics* (Reston, Virginia 2000).
46. Van der Blij *et al.*, 'A synthesis of national reports'; A.G. Howson and B. Wilson, *School Mathematics in the 1990s* (Cambridge 1986).
47. S. Prediger, M. Vigiani-Bicudo and P. Ernest, 'DG4: philosophy of mathematics education' in M. Niss (ed.), *ICME – 10 Proceedings: Proceedings of the 10th International Congress on Mathematical Education, 4–11 July 2004* (Roskilde, Denmark 2008), pp. 438–42.
48. *Ibid.* p. 441.
49. National Council for Curriculum and Assessment, *Project Maths: Information for Schools* (Dublin 2008). Online at www.ncca.ie/en/Curriculum_and_Assessment/Post-Primary_Education/Review_of_Mathematics/Project_Maths/Project_Maths_Update/Project_Maths_leaflet_for_schools.pdf.
50. A.E. Beaton *et al.*, *Mathematics Achievement in the Middle-School Years: IEA's Third International Mathematics and Science Study* (Chestnut Hill, Massachusetts 1996).
51. Prediger *et al.*, 'DG4', p. 441.

ELIZABETH OLDHAM read for her H.Dip. and MEd with Val Rice and later became a member of staff in the School of Education, TCD. She has published extensively in the area of mathematics education and has been influential in mathematics curriculum development in Ireland.

Knowledge and the Idea of the University: Val Rice and John Henry Cardinal Newman

AIDAN SEERY

On one of his last appearances in a public educational setting, following a lecture in the series to commemorate the centenary anniversary of the 1905 chair of education in Trinity, Val Rice waited, as was his custom, until the end of the question session. He then rose from his seat, placed his left hand in his blazer pocket and, with the right, brought out his signature index cards. He paused and then began his three-minute discourse (in the old-fashioned use of this term) on Newman's *Idea of a University*.

These studied actions and gestures, as well as the theme, were familiar to both his students and colleagues over the many years of his incumbency of the same chair of education celebrated in those lectures. In his thirty-nine years as Professor of Education, he embodied the now-vanished traits of the gentleman-scholar, showing a constant and growing concern for the changing nature of the university. His concern, shared increasingly by others, centred principally on the perceived decline, in stature and influence, of the teaching role in academic life. His own belief in a view of the university, primarily as a teaching institution, was at the heart of a coherent and carefully constructed philosophy of education, which he taught to generations of educators willing to engage with it.

His interest in, and frequent recalling of, Newman's idea of the university, may often have inspired a smile at the notion of a finishing school for gentlemen in mid-Victorian Oxford being held up as a model of the modern university. And while Val did often quote the well-known passage in Newman in which he describes the university as a place where 'an assemblage of learned men, zealous for their own sciences, and rivals of each other, are brought, by familiar intercourse and for the sake of intellectual peace, to adjust together the claims and relations of their respective subjects of investigation',[1] I want to suggest here that it was not a hankering back to a romantic past that ultimately determined his views (although a nostalgia for the past was not unknown in him). Rather, a close reading of Newman's text, together with the text of some of Val's lectures, suggests the tentative argument that Val shared Newman's view of the university because he shared his theory of knowledge. It is this thesis that I would like to explore in just a little more detail.

An outline of the theory of knowledge of the Discourses

In the *Discourses on the Idea of a University* the pillar of Newman's argument is his claim of the unity of all knowledge: '... the various branches of science [knowledge] are intimately connected with each other, and form one whole ...'.[2] This fundamental assumption supports the two main arguments of the *Discourses*: first, that the university should teach 'universal knowledge'[3] and second, as a consequence, that it is inconstant to exclude theology from the university curriculum. Thus, for Newman, the idea of the university is founded in a fundamental assumption about the nature of knowledge.

Newman's further argument is difficult to fault in its execution but, as with all syllogistic reasoning, the truth of the conclusions is entirely dependent on the truth of the initial premises. The argument, then, for the kind of university proposed, while being structurally sound, is really only convincing if the major premise is accepted, and Newman's theory of knowledge constitutes the major premise of the *Discourses*. For this reason, it is worth examining this assumption, in as much detail as is allowed by the text of the *Idea of a University*. This examination can then be used to throw light on the theory of knowledge, as taught by Val Rice in his lectures on rational and aesthetic knowledge.

I think that Newman's unity assumption can be read on a number of levels. First, the unity of the bodies of knowledge as a network of *relationships*: 'All that exists, as contemplated by the human mind, forms one large system or complex fact, and this, of course, resolves itself into an indefinite number of particular facts, which, as being portions of the whole, have countless relations of every kind towards each other.'[4] The claim of countless relations may seem reckless, but is explained somewhat by the further elaboration made, concerning both the functional and structural properties of the bodies of knowledge. For one, there is the constant and dynamic functional relationship of mutual revision, reinforcement and endorsement, correction and augmentation. Newman does not subscribe to the now readily accepted division of knowledge, between *Geisteswissenschaften* and *Naturwissenschaften*, made famous by Dilthey. Indeed, in his conviction of the unity and inter-relatedness of all knowledge, including revealed knowledge, Newman accepts the possibility of revelation contradicting and correcting both history and the natural sciences: 'Thus, in the science of history, the preservation of our race in Noah's ark is an historical fact, which history never would arrive at without Revelation.'[5] As each of the sciences changes and grows, so do the relations that any one science holds to another, and so the claim that the relations are countless can be justified.

If more evidence were required to support Newman's rejection of strict divisions between bodies of knowledge, then it is contained in an interesting passage that is almost postmodern in its tenor: ' ... there are no natural or real limits between part and part; one is ever running into another; all, as viewed by the mind, are combined together'.[6] This structural fluidity, in the boundaries of the bodies of knowledge, is recognized as a characteristic of the way in which the world is apprehended by the mind. It is 'as contemplated by the mind' that perceptions of the world are grasped and wrought, by the power of intellect, into knowledge. But this does not make Newman an idealist. The bodies of knowledge remain, despite their fluid boundaries, representations of objective truth. Newman is demonstrably an ontological realist, but this does not, necessarily, determine his epistemological position. What is at stake here is the claim that, because of the absence of fixed boundaries, and because of the reciprocal corrective relationships between the bodies of knowledge, no one science or way of knowing can claim to be the only possible or legitimate one. Not only that, there is the distinct danger that, in over-specialism and concentration on one view of the world, facts about the world are decided by theory. Thus, for instance, if the only view of the world that is permitted is a physicalist one, then the only facts about the world that are considered legitimate are physical facts. This restrictive view cannot, however, be warranted within a physicalist grammar. It is only by putting together the largest number of individual sciences that the knower advances towards a complete and accurate knowledge of the world.[7] It is this view that underpins the argument for the teaching of universal knowledge in a university.

Secondly, in addition to the unity of all knowledge, in the interrelatedness of all ways of knowing, Newman also claims a unity of knowledge on a *methodological* level. Common to all of the sciences are the notions of method, order, principle, reasoning and system, of rule and exception, richness and harmony.[8] Regardless of the subject studied, the student 'apprehends the great outlines of knowledge, the principles on which it rests, the scale of its parts, its lights and its shades, its great points and its little, as he otherwise cannot apprehend them'[9] and '[a] habit of mind is formed ... of which the attributes are freedom, equitableness, calmness, moderation and wisdom'.[10]

If it is the case, as argued also by Ortega and Gasset,[11] that human beings cannot live in the world without constructing an intellectual interpretation of it, then it is not surprising that all attempts to give meaning to life would share some general characteristics of human reasoning, provided they can be distinguished from mythology and superstition. On the other hand, the idea of formulating learning outcomes to include calmness, moderation and wisdom seems absurd. It is unlikely that this idea would appear in the strategic plan of a modern university and not just because they are not measurable!

Finally, on a *functional* level also, there is, for Newman, a unity of all knowledge. Reflecting Aquinas's theory of the *intellectus agens* and

Aquinas's own reliance on Aristotle, Newman claims that all knowledge is a result of the mind acting on perceptions and new ideas, in a formative exercise that reduces the mass of information both to order and to our purposes. Only then is knowledge our own.[12] As a result, learning and knowledge is never passive assimilation, and all sciences are indeed one 'as contemplated by the mind'.[13]

> The intellect of man [sic], on the contrary, energizes as well as his eye or ear, and perceives in sights and sounds something beyond them. It seizes and unites what the senses present to it; it grasps and forms what need not have been seen or hear except in its constituent parts ... It distinguishes between rule and exception, between accident and design. It assigns phenomena to a general law, qualities to a subject, acts to a principle, and effects to a cause.[14]

This activity of the mind, in shaping and adding to sense data, together with the synthesis and comparison of phenomena and abstract patterns, is not restricted to any one science or body of knowledge but is shared by all of our efforts to make sense of the coercive demands of knowledge decisions.

This theory of knowledge and mind has been challenged and rejected by many a philosopher in the last century and even before, but it is not my purpose here to rehearse these objectives, or to raise a defence of Newman's ideas. This purely descriptive treatment is to provide a platform, to examine some of Val Rice's thoughts on the theme of knowledge and the university, and it is to these that we now turn.

Val Rice on rational and artistic knowledge

The core assumption of the unity of all knowledge, found clearly in Newman's *Idea of the University*, is to be found also in the few writings of J.V. Rice. Val Rice, regrettably, published little during his career, a fact reflected upon by John Heywood in another contribution to this volume. However, in 2001, his health did not permit him to complete his lecture series to the higher diploma in education class of the year, and he produced two monographs for the use of students: one on rational knowledge, and the other on poetic and artistic knowledge. This obviously does not constitute a body of work, and with such a paucity of sources, there is a danger of over-interpretation of what is available. On the other hand, having studied and worked with Val for a number of years, I think it is possible, at least, to sketch his thoughts on epistemology from these sources.

First, it is clear that Val Rice considered the acquisition and growth in knowledge to be the central mission of education. This concern comes before any consideration of education, or schooling, as social reproduction or cultural transmission, which are deemed secondary aims. This is not to say that education can remove itself from the realms of society, politics and economics and flee to the sanctuary of the contemplation of truth. On the contrary, knowledge is a problem; we struggle to understand what it is. It comes about only in communicative, social and cultural settings, and tensions also exist between different bodies of knowledge, vying for recognition and legitimacy. To be a teacher is to grapple with these contending voices and situational complexity since, without an understanding of knowledge and its settings, there is no satisfactory or successful teaching. In the field of curriculum theory also, an understanding of the structure of knowledge, and the kinds of knowledge that are involved in the different disciplines, is required for any rational curriculum design. In Val Rice's words: 'It is therefore imperative that we should attempt to confront the problem of knowledge, and that we should attempt to understand what knowledge is, how knowledge comes about, and whether there are different kinds of knowledge ... If we understand what knowledge is and how it comes about, we will know how to teach it.'[15]

Of particular and even exclusive interest to him was the latter question of how knowledge comes about. The Aristotelian and Thomist foundations of Newman's functional unity of knowledge, in the νους ποιετικος or *intellectus agens*, is evident in Val's description of 'an active and creative element in the mind which could address a sequence of images and experiences and release what was common to them'.[16] A distinction between Newman's moulding and shaping mind, and Val's description, lies in Val's stronger realist view of the innate structure and form of objects being simply released in the encounter with mind. This places his theory of knowledge firmly in the era preceding the epistemological turn, with its shift from the idea of the world presenting itself to the mind as it is, to consideration of the conditions of the possibility of knowing the world, in perception and conceptual reason.

In contrast, too, to some of the ideas presented in *The Idea of a University*, Val's essays present the idea of the mind acting upon itself in such a way that the mechanisms at the core of the creative and knowing mind can, themselves, be known in reflection. In this claim he relies almost completely on the theory of knowledge and knowing developed by the Jesuit philosopher, Bernard Lonergan.

Val's personal and intellectual involvement with Lonergan is well known to generations of his students and colleagues, and need not be discussed here. With regard to the topic in hand, Lonergan provides a kind of second-order description of reason by claiming that, in introspection, the subject is capable of perceiving and understanding the first-order processes of the mind, in shaping, grasping, ordering and comparing phenomena in the mind, and is also capable of discovering not only patterns in the functions and processes of reasoning, but *invariant* patterns at that. This bold claim, that there are universal structures and laws that precede and guide all acts of knowing, which are epistemically accessible to the knowing subject, is the central theme in Lonergan's *Insight*, which became Val's 'knowledge bible'. Lonergan echoes Newman's unity of knowledge in mind functionality but expands the claim: 'Not only is the percept inquired about, understood, formulated, reflected on, grasped as unconditioned, and affirmed but also there is an identity involved in perceiving, inquiring, understanding, formulating, reflecting, grasping the unconditioned, and affirming. Indeed, consciousness is much more obviously of this unity in diverse acts than of the diverse acts.'[17]

So, common to all bodies of knowledge is not only the shared functions of the mind, but these functions exhibit an invariant pattern of operation, regardless of the intentional object of knowing. The same process and dynamic of insight is at work in all areas of human inquiry, from science and mathematics to history, the arts and literature, and theology, thus guaranteeing a strong version of knowledge unity.

Regarding Newman's unity of knowledge in the *relationship* of the bodies of knowledge with each other, Val Rice understandably does not pursue the idea of the 'sciences' competing, augmenting and correcting each other. Although a believer, I do not think that he would argue for the possibility of theology furnishing historical or scientific facts. On the other hand, he did teach a theory of creative invention that is based on Arthur Koestler's idea, of two 'frames of reference' coming into simultaneous focus, and a single idea that 'bisociates' them. In this process, two bodies of knowledge brought to bear on a single event or occurrence may not correct or augment each other so much as bring forth something new. This 'insight that grounds the act of creation' obviously can occur only in the situation in which the knower is exposed to different ways of seeing and knowing the world. Here again we have one more argument for a university of universal knowledge that allows the study of all disciplines.

The knowing of poetic and artistic knowledge, as taught by Val, consists also in the encounter of two ways of engaging with the world. At the level of experience, the 'buzzing, booming confusion'[18] of the world is chaotic and bewildering. In the encounter with the rational mind, this chaos is ordered by the processes of concept-formation, judgment and logic, in the attempt to make sense of otherwise meaningless tragedy. Art, which results from this tense encounter, can therefore be understood 'only in terms of an adequate theory of knowledge'[19] since it 'brings into play a unique form of knowledge'. This unique form of knowledge has a number of unusual features. Using the metaphor of physical resonance, Val Rice presumes that situations and events in the world possess a structure and order that can be understood analogously to the characteristic frequency, possessed by all material bodies, which manifests itself when the object is struck. In the tense encounter with the world, a human being is capable not only of picking up these vibrations, but of responding to them, in the way in which a second body resonates in sympathy with a first of the same characteristic frequency. As in the case of the physical event, the analogous resonance of the individual with the world releases energy, this time in the form of artistic creativity.

The metaphor is apt, at least to the degree that it suggests a response of the whole human being to the event. Artistic expression and experience is a matter not only of emotion and feeling, it is a physical and cognitive response also. Equally, the knowledge gained in encounters with art is not solely subjective; art says something about the world. The use of this metaphor indicates a fundamentally naturalist, and essentialist, understanding of artistic and poetic engagement with the world. There is the suggestion of an underlying order and harmony in the world, which is reflected in the order and harmony of human emotion and cognition. The resonance of the two reveals the inner structure of both, so that in art and poetry, something of the world and something of 'the intimate subjectivity of a living human being' is revealed.[20]

However one might view the metaphysical assumptions at the core of this theory of knowledge, in the light of linguistic, phenomenological or postmodernist objections, the similarities between Val Rice's and Newman's positions seem clear. Both are metaphysical realists, and both believe in the possibility of grasping how the world really is, by means of reason, empathy and cognition. The bodies of knowledge are various in perspectives, but come together in an actively unifying human consciousness.

The consequences for the university, and specifically for teaching, are also clear. If there are common procedures and functions, in the act of coming to know, in all bodies of knowledge, then an understanding of these can form the basis of a science of teaching. For Val Rice, this was central to his theory of teaching. The act of human insight, applied to the levels of both phenomenal experience and the relationships between the bodies of knowledge, 'confers a startling unity and simplicity on the teaching process'.[21] Teaching is the act of bringing the student to an understanding of the connection between data, and an understanding of the relationship between the different bodies of knowledge. This can be achieved only if the student is exposed to different ways of seeing and grasping the world: the scientific, mathematical, artistic and poetic lenses of the human view. The university is the place and space in which these lenses are polished to the highest degree of clarity, yielding a more defined and differentiated picture, not only of the world but of the self.

The theory of knowledge and education outlined here sits uneasily with, or is firmly rejected by, many who consider its metaphysics and epistemology as refuted by much of the philosophy of the twentieth century. It is, indeed, a long way from contemporary, more reductionist positions of education as socialization and knowledge as commodity. On the other hand, there are recent indications, that current sociological, psychological and economic theories of education and learning are not rich enough to provide human beings even with some rudimentary repertory of ideas, interpretations and meanings, to inform the pressing moral, social and even economic decisions demanded by 'the coerciveness of life's demands'.[22] Val Rice's views and approach have suffered, as a result of what many regard as the 'death of metaphysics', and the failure of the modernist project, but there are elements of his and Newman's views, on education and knowledge, to which we may well return.

NOTES

1. J.H. Newman, *The Idea of a University*, ed. M.J. Svaglic (Indiana 1982), p. 76.
2. *Ibid.* p. 54.
3. *Ibid.* p. 15.
4. *Ibid.* p. 33.
5. *Ibid.* p. 54.
6. *Ibid.* p. 34.
7. *Ibid.* p. 35.
8. *Ibid.* p. xliv.
9. *Ibid.* p. 76.
10. *Ibid.*
11. José Ortega and Gasset, *The Mission of the University* (London 1946), p. 65.
12. Newman, *The Idea of a University*, p. 101.
13. *Ibid.* p. 33.
14. *Ibid.* p. 56.
15. J.V. Rice, 'Rational knowledge' (unpublished lecture notes, TCD 2000), p. 1.
16. *Ibid.* p. 10.
17. B.J. Lonergan, *Insight: A Study of Human Understanding* (London 1957), p. 325.
18. William James quoted in J.V. Rice, 'Poetic and artistic knowledge' (unpublished lecture notes, TCD 2000).
19. *Ibid.* p. 5.
20. *Ibid.* p. 8.
21. Rice, 'Rational knowledge', p. 13.
22. Ortega and Gasset, *The Mission of the University* (Norton 1944), p. 72.

Educating for Consistency in Knowing and Doing

RAYMOND TOPLEY

This paper in honour of the memory of Professor Valentine Rice centres upon a particular question that he posed to Bernard Lonergan, during an extensive interview in March 1980. The paper will begin, however, with reference to Lonergan's challenging invitation to teachers, some decades earlier, to give practical expression to the theoretical material he was placing before them. It will then go on to highlight Val Rice's fruitful response to this challenge, and will proceed from there to identify his own particular educational concern, arising from his familiarity with Lonergan's work. That work will be the focus of the next part of the paper, designed to ascertain the attraction of a philosopher like Lonergan for an educator like Rice. The remaining part will propose a teaching strategy, inspired by a Lonerganian perspective, as a considered response to Rice's concern regarding educating for consistency in one's knowing and doing.

Lonergan's challenge to educators

In 1959, Bernard Lonergan conducted a two-week summer school on the philosophy of education in Cincinnati, Ohio. The lectures delivered on that occasion were later published under the title *Topics in Education*.[1]

The stated intent of the programme was to assist the participants in appreciating what a Catholic philosophy of education might look like. The audience was comprised mainly of personnel from religious orders. The organizers, and Lonergan himself, were conscious that such a group, at that time, would not possess an extensive background in philosophy. Accordingly, Lonergan looked upon the occasion as an opportunity for initiating a dialogue between the philosopher and the educator. It would be his role to present the theory, and it would be up to those present to discern its practical relevance to education. At the outset he articulated his understanding of the respective tasks ensuing as follows:

> I am not a specialist in education, but I have suffered under educators for many years, and I have been teaching for an equally long time ... I speak about philosophy and its relation to theology and concrete living. But most of the concrete applications, the ironing out of things, will have to be done by you who are in the fields of education and the philosophy of education.[2]

In stating the case in such a straightforward manner. Lonergan was clearly laying down a challenge for educators – and not just for those present – in respect of the pioneering work he himself was engaged in, particularly in relation to the nature of methodology, human knowing and human authenticity. It was his expressed hope, as we can see, that educators would take seriously their side of the bargain in 'ironing out' concrete and practical educational applications of his discoveries and insights. As to how responsive the educational community has been to this challenge, the findings are not as encouraging or as immediate as one might have hoped for, given the extent of Lonergan studies worldwide. Moira Carley, at the outset of her own Harvard-based doctoral work on Lonergan, discovered that of seventy-two doctoral theses directly concerned with Lonergan's work up to that time (1989), none applied his thought to teaching. Understandably, she concluded that 'the application of Lonergan's work to teaching in general has yet to be done'.[3]

Rice's response and concern

A notable exception to this seeming neglect, however, was to be found at Trinity College Dublin, due to the enthusiastic endorsement of

EDUCATION FOR CONSISTENCY IN KNOWING AND DOING

Lonergan and his work by Professor Valentine Rice of the Department of Education. During the final quarter-century of his tenure as head of the department, until his retirement in 2005, he oversaw the completion of over a dozen pieces of research in the area of Lonergan studies, at both masters and doctorate levels.[4] With the exception of one earlier contribution, this remarkable series of Lonergan-focused theses began, effectively, in 1980. Also in March of that same year, Val held the first of fifteen interviews with Lonergan, the last of which was completed in September 1981, just three years before the renowned Jesuit passed away at the age of eighty.[5] While the general intent of the interviews was to source material for a biographical project on Lonergan, the transcripts also contained pointers to the interest that Lonergan held for an educator such as Val. Here it has to be borne in mind that Professor Rice approached Lonergan not from the perspective of philosophy, theology or economics – all fields in which Lonergan possessed an acknowledged expertise – but from that of education.

Furthermore, an educator approaches the likes of Lonergan much the same way as one would approach a well in a desert, bucket in hand – namely with a view to taking away from the encounter something of practical use for one's educational endeavours. That Val was similarly preoccupied is evident from the very opening interview that he conducted with Lonergan. He clearly declared that he was coming to the master 'from the point of view of education'.[6] He then revealed his principal interest, as an educator, in Lonergan's work, by articulating the following queries:

> It seems to me ... there's first of all the importance of encouraging insight in young people, and there is, secondly, the business of getting them to achieve consistency between their knowing and their doing. The one is the intellectual side of education, the other is the moral. Have you any ideas as to how one could go about both? First of all, how can one encourage young people, or old people, to achieve insight? Is there any programme that can be followed? Any set of exercises, any advice?[7]

Lonergan, in respect of the first question, about how to encourage people to gain insight, tersely replied, 'Set them problems.' This seemed to satisfy his interlocutor. However, Val's search for direction as to how learners might be brought to a level of consistency between their knowing and their doing did not quite elicit the kind of response he was so anxiously seeking. This is evident from the fact that Val had to raise or allude to this particular issue no less than six times during the course of this single interview![8] After the fourth time, for instance, while still searchingly enquiring, 'What can we do to encourage that [consistency in knowing and doing] in education?'[9] he resigned himself, for the time being, to simply suggesting they move on to his next question.

It is clear from the above that in respect of Lonergan's work this particular issue loomed large for Rice. He wished to discover how, through the instrumentality of education, learners could be helped to achieve consistency between knowing and doing, and thereby realize and constitute themselves as authentic human subjects. Further indication as to the importance of this question for him is evident from notes, taken by students, during his College courses and lectures.[10] But why, one might ask, did Val Rice look to Bernard Lonergan for light in the resolution of such an issue? To answer this question one would need to recall, firstly, the impact made by Lonergan on the intellectual scene in his day and, secondly, to note, particularly, his contribution in clarifying, with striking methodological precision, the workings of the human mind, and the inter-connectedness of the cognitional and the volitional in the make-up of the human person. And so to a snapshot of Lonergan and his principal writings.

Lonergan's contribution

Born in Canada in 1904, Bernard Lonergan joined the Jesuits soon after leaving school. Quite early on in his academic career, when studying at Heythrop College, England, he revealed in a letter to a confrere: 'The theory of knowledge is what is going to interest me most of all.'[11] This interest provided an intellectual focus for him, and eventually culminated in his best-known work, *Insight: A Study of Human Understanding* (1957). It was followed, some years later, by his other major work, *Method in Theology* (1972). Either side of these undertakings, and in between, he produced many other writings in the areas of philosophy, theology, education and economics. An appreciation of the reception accorded Lonergan and his endeavours may be glimpsed by recalling observations from both admirers and critics alike. Even a brief selection will reveal Lonergan as one of those figures loved and loathed in almost equal measure. John Macquarrie is reported to have described *Insight* as a jungle of a book while others complained of Lonergan's propensity for excessive analysis and obfuscation.[12]

On the other hand, admirers swoon at the thought of him. '*Insight* is a breathtaking work,' declares Mark Doorley,[13] while Terry Tekippe described himself as 'a disciple unduly smitten with the brilliance of Lonergan's thought'.[14] Fellow Jesuit, William Van Roo, although critical of certain aspects of his work, admits that Lonergan's 'metaphysics is a magnificent work of human reason'.[15] Part of the problem with tackling Lonergan, particularly using *Insight* as a portal, is the demanding nature of the engagement. Countless readers have found the plethora of exercises unrealistically demanding, unnecessarily time-consuming and too high a price to pay for accessing the heart of what Lonergan is about. Fred Crowe, long-time colleague and disciple of Lonergan, probably had something of this in mind when, anecdotally, he noted, 'If you want instant results, get out of the Lonergan business.' Lonergan himself never apologized for setting the intellectual bar high. Neither did he shirk such challenges himself, spending 'years reaching up to the mind of Aquinas'[16] and declaring:

> There is a disinterestedness and an objectivity that comes only from aiming excessively high and far, that leaves one free to take each issue on its merits ... to seek no greater achievement than the inspiration of the moment warrants, to await with serenity for the coherence of truth itself to bring to light the underlying harmony of the manifold whose parts successively engage one's attention.[17]

However, anyone regarding this as too exalted an ideal will be encouraged by Hugo Meynell's comforting and encouraging observation that 'the basic principles of Lonergan's philosophy are not at all difficult to grasp'.[18] This upbeat note provides an opportune cue for grappling with these principles and exploring the extent to which they might contribute towards unlocking Val Rice's 'consistency' query noted above. The engagement will bring us face to face with Lonergan on methodology, cognition and authenticity.

Lonergan was happy to be described as a 'methodologist'.[19] With his interest in mathematics and science, particularly, he was partial to a methodical way of going about his scholarly and professional business, and he liked to say from time to time, 'It never hurts to know what you are about.'[20] In the opening chapter of *Method in Theology*, he outlines his search for what he terms a 'transcendental method', which he describes as 'a basic pattern of operations employed in every cognitional enterprise'.[21] He finds such a pattern in the operations of the human mind, an examination of which leads him to the conclusion that the human subject, in coming to know and act, progresses along four distinct levels of consciousness. A study of these levels and their implications will supply the key to unlocking Rice's question of Lonergan, regarding the promotion of consistency between one's knowing and one's doing.

In addition to naming and commenting on the levels, it should also be noted that each of them also requires the observance of a particular imperative, or 'must do', if the human subject is to participate, as genuinely and as authentically as the level in question requires. Accordingly, in the accounts of the levels that follow, the respective imperatives will be identified. The four levels of consciousness may be named respectively as the experiential, the intellectual, the rational and the responsible. A detailed look at the structure will reveal the nature of each of the levels in clearer light.

Lonergan's levels

THE EXPERIENTIAL LEVEL

This is the level at which the principal operations, on the part of the human subject, are those pertaining to the senses, namely seeing, hearing, tasting, touching and smelling, or, alternatively, remembering sense experiences from the past or imagining them in the future. The only requirement on the part of the person, at this juncture, is to 'be attentive', nothing more, nothing less. Once the required attentiveness is achieved, the mind takes over, conjuring up questions in search of answers. This propels the person to the next level.

THE INTELLECTUAL LEVEL

This level is driven by curiosity, that is, the natural drive to uncover and reveal what is hidden. Questions in search of meaning arise such as 'What is it?', 'How is it?', 'Where?', 'When?', and the like. Here, the person is seeking insight. Genuine insights are not easily come by, but it is important that the person continues to engage and puzzle until one emerges, by way of release of tension, to the question posed or issue being considered. The operations at this level are those of puzzling, wondering, questioning, sorting out, joining up the dots, looking for the missing link and making connections: in other words, seeking coherence. The imperative at level two is to 'be intelligent'. The restless searching is satisfied with nothing less than a solution. Once one is found and articulated, then the transition to level three beckons.

THE RATIONAL (OR REASONABLE) LEVEL

This is characterized by a reality check. Questions such as 'Is it so?' or 'Is it not so?', 'Is it true?' or 'Is it false?', are asked. The operations here are those of checking, weighing up the evidence, judging the facts and the procedures. The answer is a simple yes or no. If the person is not sure, and unable to make such a judgment of fact, then there is no option but to return to the previous level and renew the search for insight. At level three, the person sets some conditions that need to be fulfilled, in order for an affirmative answer to be given. Among the concerns are not just the answers arrived at from the previous level, but also the question of proper procedure. So one wonders, 'Was anything important left out, in coming to the solution arrived at?' In other words, bias has to be detected, and eliminated, if the truth of a situation or puzzle is to be reached. Once the person can honestly and authentically declare, 'It is so' or 'It is true', then the work of the level is complete. The search is over and the imperative, 'Be reasonable', has been duly honoured.

This is as far as Lonergan went in *Insight*. He had studied the question of what constitutes knowledge, and discerned that it entailed three levels of consciousness, namely, observation of data, followed by the identification of a solution, and concluding with an assent to the solution arrived at. This constituted his cognitional theory. However, Lonergan's later concern was with the totality of human subjects, and the reality of their being. As such, then, his agenda comes to encompass not just knowing, but also doing. Truth was but the gateway to goodness. The truly authentic human subject, he believed, was one who not only knew what was right and correct, but who also committed to achieving the good arising from the truth ascertained. In *Method in Theology* (1972), particularly, he spelt out what he understood by a fourth level.

THE RESPONSIBLE (OR MORAL) LEVEL

It is here, on level four, that the person deliberates on the various courses of action possible, in light of the truth apprehended at the previous level. This, in turn, leads to decision, which, ultimately, points to corresponding action. The operations at this level are those of deliberating, evaluating, deciding and doing. The imperative required is, 'Be responsible.' At this level, Lonergan understood human subjects as constituting themselves and their worlds. Here, truth finds its natural fulfilment in the doing of the good. The assurance that a person successfully achieves, at this juncture, derives from the faithful observance of the four transcendental precepts, or imperatives of attentiveness, intelligence, reasonableness and responsibility. It is these that propel the person from one level to the next. They are the soul of the process. This leads to the question of how human subjects and learners can be formed, or educated, in the practice of the transcendental imperatives. In this respect, the observation of Meynell to the Philosophy of Education Society of Great Britain, in 1976, is worth recalling: 'The cultivation of these four dispositions, the inculcation of what Lonergan has called "the four transcendental precepts", "Be attentive, Be intelligent, Be reasonable, Be responsible" is, I shall argue, the basic aim of education.'[22]

This is quite a claim, and derives directly from Lonergan's analysis of the human condition, and the struggles entailed in knowing the truth and doing the good. If this claim can be sustained, then there arises the question of how, practically and effectively, may these imperatives be delivered on in the classroom? The answer, which this paper proposes, is straightforward enough but potentially very effective. The imperatives may be activated by a distinctive type of question at each of the four levels. They might very well be termed 'trigger questions' as they are designed to trigger, in learners, the required imperatives, one per level.

Conveniently, the four sets of questions all begin with a word whose initial letter is 'R'. At level one, one may utilize simple 'recall questions' (who, what, when, where, how) to check if attentiveness has, indeed, occurred. At level two, search or 'research questions' (What do you make of all of this?, Can you detect any connections with what you already know?, What does it mean?) enable and promote the exercise of intelligence and enquiry, and so assists in quarrying meaning from the data provided at the opening level. 'Reality questions' (Is it so?, Is it real?, Is it true?) follow at the next level, requiring learners to be reasonable and rational. At the fourth level, 'response questions' (How do you think you might act in similar circumstances?, What decision do you think you should make?) of evaluation, deliberation and decision, arise, which feed into responsible moral activity.

Fidelity on the part of the teacher, in skilfully posing such trigger questions, will effectively contribute to the exercise of the transcendental imperatives by learners, and so promote consistency between knowing and doing. Now, it is one thing to theorize about such matters. It is a qualitatively different matter to demonstrate, in detail, how such theory may be translated into educational practice. This is what it is now proposed to undertake and, in so doing, to illustrate how Lonergan's cognitional and behavioural theory may work effectively in classroom practice.

The subject area chosen is moral education, and the topic is the universal aspiration to assist one's neighbour. Overall, the intent is to bring the learner from initial apprehension of data, to ultimate decision and doing. Structurally, the lesson will follow the normal layout of a teaching plan, complete with statement of aims and provision of a basic teaching strategy. However, the teaching strategy in this instance will be an illustration of how consistency between knowing and doing, on the part of learners, can be achieved by means of a methodology rooted in Lonergan theory.

APPLICATION OF LONERGAN'S LEVELS OF LEARNING TO MORAL EDUCATION[23]

Task: An illustration of Lonergan's learning levels in action.
Subject: Moral education.
Topic: Development of an attitude towards helping one's neighbour.

Story: The Samaritan who helped his neighbour (Luke 10: 25–37). This story is chosen because of its nigh-universal familiarity to most readers. Also, it is being dealt with solely as a human story and not as a religious one. So it will refrain from making reference to the identity of the original storyteller or to any religious interpretation.

Age-range: From ten years or so upwards to adulthood.

Methodology: Lesson to be structured in accordance with Lonergan's levels of consciousness, to utilize the construct of 'trigger questions', and to activate the transcendental imperatives, which are to be attentive, intelligent, reasonable and responsible in progressing from knowing to doing.

Aims

Cognitional: That the learners would hear and engage meaningfully with this story and, in so doing, come to discern its moral lesson for themselves.

Behavioural: That in light of their engagement with the story, they would come to a decision as to how to act responsibly in the future in respect of their neighbour.

Note: abbreviations in use: T = Teacher; Ls = Learners; Qs = Questions.

Level 1: The experiential level
T presents story to the learners.
Ls are attentive by listening to the story.
T applies attentiveness test by posing recall Qs such as:
Who is in the story? What happened? Where, when, etc.
Ls' answers provide evidence of attentiveness or otherwise.

Level 2: The intellectual level
T, by use of research Qs such as the following, enables learners explore the meaning of the story:
Why do you think people acted as they did in the story?
What do you think is the most important part of the story?
Ls explore the story by answering the teacher's questions.

T then invites Ls to pose their own questions about the story. Ls, ideally, will articulate some questions of their own.

Level 3: The rational level
T sums up the findings emerging from the previous level and invites Ls to check that they are in order, by posing reality Qs such as:
Is it true that someone was genuinely helped in the story?
Is it true that this kind of thing can happen in real life?, i.e. that it is about a person who helps someone, a total stranger, who is in difficulty?
Has anything important been left out in our checking?
Ls make a judgment on the group's summing up of the story.

Level 4: The responsible level
The purpose of this level is to move towards decision, in light of what transpired at the previous levels. However, one must take into account here the developmental stage of the particular group of learners, and so proceed gently and gradually. Teachers need to be careful not to challenge children too directly or too hastily. Rather than directly asking, 'What will you do in future about something like this?', it is advisable to proceed by means of a more indirect incremental path, and place the learners within the story, before eventually, tentatively, asking them to consider how they themselves might act when face to face with someone in need. The following procedure respects these principles.

(a) Evaluation:
T directs Ls' gaze to the main character in the story and begins the process of incremental response Qs:
Was the man right to help the stranger in need? Yes?/No?
T follows this up with the 'justification question', Why?/Why Not?
(b) Decision:[24]
Imaginary: If you had been there how, do you think, you might have acted?
General: When you find yourself in a situation something like this, how do you think you might like to act if you had the chance – like

the one who helped or like the one who passed by?
Particular: Name someone you know whom you think you could help. If you feel you would like to do something, name the place and the time and the action you could do to help them.
(c) Doing:

In a sense, the classroom activity can only go as far as the threshold of doing, as the action element, in reality, is usually something that is located in the future and, for the most part, outside the confines of the classroom. Also, the autonomy of the individual needs to be protected, as he or she has a right to the freedom to carry through on their decisions or not. However, depending on the topic in question, and also on the degree of trust and openness within the group, there may be merit in returning to the topic at some stage in the future, and allowing those, who so wish, to say how they may or may not have responded in real-life situations to the decisions they made in the original lesson on the topic in question.

Before concluding, there is another possibility worth considering, whose appropriateness again depends on several factors. This is the possibility of classroom engagement in some form of artistic or educational expression of the decisions made by the learners, e.g. writing about them, making a drawing of themselves performing them, or acting them out. All such activities tend to function as reinforcement strategies and are a legitimate form of educational activity.

Concluding comments

This paper began by noting Bernard Lonergan's inviting educators to apply his theories to the practice of education. It also noted the response of Professor Valentine Rice to this challenge, regarding the identification of an educational approach to enabling learners achieve consistency between their knowing and doing. We then considered Lonergan's contribution to this question, particularly in terms of his cognitional investigations and levels of consciousness construct. Finally, the paper proposed a detailed educational application of Lonergan's cognitional and behavioural theories to moral education, as a reasoned response to

Rice's concern. This endeavour gives rise, now, to a number of questions. In the first instance, is such a form of teaching workable and secondly is it worthwhile? A third question might be: is it an adequate response to the initial question, raised with such insistence by Val Rice, during his March 1980 interview with Bernard Lonergan?

Concerning the first question, as to the workability and practicality of the application of Lonergan's theory proposed here, the following data is provided. During the 1990s, this writer had the opportunity of delivering courses on educational practice to primary-school student teachers in three different colleges of education in Ireland.[25] The courses included an exposition of Lonergan's cognitional theory, along with applications of that to teaching, on the lines proposed above, not just in respect of moral and general education but also in respect of religious education. The feedback from the students, at the conclusion of teaching practice, was extremely positive and encouraging, as evident from the following selection:[26]

> I was surprised how well the Lonergan lesson went. LM (f), grad. dip. 1996, 9-year-olds. I was very pleased with the Lonergan method and how it worked. It grabbed attention in a very positive way. I personally got huge satisfaction out of teaching RE to an older class and the deeper interaction. AS (f), grad. dip. 1996, 11-year-olds.
>
> Using these methods had a terrific sense of achievement. The lesson went very well – although it took quite a long time to plan. I could see when the children made the connections and had 'insights' – their faces do light up. I'm glad I got the opportunity to teach one of these lessons – it's good to see the children eagerly getting involved. I was actually surprised by some of the replies and stories the children told. CL (f), grad. dip. 1996.
>
> Lonergan worked quite well – my classes usually ended up going through all the checking and deciding stages automatically. OC (f), BEd3, 1997, 12-year-olds.
>
> The children put some thought into their various points of view. One child's question almost knocked me and were it not for a slightly sarcastic bit of help from another pupil I might well have been stuck for words. I felt like a pupil who had just learned a valuable lesson. JK (m), BEd3, 1997, 11-year-olds.
>
> The Lonergan method was great fun! The children loved voicing their opinions – some were wary at first, but when they realized any opinion was accepted they all joined in and enjoyed the lesson. It is definitely a refreshing change. LD (f), BEd3, 2000, 11-year-olds.

The Lonergan method gave me a whole new insight and perspective into the delivery of a parable and story and really focused the children's minds and provoked their thinking and made for some great class debate and conversation. SH (m), BEd3, 2000, 12-year-olds.

I was amazed at some of the responses given by the children in the response part of the lesson. The children were divided in half re whether the father was right in welcoming back the son. One response given by a child was, 'The father was correct in welcoming back his son because otherwise he would lose his son as well as his money.' This level of maturity was not shown by the child before this and I was delighted that the Lonergan method allowed the children to reach this level of maturity. MK (m), BEd3, 2000, 9-year-olds.

The second question is that of the worthwhileness of the approach. While the above feedback from student teachers also provides positive support for this, there is need to consider the matter at a more theoretical level. Lonergan judged the success or otherwise of his theories on method in this area, on whether or not they contributed to promoting the authenticity of the human subject. So, one needs to apply here the 'authenticity test'. Lonergan placed a premium on authenticity, as is clear in his volume, *Method in Theology*: 'The basic idea of the method we are trying to develop takes its stand on discovering what human authenticity is and showing how to appeal to it ... it is a powerful method, for man's deepest need and most prized achievement is authenticity.'[27]

This, in turn, leads to the issue of how authenticity is appealed to and achieved. Lonergan clearly indicates that one 'achieves authenticity in self-transcendence',[28] that is, by the faithful observation of the transcendental precepts of being attentive, intelligent, reasonable and responsible. Such fidelity sees the human subject operating at the fourth level of responsibility, where decisions have to be faced: 'One has to have found out for oneself that one has to decide for oneself what one is to make of oneself; one has to have proved oneself equal to that moment of existential decision; and one has to have kept on proving it in all subsequent decisions, if one is to be an authentic human person.'[29]

Elsewhere, Lonergan, in reiterating the necessity of responsible action (level four), following on from reasoned apprehension of, and assent to, the truth (levels 1–3), cements the notion of consistency between knowing and doing at the heart of Val Rice's concern, and also points to the constitutive nature of the method, both for the individual and for his or her world, when he says: 'The subject moves to a further dimension of consciousness as his concern shifts from knowing being to realizing the good ... On this level subjects both constitute themselves and make their world.'[30] One realizes oneself, therefore, as an authentic or inauthentic human being, through the making of choices.[31] But a further question may be posed here, given the feedback above in relation to young learners, as to whether or not it is possible or, indeed, advisable, to endeavour to promote authenticity among children. Lonergan himself endorses such work with children, observing that:

> The emergence of the fourth level of deliberation, evaluation, choice is a slow process that occurs between the ages of three and six ... the child gradually enters the world mediated by meaning and regulated by values and, by the age of seven years, is thought to have attained the use of reason ... Still this is only the beginning of human authenticity.[32]

This view, that children are capable of engaging, in some degree, with what Lonergan's various levels of consciousness entail, is endorsed by educationalist Professor Thomas Groome of Boston College, who notes:

> From about the age of twelve on a person can begin to reflect critically in a qualitatively improved way. But developmentally a person is capable of engaging in reflective knowing before that stage. From an educational perspective, that reflective dimension of knowing must be promoted and encouraged at the earlier stages of cognitive development if the person is to have the likelihood of full critical reflection later on. Critical reflection needs to be encouraged from the beginnings of intentional education.[33]

In light of the above observations from theorists and practitioners, it may be suggested, with a degree of confidence, that the practical educational application of Lonergan's theory, presented here, is a worthwhile and workable response to Val Rice's question to Bernard Lonergan, in March 1980, concerning consistency between knowing and doing and its promotion through educational endeavour.

APPENDIX: LONERGAN-RELATED THESES DIRECTED BY PROFESSOR VAL RICE IN TCD

MEd Theses
- *1974* A. O'Mahony, 'The question asking process in the context of learning'.
- *1980* D. Hickey, 'Intellectual conversion and education: a study in the philosophy of Bernard Lonergan'.
- *1980* M. Vaughan-Dagg, 'An inquiry into the implications of Bernard Lonergan's *Cognitional Theory* for science education'.
- *1981* S. O'Raghallaigh, 'Some implications of Bernard Lonergan's philosophy for the teaching and learning of mathematics and for the curriculum in Irish post-primary schools'.
- *1983* H. Delaney, 'To the threshold of insight: a study of the imagination in Aristotle, Aquinas and Lonergan'.
- *1986* B. Hennigan, 'Knowing and education: a model of education based on the philosophy of Bernard J.F. Lonergan, SJ, and the psychology of Jerome S. Bruner'.
- *1988* A.J. McGovern, Epistemology and history: a study in the philosophy of Bernard Lonergan'.
- *1989* E. Mulvihill, 'Insight and counselling'.
- *1990* C.M. Bray, 'Social process and social education: a study in the philosophy of Bernard Lonergan'.
- *1991* D. Farrell, 'Education and disadvantage: a study in the philosophy of Bernard Lonergan'.
- *1991* J. Hever, 'Marist values in education: a study in the philosophy of Bernard Lonergan'.
- *1997* S. McDermott, 'Intentionality in learning and education: a study in the philosophy of Bernard Lonergan'.

PhD dissertations
- *1989* S. Breathnach, 'Communication and method: studies in the philosophy of Bernard Lonergan'.
- *2007* S. McDermott, 'Intentionality, intersubjectivity and subjectivity: a study in the philosophy of Bernard Lonergan'.

NOTES

1. Bernard Lonergan, 'Topics in Education', *Collected Works of Bernard Lonergan*, eds, Frederick E. Crowe and Robert M. Doran, vol. 10 (Toronto, 1993).

2. Bernard Lonergan, *Topics in Education*, p. 24.
3. Moira Teresa Carley, 'Bernard J.F. Lonergan, SJ: on teaching' (unpublished EdD thesis, Harvard University 1989).
4. A full listing of these pieces of work is to be located as an appendix to this essay.
5. Sometime after the death of Val Rice, in 2006, Philip McShane came into possession of the typed folders of these interviews. Copies may be located in some of the Lonergan Centres around the world, including the one in Milltown Park. We are indebted to Dr McShane for diligent retrieval and selfless dispersal of same.
6. Transcript of V. Rice's interview with B. Lonergan, 12 March 1980, p. 1.
7. *Ibid.* p. 4.
8. *Ibid.* pp. 4, 5, 6, 6, 20, 21.
9. *Ibid.* p. 6.
10. Lecture notes taken by Therese Dooley, TCD MEd student, which contain the line: 'Lonergan: person who has achieved consistency between knowing and doing', 13 Jan 1994. Viewed in March 2008.
11. Pierrot Lambert, Charlotte Tansy and Cathleen Going, *Caring about Meaning: Patterns in the Life of Bernard Lonergan* (Montreal 1982), p. 142.
12. Bernard Lonergan, 'Cognitional Structure' in Crowe and Doran, *Lonergan*, vol. 4, p. 205. Lonergan himself informs readers, 'I have been told that my view of human knowing as a dynamic structure has been pronounced excessively obscure.'
13. Mark Doorley, *The Place of the Heart in Lonergan's Ethics* (London, 1996), p. xiv.
14. Terry J. Tekippe, *What is Lonergan Up To in Insight? A Primer* (Collegevillle, Minnesota 1996), p. 159.
15. William A. Van Roo, 'Lonergan's method in theology' in *Gregorianum*, 55/1 (1974).
16. Bernard Lonergan, 'Insight: a study of human understanding' in Crowe and Doran, *Lonergan*, vol. 3, p. 769.
17. Bernard Lonergan, 'Grace and freedom: operative grace in the thought of St Thomas Aquinas' in Crowe and Doran, *Lonergan*, vol. 1, p. 144.
18. Hugo Meynell, *An Introduction to the Philosophy of Bernard Lonergan* (London 1976), p. 2.
19. Lambert *et al.*, *Caring about Meaning*, p. 220.
20. Terry Tekippe, *Theology: Love's Question* (London 1991), p. 124.
21. Bernard Lonergan, *Method in Theology* (Toronto 2003), p. 4.
22. Hugo Meynell, 'On the aims of education', *Proceedings of the Philosophy of Education Society of Great Britain*, x (July 1976).
23. Tom Daly, 'Learning levels' in William Danagher (ed.), *Australian Lonergan Workshop* (New York 1993), p. 233. Daly argues persuasively in favour of

'levels of learning' terminology, in respect of Lonergan's 'levels of consciousness'. Lonergan's theory, he claims, is 'a theory of learning – in a serious sense of the word, a theory of coming into the possession of knowledge'.
24. 'If', 'When', 'Name': these three terms may be utilized as support, or crutch questions, enabling a teacher to progress a lesson incrementally from the imaginary, through the general, to the particular.
25. The colleges in question were St Patrick's College, Drumcondra, a college of Dublin City University; Mary Immaculate College, a college of the University of Limerick; and Coláiste Mhuire, Marino, with links to Trinity.
26. In this instance, the selection is confined solely to feedback from the Coláiste Mhuire students, by virtue of their association with Trinity, where they would also have had Professor Rice as a lecturer in the philosophy of education. Coding indicates and includes: the initials and gender identity of contributors, programme year identity (BEd3/grad. dip.); and calendar year, as well as, in some instances, the age group of children addressed. The students used the term, 'Lonergan method', to describe teaching according to Lonergan's levels of consciousness, irrespective of whatever curriculum subject was being taught at the time.
27. Lonergan, *Method in Theology*, p. 254.
28. *Ibid.* p. 104.
29. *Ibid.* p. 121.
30. Lonergan, 'Cognitional Structure', p. 219.
31. Lonergan, *Method in Theology*, p. 38.
32. *Ibid.* p. 121.
33. Thomas H. Groome, *Christian Religious Education: Sharing our Story and Vision* (London 1980), p. 237.

RAYMOND TOPLEY was head of the Department of Religious Studies and Religious Education at St Patrick's College, Drumcondra, and was a Fellow of the Lonergan Institute of Boston College. He made a particular study of the practical application of Bernard Lonergan's cognitional theory to moral and religious education and shared a long-time interest with Val Rice in Lonergan's works. He died in 2009.

Toward an Interpretation of the Work of Art

VALENTINE RICE

The concern of this paper is essentially philosophical.[1] We live at a time when, happily, new attention has been directed to the identification and development of talent in the arts. I would like to suggest that these statistical and methodological studies may usefully be complemented by an enquiry into the nature of the artistic product. Such an enquiry may not merely respond to what Bernard Lonergan terms 'the unrestricted desire to know', it may also serve to focus practice and to clarify its directions. Accordingly, it seems worthwhile to ask what is a work of art, what processes went into its creation, and in what sense, if any, it may be said to communicate and have meaning. I would like to suggest, also, that one must seek for an interpretation of art more fundamental than that which is offered by the wasteland of Behaviourism. It seems rather inadequate, for example, to define poetry as 'a kind of applied psychology', and to centre a theory of art on the assumption that 'the stimuli of poetry elicit responses in such a way as to organize our impulses toward action'.[2] Accordingly, what is attempted below is a personal exploration, which acknowledges a fundamental debt to the philosophy of Jacques Maritain.

Let us begin by noticing the pervasiveness of art in the world in which we live. There is literature, both oral and written; we are all familiar with poetry, with the novel, the short story, the essay. There is drama, an artistic form that is allied to literature; it is significant, however, that in drama, the text requires execution for completeness. Then there are the worlds of painting, of sculpture and of the dance. There is the world of music, with its variety of forms, both vocal and instrumental. As in the case of dramatic art, two levels of artistic achievement are involved in music. There is an artistry that relates to the composition and an artistry which relates to the execution. We may admire the creative freshness of Vivaldi or Dvorak, but we must equally admire the artistry of John McCormack, as he takes a simple ballad like 'Off to Philadelphia in the morning' and fashions it into a thing of lasting beauty.

Equally, one thinks of the art that relates to building. The art of architecture does not necessarily involve a professional architect: in the old farmhouses of the Irish countryside, there was a marvellous use of local materials, to produce a home that was, at once, functional and in harmony with the landscape. There is the art of making furniture: we are all familiar with the names of Chippendale, Shereton and Buhl. There is the art of designing and making clothes. There is the art of cooking, an art that is quite fundamental to human welfare. I would suggest, indeed, that there is no single human activity that cannot become the subject of an art. And following Oscar Wilde, even the living of one's own life can become an art form.

Art is as varied, therefore, as the multifarious activities of the human being, who tells stories, makes images of reality, plays music, builds places to live in and things to sit on, prepares food and tills the ground. We are well aware that any one of these activities may be carried out at a routine level, or with a high degree of skill. I want to suggest that it is skill, or technique, that distinguishes the work of art from the routine performance. The work of art is supremely well done: it is technically first-rate. 'A painting,' says Degas, 'is something which requires as much knavery, trickery and deceit as the perpetration of a crime.' The mediaevals recognized the role of technique, in art, when they defined art as *recta ration facibilium*, the right way of making things. And it is no accident that the Greeks had the same word for 'art' and 'technique' and that their word *poiema* has to do with making.

TOWARD AN INTERPRETATION OF THE WORK OF ART

The technical mastery of the medium – whether it be paint, or stone, or language – involves protracted effort. In the process, one will be well advised to profit from the experience and discoveries of others. Human progress is culturally cumulative. All that we can achieve technically in painting, in music, in mathematics, in cuisine, is due to the accumulation of individual discoveries, made by particular human beings, at specific points of time. Where, for example, would modern music be without the innovations in harmony of the last five hundred years? Where would painting be without the early-Renaissance experiments in perspective, or the insights into colour and light of the Impressionists? I suggest, therefore, that high achievement, in any field of art, is dependent on the mastery of a technique, which incorporates the experiences of those who went before us, and which, indeed, takes account of the work of those who are presently active in the field. This, ultimately, is the justification for art schools, for technical institutes, for universities and for pleasant occasions such as Listowel Writers' Week.

At this stage I would like to make two further observations on technique. The first is the salutary point made by Chardin to the jury of the Salon in 1765: 'He who has not felt the difficulties of his art does nothing that counts; he who ... has felt them too soon does nothing at all.' The second is that once one has become master of one's medium, one can extend the technique, or even ignore the rules creatively. Here is Van Gogh describing the completion of a portrait:

> I should like to paint the portrait of an artist friend, a man who dreams great dreams, who works as the nightingale sings, because it is his nature. He'll be a fair man. I want to put into the picture my appreciation, the love I have for him. So I paint him as he is, as faithfully as I can to begin with. But the picture is not finished yet. To finish it I am now going to be the arbitrary colourist. I exaggerate the fairness of his hair, I come even to orange tones, chromes, and pale lemon yellow. Beyond the head, instead of painting the ordinary wall of the mean room, I paint infinity, a plain background of the richest, intensest blue that I can contrive, and by this simple combination of the bright head against the rich blue background, I get the mysterious effect, like a star in the depths of an azure sky.[3]

I now want to point to a traditional distinction, which is of paramount importance: this is the distinction between the fine arts and the useful arts. All arts involve technique, but the arts fall into two broad categories. On the one hand, there are the arts based on practical activities – building, the making of furniture, clothes and so on – which can be brought to a high degree of sophistication. On the other hand, there are the activities of poetry-writing, the writing of novels or short stories, the composing of music, painting, sculpture. To these, during the past three hundred years, it has been customary to give the name 'the fine arts'.

The fine arts are essentially non-practical although, of course, they are not entirely devoid of function. To a far greater extent than the useful arts, however, they seem to involve the free play of human intellect over and above what is required for survival; in many ways they resemble the free play of children. What is particularly significant about them is that they relate to communication between people: you assume a public when you write a poem or paint a picture. We are not prepared to concede that the same is true of arts such as fashion design or cuisine, or the finest architecture or furniture-making.[4] Indeed, the distinction between the useful arts and the fine arts might appropriately be restated as a distinction between the silent arts and the arts of meaning.

The two categories, of course, are not mutually exclusive. Historically, the fine arts arose out of the useful arts; in the historical evolution of mankind, as Maritain has pointed out, *homo faber* has carried on his shoulder *homo poeta*.[5] The stories of Scheherazade had, in their time, a very practical purpose. Irish bardic poetry had its origins in the need to crystallize, orally, the memory of historical events and tribal obligations. The wall paintings of Altamira, in all likelihood, were created to serve some immediate magical function. And many portraits have been painted that never transcended the practical function of providing a likeness.

I have suggested that the fine arts emerge from the free activity of the human spirit, and that they are essentially activities of free intellectual play, after the business of survival has been taken care of. One tells stories as opposed to talking business. One plays music. One paints pictures, which, in the final analysis, are of no use in terms of food and shelter. One creates dreams, a reflection of life, instead of living life itself. I have suggested also that the fine arts are related to the human urge to communicate. Much of political theory is based on the assumption that human beings need one another because of their limitations.

That is undoubtedly true: we can achieve more by standing together and allowing each man to specialize, rather than by obliging each man to grow his own food and make his own clothing. But it is even more true that we need each other because the human spirit is rich, and needs to overflow in communication, both intellectually and emotionally. If we understand this we can understand why the poet needs to lay bare his heart, why the philosopher needs an audience, why men go to pubs and why women talk over the garden wall.

To sum up, I have argued that all works of art involve technique or craftsmanship, and that certain arts, the fine arts, carry meaning. I now want to suggest that we can understand the meaning that attaches to the fine arts only in terms of an adequate theory of knowledge. In short, I want to suggest that poetry, music, theatre and painting speak to us in a unique way only because the process of poetic and artistic creation brings into play a unique form of knowledge.

The human being is inserted into the world; his life is a process of grappling with, of coping with, that world. We come to know that world in various ways; we react to it, we act upon it. We are all familiar with traditional accounts of the central elements in the knowing process. As the basis of all knowing there is sense perception – our experience of the world through our eyes, our ears and touch receptors. We encounter the 'buzzing, booming confusion' of William James, and we order it into patterns of space and sound and colour. Associated with sense perception is the automatic formation of images of what we have experienced. These images are more or less proximate to consciousness, depending on the intensity of the original experience, or the degree of reinforcement that has taken place. The image is always singular, in that it relates to a particular object: one can readily, for example, summon up the image of an absent friend. If one has any doubts about the automatic production of images, one has merely to indulge in the personal experiment of placing oneself mentally in the kitchen of the home in which one lived as a child. The form of the room comes back to one – the colour on the walls, the size and place of the windows, the texture of the curtains, the shape of the fireplace. One image links with another until the whole is surveyed. Yet none of these things were consciously committed to memory.

Overlaid upon sense perception, with its associated images, are the three processes that we associate with human reason – concept formation, judgment and logic. These three processes, in turn, are related to the reflexive capacity of the human mind, which can return on itself so as to survey its own contents. Comparison of images and sense impressions yields the concept, the universal idea, which refers validly to a variety of particular objects. We have, for example, concepts of 'man', of 'woman', of 'house', of 'justice'. Universals are fundamental to the development of language, because of the economy which they permit: language would be impossibly cumbersome if every tree and cow had separately to be named. Similarly, reflexive comparison of concepts, or of concepts with images or sense impressions, yields the judgment that consists essentially in the recognition of relationship of identity or non-identity, consistency or non-consistency, between the elements compared.[6] And so one judges that 'all men are mortal' or that 'this is a painting by James Arthur O'Connor'. By a similar reflexive activity, judgments may in turn be compared from the point of view of consistency or non-consistency, and so the concatenation of judgments in logic becomes possible. Thus, in a basic paradigm we argue: 'All men are mortal. John is a man. Therefore John is mortal.'

The cognitive processes that I have outlined above, however sketchily, are spontaneous human processes. They are used in everyday life, in buying and selling, and coping with the world. Some men – mathematicians, scientists, economists, philosophers, for example – develop the rational superstructure to a high degree of sophistication, but one is still dealing with common human operations. They are cognitive processes, of which we may be justly proud, because they have made possible the technical sophistication of our culture. They underlie our definition of man as a rational animal and, as a consequence, we often tend to think that an account of human knowledge, in terms of these rational processes, is the whole story. I want to suggest that we need to complement this account by an insistence on another dimension of human knowledge, on what might be termed a para-rational or left-handed form of knowledge, which, like the rational processes, is common to all of us, but which is particularly developed in the poet or artist.

Let us begin by noting the physical phenomenon of resonance. If one tunes a violin and then sounds an A somewhere in the vicinity, the violin will begin to vibrate in sympathy with the external sound. I suggest that something similar happens to us in our encounter with the world and that it constitutes the basis of the artistic experience.

We move through the world, through a flow of sense impressions, images and ideas. Is it not a fact of experience that, from time to time, through the sensory flow, one feels shaken by a feeling of union, or sympathy, with reality? It is essentially a feeling of resonance, by which some aspect of reality strikes an answering chord within one's being. You feel in a wordless way that you know; you feel that you are profoundly aware and you feel compelled to express the experience. It may be that you come over the hill at Bearna and see the great plain of Limerick before you, and you want to photograph or paint it. Or it may be some human situation, with which you empathize, and you feel that you must give expression to it, in a poem or a play or a short story. In all cases there is a tension; there is a load that must be set free, and ideally it will be set free in a work of art.

The tragedy is that most of us do not have the technical ability to follow through. You try to capture the view from Bearna, and the photograph is flat and uninteresting. You try to paint a picture and the paints become muddy and indistinct. You try to work with words, and find you cannot get the proper flow. You try to make a melody, and find you are merely stringing banalities together. It is not so for the artist. He has the insight; indeed, it is probable that his sensibility is more developed than that of the ordinary man. But he also has the technical ability to express his insight in a completed work of art. The work of art involves, therefore, a combination of intuition and technique. If either is lacking one does not have a work of art. We are all familiar with the problem of insight unsupported by technique. Equally, however technically competent a work may be, it is not a work of art unless there is a worthwhile insight at the centre.

Artistic activity is thus essentially creative. The feeling of resonance yields an insight below the level of words, which in turn results in the production of an artistic object – a painting, a carving, a piece of music, a poem. Here there is indeed a significant analogy with the process of rational knowledge. The activity of rational knowledge terminates in the production of a concept or a judgment; the activity of artistic knowing terminates in the production of a work of art. And both communicate.

Something new, the work of art, has therefore been brought into existence. What is this new thing, this work of art? We can admit that it is something personal, since it has been shaped by a particular human being. We know that it has a role to play in communication since it was conceived of an urge to share. But why should it assume its particular shape or form? Let us return to the tension in the artist, which demands expression. In his encounter with the world, sense impressions, images, ideas form in him. As a result of this, from time to time he experiences the resonance to which I have alluded above, the pregnant sympathy between his own subjectivity and some aspect of the outside world. In giving expression to this resonance he finds that concepts and logical propositions of the kind used by scientists, economists and mathematicians, are not enough. As laws will not span the totality of human morality, so he finds that concepts and logic will not span the delicacy and profundity of what he has felt. And so he must create another thing that will communicate – the artistic object. It may not use words at all: it may be a piece of music, or a pattern of paint on a canvas, or a carved stone or piece of wood. If he uses words, as in a poem or a play or a novel, he will use them in a special way, so that the meaning of the work as a whole – the integral meaning – is greater than the sum of the literal meanings of any sentences used in the course of the work.

Finally, the insight itself may be clarified for the artist only as the work progresses. The original resonance that demands expression may be obscure and general. Frequently, it is only as the work proceeds that the artist comes to know the details of the correspondence, as, within his consciousness, reality and his own subjectivity emerge together from sleep.

And what do we, in turn, obtain by encountering the artistic object – the poem, the play, the story, the painting, the piece of music? If the analysis I have given above is correct, and if we are open to the effect of the work of art, we obtain a double knowledge that is quite unique. The work of art expresses simultaneously an insight into some aspect of reality and the intimate subjectivity of a living human being. As a consequence, we obtain through an encounter with it an insight into some aspect of reality, together with an understanding of the heart of man himself, which might not be possible to obtain by any other means. Here is what Maritain has to say on the subject:

> An act of thought which by its very essence is creative, which shapes something in existence, instead of being shaped by things, what does such an act express and manifest when it produces the work if not the very being and substance of the one who creates? But the heart of man is obscure to himself; it is only by receiving and suffering things, by awakening to the world, that our substance awakes to itself. The poet can express his own substance in a work only if things resound in him, and if, at the same awakening, they and he emerge from sleep. All that he discerns and divines in things is thus inseparable from himself and his emotions and it is actually as part of himself that he discerns and divines it, and in order to grasp obscurely his own being through a intuition or emotion, is an obscure grasping of himself and things together in a knowledge by union and con-naturality, which only takes shape, bears fruit and finds expression in the work.[7]

The cognitive content of the work of art, the unique knowledge that the work of art conveys, is the best argument for the presence of the arts in life and in education.

Finally, I should like to advert briefly to two matters. First, the universal dimension of meaning implicit in the work of art, and second, the relationship between art and beauty. The question of universality was raised a long time ago by Aristotle when he argued that poetry was of richer worth than history, since history, as he understood it, related to particular events while poetry made statements of universal human import. The question emerges again whenever we investigate the difference between a good portrait and a likeness, or the difference between one of Paul Henry's Connemara landscapes and a photograph of the same scene. According to the interpretation of the work of art given above, the work of art conveys to us a double knowledge; it bisociates an insight into some aspect of reality with an insight into the subjectivity of the poet or artist.

But this basic meaning is essentially particular and is hardly sufficient to explain both the appeal and the relevance of the work of art to men and women who are separate in time and space from the context in which it was originally produced. I want to suggest therefore that the artist encapsulates in his creation a dimension of meaning over and above the particular meaning that is central to the work. Paul Henry's painting speaks not merely of Paul Henry and of a fine day in Connemara, but also of anyone face to face with sky and moor and mountain.

Sean O'Casey wrote plays about life in a Dublin slum, but the works speak also of the universal human condition. And so, as Maritain says, the work of art makes present to us 'together with itself, something else, and still something else, and still something else indefinitely, in the infinite mirrors of analogy'.[8] There is again a significant parallel with the process of rational knowing. In both cases the universal is reached through abstraction: painting and drama, for example, are selective in their use of material. Furthermore, as Lonergan has pointed out, rational insight pivots between the concrete and the abstract. The problem presented to Archimedes was concrete. His solution dealt with the immediate problem but possessed a relevance and a significance infinitely wider than its original application.[9]

There remains the question of beauty. Our common-sense understanding of things posits a relationship between art and beauty, but common-sense understandings can be notoriously wide of the mark. Certainly there can be no question of requiring that the content of the work of art be beautiful or pleasing in the conventional sense in which these works are used; otherwise we should have to refuse the name of art to Goya's indictments of war and to two thousand years of effort to convey the sufferings of Christ. Our common-sense expectation must therefore be refined; insofar as beauty relates to a work of art it would seem that it relates to its form rather than to its content. We indeed expect a work of art to exhibit certain qualities of balance, arrangement, rhythm and harmony. And when we set out to fashion something, do we not find that the very material makes its own aesthetic demand? One begins to paint a picture and the shapes and colours force their own arrangement within the space of the rectangle. One tries to work with language, and the words demand their own cadence and balance.

I want to suggest that the work of art reaches towards beauty because of an intimate and fundamental relationship between being and beauty. The mediaeval Scholastics affirmed that all being is beautiful, and that being and beauty are convertible.[10] In the face of the evil and ugliness in the world this may seem to be an uncritical and unwarranted position. But then one remembers that the sky is beautiful, that lakes and trees and flowers and mountains are beautiful; one thinks of the beauty of a horse, of a tiger, of a human face or body. One recognizes that there is no reason at all why any of these things should be beautiful, that their beauty is a glorious bonus of existence, and one begins to feel that the mediaevals may have been right after all. In such a view of things evil and ugliness appear as a defect in being, as a wound in existence, as an absence where there should be found fullness. If we now apply this thinking to the work of art we find that in artistic creation a man or a woman brings a new being into existence. And so, as if by an inner law that emerges from the material of the work of art, this new being strains toward beauty.

A brief summary of the argument may be appropriate in order to bring this investigation to a close. I have sought for an interpretation of work that would be relevant to the variety of art forms, from poetry to furniture-making to painting. I began by pointing to the pervasiveness of art, and by noting that any human activity, provided it is carried out with sufficient skill, can become the subject of an art. This led to the suggestion that in all art, technique is essential; there may be a technique without art but there is no art without technique. I then went on to suggest that, within the broad field of the arts, a distinction must be made between the useful arts and the arts of meaning. I suggested that we can understand the meaning that attaches to works of art, such as poems and plays and paintings, only by reference to a theory of knowledge. In the process of artistic creation in these fields, I suggested, there occurs a resonance between some aspect of reality and the artist's subjectivity. The work of art crystallizes and expresses this resonance, so that by encountering it, we obtain a double insight – into some aspect of reality and into the intimate subjectivity of the human being. Finally, I pointed to the relationship between art and beauty and suggested that it can be understood in terms of a more fundamental relationship between being and beauty. In the work of art a man or woman brings a new being into existence. And so art must engender in beauty.

NOTES

1. This essay is a version of a set of lecture notes by Val Rice, titled 'Poetic and Artistic Knowledge', 2001.
2. Robert Goldwater and Marco Treves (eds), *Artists on Art* (London 1976), p. 308.
3. Vincent van Gogh to Hugo van Gogh, Arles, August 1888, *Letters* (London 1997).
4. A fine cabinet may indeed *say*, if we are prepared to use the word analogically, 'I am beautiful.' 'I am well made.' However, a poem or a painting may make a similar statement. What is suggested here, is that a second and more fundamental level of meaning may be predicated of the poem or painting, of a kind which can in no sense be predicated of the cabinet.
5. Jacques Maritain, *Creative Intuition in Art and Poetry* (New York 1953), p. 45.
6. The term 'judgment' is used here in a broader sense than that used by Bernard Lonergan, who restricts the use of the term to the intellectual act, by which an essentially hypothetical construct is deemed to coincide with reality.
7. Jacques Maritain, *The Range of Reason* (New York 1952), pp. 17–18.
8. Maritain, *Creative Intuition*, p. 128.
9. Bernard J.F. Lonergan, *Insight: A Study of Human Understanding* (London 1957), pp. 4–5.
10. *Omne ens est pulchrum; ens et pulchrum convertuntur* (Whatever is beautiful; being and the beautiful are interchangeable).

Resilience: Ordinary Magic

EILEEN DOYLE

This article presents the construct of resilience in its historic setting, considers, among others, the contributions of Werner, Garmezy and the University of Minnesota, Luthar, Kim-Cohen, and the caring adult, and examines the implications of a number of research projects.

Introduction

Adversity in life is inevitable. Each of us has differing degrees of vulnerability when faced with risk factors. How an adult may respond to problems, challenges and difficult situations therefore varies. Some respond in a reactionary and aggressive manner, others freeze; some are devastated while others seem to cope, find enjoyment or even thrive. Coping means managing the personal reality, past, present or future.[1] Resilience was of interest to health and social workers from the 1940s and the spotlight was on at-risk children.[2] The construct of resilience, developed from the sixties and seventies, continues to be used mainly in relation to children. In the eighties the resilience of the workforce of the downsizing Illinois Bell Telephone was studied.[3] From this grew The Hardiness Institute. Since the nineties attempts have been made to apply the construct of resilience to careers and guidance counselling for adults.[4] Resilience is a way of thinking, acting and behaving in relation to risk. Boris Cyrulnik believes that it is about living[5] and may therefore be applied to adult adaptation.

Defining resilience

The term resilience is broad and connotes the ability to bounce back, to recover from, and to withstand disappointment, shock or suffering. The notion of 'bouncing back' is questionable because the child or adult will not be the same after the experience. Essentially, resilience is about positive adaptation in the face of risk or adversity.[6] For nearly forty years, research has sought to define the construct of resilience.[7] Before then a deficit model prevailed in relation to at-risk children. There is general agreement that resilience is not static and that an individual's resilience may vary at different developmental stages. A number of educators and social psychologists have used social and curriculum interventions to develop coping skills in children so as to promote adaptation and mental health.[8] This is grounded in the importance of early childhood experience of parental/adult influences, of social, environmental and educational aspects.[9] The contribution that a supportive teacher can make in the lives of high-risk children was documented by Emmy Werner in her study of Hawaiian children on the island of Kauai.[10] Durlak's analysis of 1200 studies on child adjustment confirmed the importance of the caring teacher.[11] Cyrulnik's recent work on resilience gives testament to 'teachers' power to influence human souls'.[12] Moreover, he states that 'Even when they were not verbalised, their subjective values influenced the existential choices made by the children in their care.'

Emmy Werner's study

Werner set out to study the cohort of babies who had been born in 1955 on the island of Kauai. This 35-year study initially focussed on 201 children born into poor living conditions, at high risk of psychological disorder due to addictive parents, mental illness, and separated parents. However, 35 per cent of the cohorts developed positively.[13] While two-thirds of the children were not resilient through childhood they became so in adulthood. Thus a total of 78 per cent of the original group developed well. The researchers became fascinated by the children who seemed to recover from their adversities; Werner described them as 'vulnerable but invincible'. Elwin James Anthony[14] had described 'the invulnerable child' in 1982. Werner went further and identified the processes involved in this invulnerability, thereby promoting an understanding of resilience. Analysis of the data showed Werner that children were resilient because of 'protective factors'. These included a relationship with a significant or caring adult, not necessarily a parent but an adult with a determining influence, the skills of problem-solving rather than avoidance, social interaction, and participation in local or community activities. Nowadays there remains a question about the association between risk and protective factors.[15]

Werner summarized a resilient person as one who 'loves well, works well, plays well and expects well'. In other words, the resilient one experienced a caring relationship, a desire to succeed, the ability to do so, the capacity to enjoy, have fun and interests, and possessed a positive attitude about the future. Theoretically, resilience seems to necessitate a healthy lifestyle, alertness to the connection between thoughts and emotions, the ability to think or reflect, and the courage to make a choice or decision, however small. Other aspects of the research that merit attention are the effects of belief systems[16] and the importance of being able to read. Lyubomirsky[17] has examined the role of spirituality and religious belief in adult coping, a factor noted by Werner and Smith[18] among women whose ability to deal with adversity was helped by faith and prayer. The current research by Lyubomirsky *et al.*[19] seems to affirm the relevance of personal faith and religious conviction.

Negative influences on resilience were found to be violence, whether physical or sexual abuse, exposure to alcoholism, and homelessness. Protagonist of Positive Psychology Martin Seligman[20] concentrated on individual attribution of negative events; what he termed the 'explanatory style' was a contributor to 'the optimistic child'. Cyrulnik's continuing work on overcoming trauma highlights the human potential for self-management and growth.[21] Werner's study had shown that resilient children were problem-solvers who could attract positive attention and who tended to perceive life experiences as challenges rather than problems.[22] Human interaction facilitates development through possible close relationships with a parent, teacher, friend, neighbour or social group.

Michael Rutter clarified the concept of risk resilience within the individual and the family[23]. His earlier study[24] promoted the concept of effective schools as organizations where positive expectations and the highest standards of behaviour were espoused by teachers and communicated to students.[25] The term 'hardiness' is used mainly in relation to adults and stress.[26] The growth of Positive Psychology since the sixties has resulted in a looser interpretation of terminology. Nevertheless, psychologists Seligman, Diener, Lyubomirsky, Csikszentmihalyi, and their ever-growing number of students and colleagues, seek a more precise use of terms and definitions. Sexual abuse and sexual exploitation have presented in resilience and risk studies from the late eighties.[27]

Resilient children

Norman Garmezy at the University of Minnesota pursued research on able or competent children to counteract the prevailing emphasis on at-risk children.[28] His research, continued by Anna Masten,[29] has contributed significantly to promoting awareness of the construct of resilience through the National Resilience Resource Centre. Project Competence was a longitudinal study of 205 urban children. Their abilities, families, social contexts and risks or adversities at developmental stages were documented. The working definition of resilience was 'competence in the face of adversity'. The study showed that resilient children were effective problem-solvers who could learn, had caring adults in their lives, whose self-esteem was positive, who tended to be involved in activities at home, in school and in their local communities. Resilience in childhood and adolescent years was a positive predictor of competence in adulthood. An important aspect identified by Luthar et al.[30] was that some seemingly resilient adolescents were internalizing problems. Werner and Smith[31] found that children who had effective parenting and better cognitive skills continued to be resilient in adult life. Masten et al.[32] also found that some at-risk individuals could have a second chance. Thus, life-altering events such as a career choice, breaking away from negative peer influences, a positive life partner proved to be significant.

The findings by Masten et al. are consistent in identifying protective factors for developing resilience. What is striking is that resilience is nurtured from quite ordinary, even pedestrian, experiences, what Masten called 'ordinary magic'.[33] Like other researchers[34] the Minnesota study acknowledged the role of effective, caring adults, intellectual skills, self-efficacy, effective schools and other socio-economic advantages. Masten[35] avers that: 'Resilience does not come from rare and special qualities, but from the everyday magic of ordinary human resources in the minds, brains and bodies of children, in their families and relationships, and in their communities.'

Masten's work illustrated the need to shift attention from prevention strategies to systemic promotion of competence and healthy development in children. That is not to advocate ignoring risk prevention. The challenge is to emphasize a positive approach. Masten[36] identifies intervention strategies from the research on resilience:

1. Risk-focused strategies include prenatal care, effective transitions between school stages, prevention of homelessness through effective housing policies.

2. Asset-focused strategies that enrich childhood experiences are co-curricular activities, literacy programmes for parents, parenting programmes etc.

3. Process-focused strategies promote attachment relationships, effective mentoring and coaching programmes, enabling children to develop skills and talents that add to their self-efficacy.

Masten warns of the potential dangers of resilience models. The greatest danger is to assume that children are naturally resilient. The relevant literature clearly shows the centrality of the adult role, whether parents, teachers or significant others.[37] Another danger is to assume that one size fits all. Each child is unique and has specific experiences of family, school, relationships. The final danger is that an emphasis on strengths-based strategies for resilience could ignore preventable risks. Masten cites the following examples where government policies may affect such risks: interventions to prevent premature birth, disease, family violence, hunger and homelessness.

Resilience: definition and prevailing issues

Defining resilience is not without controversy and its refinement continues.[38] A self-confident child will manifest resilience only in the context of risk or adversity. Resilience is not to be confused even with overt self-confidence. Indeed, the research seems to suggest that resilience itself has not (to date) been 'measured'; it has been 'inferred', whether by its absence or presence. A working definition is given by Luthar as 'a dynamic developmental process reflecting evidence of positive adaptation despite significant life adversity'.[39] Resilience is not about any single human attribute. Neither is resilience static. It is not something that is in the individual personality, though the debate has already begun on temperament, genes, adaptation and the 'science of human strengths'.[40] Resilience is 'a process that emerges from the dynamic interaction between persons in their environments'.[41] By definition, therefore, resilience requires adversity. Successful outcomes from competence to deal with risk are the criteria by which resilience may be inferred. This obviously muddies the waters of a desirable agreed definition.

The initial emphasis in resilience research was on individuals who were exposed to extremes of poverty, stress and/or early trauma. The approach was therefore from a perspective of weaknesses and helplessness. From the seventies the work of Garmezy[42] included a focus on protective factors in relation to high-risk individuals and in the context of schizophrenia. The recent work of Masten[43] has built on this 'strengths' approach. As a result the focus now is on identifying preventive measures to enable children to function and adapt. A strengths-based approach considers relevant protective factors to be a combination of the individual's internal (or genetic?) resources as well as the people, organizations and activities that may contribute to resilience. The research as to whether resilience is innate or learned continues and in 2009 is neither complete nor strongly on track.[44] That is not to deny a wide span of research, particularly in the English-speaking academic world. In this context Nan Henderson's Resilience Wheel[45] is helpful. If resilience is acquired, this strengthens the role of education and targeted well-founded programmes that promote problem-solving and social interaction skills. Examples are the START programme in Australia, the RIRO curriculum programme in Toronto, Seligman's PENN programme in the US,[46] the PATHS curriculum[47] and the intervention strategies of Daniel and Wassell[48] in the UK. The relevance of temperament to resilience is not yet sufficiently researched.

A way forward

Biological and genetic aspects have not figured significantly in the research though one recent study attributes 70 per cent of resilience in children to genetic effects.[49] This lacuna has been noted by Luthar[50] among others[51] who highlight the relevance of an inter-disciplinary longitudinal framework to research risk, resilience and the total spectrum of personality, temperament etc. Such a model would include advances in neuroscience[52] and be a resource for learning programmes and 'therapeutic interventions'.[53] This would advance the understanding of why and how individual response to adversity varies and whether or not resilient adaptation may be beyond some human beings.

The power of the individual's social environment to affect levels of resilient adaptation might therefore be informed by modern neuroscience.[54] Nonetheless, understanding risk and resilience within a framework of genetics is not an end in itself. It could be a basis for the development of interventions whether through the school curriculum or more generally through social, guidance and counselling services. During the nineties the concept of resilience was popularly applied if not purloined by a number of career specialists. At the same time in the United States, Professor Al Siebert[55] established The Resiliency Centre as an online service to include training and support for adults dealing with varying levels of stress. Siebert's initial focus was on problem-focused mechanisms for coping with stress, risk and adversity. Nicholls and Polman[56] take a similar approach.

Risk factors: how many and how much

Research suggests that one risk factor alone is unlikely to have a long-lasting negative effect on children. Cumulative adversity when children are reared in disadvantaged and dysfunctional homes where parenting is inadequate and the culture is one of disharmony, rows and possibly violence may contribute to negative outcomes. Nearly twenty-five years ago, Rutter[57] advocated developing 'protective factors' to counteract the impact of family adversity. More recently Fergusson and Horwood[58] propose the term the 'resilience factor' to encompass both protective and compensatory processes in dealing with cumulative adversity. Their work is important because it analyses data from a 21-year longitudinal study in Christchurch, New Zealand, begun in 1977. This CHDS (Christchurch Health and Development Study) involved 1265 urban children. The cohort was studied systematically to age sixteen years and again at eighteen and twenty-one. A comprehensive range of research sources included interviews with parents, psychometric tests, school reports, self-reports, medical and police records. In essence this study sought to understand and analyse human responses to adversity at varying stages and situations. The shift from a negative mental disorder approach to a strengths-based approach is the outcome of decades of research on resilience. The impact has been well described by Coatsworth and Duncan:[59]

The theoretical, empirical and applied underpinnings of resilience have provided an excellent foundation for wide ranging systems change in how we approach the prevention and treatment of mental-health problems throughout the lifespan. It leads directly to a strengths-based approach to interventions with the main goals of fostering development by assuring that all social ecologies are filled with supportive resources and protective factors that nurture inherent human adaptive systems.

Resilience: conclusion and beginning

Research continues on the construct of resilience and not only in relation to children. One emerging aspect is gender. A recent study has found that girls were more resilient than boys in adolescence and early adulthood.[60] Another is the effect of belief systems, religious affiliation and spirituality, initially identified by Werner.

While no single agreed definition of resilience exists, to date the extent of continuing research is impressive. The older deficit model approach has been replaced by a positive mindframe that may be further enriched. Morale[61] stresses the importance of community resilience, especially in the context of South America where the culture of community is strong.

The largest body of the research so far has come from the US and Canada although some important work is emerging from the UK and

France in particular. On the outer periphery, perhaps, is what has been learned since the sixties in the field of Positive Psychology. The work of Seligman *et al.* could cloud the lens on resilience in children and young people and questions persist about an agreed definition. For research purposes this means clarifying risk, protective factors, and what precisely is being measured. There is no straight line to resilience. Where a curriculum, social, preventive and intervention measure is the route of the caring professions, research will need to include 'sleeper effects', or those possible positive outcomes that emerge only after the interventions. Cyrulnik[62] applies the image of knitting to the daily human challenge of living. He points to the importance of hope and the ability of the child or the adult to manage their vulnerability: 'The world may taste the same but we have to resolve the problems of our age in every chapter of our stories. Knit one stitch for our past and our subjective life, another for our culture and those who are close to us. That is how we knit our lives.'

Nearly a century earlier the poet Robert Frost (1874–1963) captured the essence of resilience in 'A Soldier':

> But this we know, the obstacle that checked
> And tripped the body, shot the spirit on
> Further than target ever showed or shone.

Resilience is a challenge to the University of Dublin, Trinity College, through current and future masters in education postgraduates to research, reflect, publish, and in the attributed words of Professor J. Valentine Rice, 'to ensure that your research makes a difference and does not gather dust on university shelves'. The 'prize' could be increased resilience in children, not to mention adolescents, adults and communities in Ireland and worldwide.

NOTES

1. R.S. Lazarus and S. Folkman, *Stress, Appraisal and Coping* (New York 1984).
2. K. Cairns, *Attachment, Trauma and Resilience: Therapeutic Caring for Children* (London 2008); B. Benard, *Resiliency: What we have Learned* (San Francisco 2004); J. Barlow *et al.*, *A Systematic Review of Reviews*

of Interventions to Promote Mental Health and Prevent Mental Health Problems in Children and Young People (Brighton 2007).
3. S.C. Kobasa, 'Stressful life events, personality and health: an inquiry into hardiness', *Journal of Personality and Social Psychology*, 37 (1979), 1–11; S.R. Maddi, and S.C. Kobasa, *The Hardy Executive: Health under Stress* (Illinois 1984).
4. W. Bancroft, *Sustaining: Making the Transition from Welfare to Work*, SRDC Working Paper Series (Montreal, QC: Social Research and Demonstration Corporation 2004); Benard, *Resiliency*; W. Borgen, N.E. Amundson and E. Tench, 'Psychological wellbeing throughout the transition from adolescence to adulthood', *The Career Development Quarterly*, 45 (1996), 189–211. Canada Career Development Foundation (CCDF), *Applying the Construct of Resilience to Career Development: Lessons in Curriculum Development* (Montreal 2007).
5. B. Cyrulnik, *Talking of Love: How to Overcome Trauma and Remake your Life Story* (London 2005); B. Cyrulnik, *Resilience: How your Inner Strength Can Set you Free from the Past* (London 2009).
6. J. Kim-Cohen *et al.*, 'Genetic and environmental processes in young children's resilience and vulnerability to socio-economic deprivation', *Child Development*, 75, 3, May (2004), 651–68; A.S. Masten and J.L. Powell, 'A resilience framework for research, policy, and practice' in S.S. Luthar (ed.), *Resilience and Vulnerability: Adaptation in the Context of Childhood Adversities* (New York 2003).
7. Suniya S. Luthar, *Resilience and Vulnerability: Adaptation in the Context of Childhood Adversities* (New York 2003); M.O. Wright and A.S. Masten, 'Vulnerability and resilience in young children' in J.D. Noshbitz *et al.* (eds), *Handbook of Child and Adolescent Psychiatry* (New York 1997); A.S. Masten and Abigail H. Gewirtz [Internet], 'Resilience in development: the importance of early childhood' in R.E. Tremblay, R.G. Barr and R. de V. Peters (eds), *Encyclopedia on Early Childhood Development* (Montreal, Quebec: Centre for Excellence for Early Childhood Development 2006). Online at www.child-encyclopedia.com/Pages/PDF/Masten-GewirtzANGxp.pdf; Sam Goldstein and Robert B. Brooks, *Resilience in Children: Handbook* (USA 2006); A.S. Masten *et al.*, 'Resilience in development' in C.R. Snyder and S.J. Lopez (eds), *The Handbook of Positive Psychology* (New York 2009).
8. Luthar, *Resilience and Vulnerability*; Barlow, *A Systematic Review*.
9. D. Cicchetti *et al.* (eds), *The Promotion of Wellness in Children and Adolescents* (Washington DC 2000); Luthar, *Resilience and Vulnerability*; A.S. Masten and J.L. Powell, 'A Resilience Framework for Research, Policy, and practice' in Luthar, *Resilience and Vulnerability*, pp. 1–25.
10. E.E. Werner and R.S. Smith, *Vulnerable but Invincible: A Longitudinal*

Study of Resilient Children and Youth (New York 1982); E.E. Werner and R.S. Smith, *Overcoming the Odds: High Risk Children from Birth to Adulthood* (New York 1992).

11. J.A. Durlak and A.M. Wells, 'Evaluation of indicated preventive intervention (secondary intervention) mental health programmes for children and adolescents', *American Journal of Cunmmunity Psychology*, 26 (1998), 775–802.
12. Cyrulnik, *Resilience*.
13. Werner and Smith, *Vulnerable but Invincible*.
14. E.J. Anthony, 'The Syndrome of the Psychologically Invulnerable Child' in E.J. Anthony and C. Koupernik (eds), *The Child and his Family* (New York 1974), pp. 529–44; E.J. Anthony, 'Risk, Vulnerability and Resilience' in E.J. Anthony and B. Cohler (eds), *The Invulnerable Child* (New York 1987), pp. 3–48.
15. Luthar, *Resilience and Vulnerability*; I. Schoon, S. Parsons and A. Sacker, 'Sociometric adversity, educational resilience, and subsequent levels of adult adaptation', *Journal of Adolescent Research*, 9, 4 (2004), 382–404; N. Garmezy and M. Rutter, *Stress, Coping and Development in Children* (New York 1983); S.S. Luthar, D. Cicchetti and B. Becker, 'The construct of resilience: a critical evaluation and guidelines for future work', *Child Development*, 71 (2002), 543–62.
16. E.E. Werner and R.S. Smith, *Journeys from Childhood to Midlife: Risk, Resilience, and Recovery* (New York 2001).
17. S. Lyubomirsky, *The How of Happiness: A Practical Guide to Getting the Life you Want* (London 2007).
18. Werner and Smith, *Vulnerable but Invincible*.
19. S. Lyubomirsky, K.M. Sheldon and D. Schkade, 'Pursuing happiness: the architecture of sustainable change', *Review of General Psychology*, 9 (2005), 111–31; Lyubomirsky, *The How of Happiness*.
20. M.E.P. Seligman et al., *The Optimistic Child* (New York 1995).
21. Cyrulnik, *Talking of Love*; Cyrulnik, *Resilience*.
22. Werner and Smith, *Vulnerable but Invincible*.
23. M. Rutter, 'Resilient children', *Psychology Today* (1984), 57–65.
24. M. Rutter et al., *Fifteen Thousand Hours* (Massachusetts 1979).
25. M. Rutter and B. Maughan, 'School effectiveness findings, 1979–2002', *Journal of School Psychology*, 40 (2002), 451–75; M. Rutter, 'Genetic Influences on Risk and Protection: Implications for Understanding Resilience' in Luthar, *Resilience and Vulnerability*, pp. 489–509.
26. S.R. Maddi and S.C. Kobasa, *The Hardy Executive: Health under Stress* (Illinois 1984); S.C. Kobasa et al., 'Effectiveness of hardiness, exercise and social support resources against illness', *Journal of Psychosomatic Research*, 29 (1985), 525–33; S.R. Maddi, 'Hardiness training at Illinois

Bell Telephone' in J. Opatz (ed.), *Health Promotion Evaluation* (Stephens Point, WI 1987), 101–15; S.R. Maddi, 'The story of hardiness: twenty years of theorising, research, and practice', *Consulting Psychology Journal*, 54 (2002), 175–85; S.C. Funk, 'Hardiness: a review of theory and research', *Health Psychology*, 11 (1992), 335–245; S. Goldstein and R.B. Brooks, 'Why study resilience?', *Handbook of Resilience in Children* (New York 2006), pp. 3–16.
27. K.E. Bolger, C.J. Patterson and J.B. Kupersmidt, 'Peer relationships and self-esteem among children who have been maltreated', *Child Development*, 69 (1998), 1171–97; D.M. Fergusson and L.J. Horwood, 'Resilience to Childhood Adversity: Results of a 21-year Study' in Luthar, *Resilience and Vulnerability*, pp. 130–55; E. Morale, *Approaches Based on Resilience* (Paris 2007).
28. N. Garmezy, 'Stress-resistant Children: The Search for Protective Factors' in J.E. Stevenson (ed.), *Recent Research in Developmental Psychopathology. Journal of Child Psychology and Psychiatry, Book Supplement* (Oxford 1985), pp. 213–33; N. Garmezy, 'Resiliency and vulnerability to adverse developmental outcomes associated with poverty', *American Behavioral Scientist*, 34 (4) (1991), 416–30; A.S. Masten, K.M. Best and N. Garmezy, 'Resilience and development: contributions from the study of children who overcome adversity', *Development and Psychotherapy*, 2 (1990), 425–44; Benard, *Resiliency*; B. Benard, 'The Foundations of the Resilience Paradigm' in N. Henderson (ed.), *Resilience in Action: Practical Ideas for Overcoming Risks and Building Strengths in Youth, Families, and Communities* (California 2007), pp. 3–7; E. Werner, 'How Children Become Resilient: Observations and Cautions' in Henderson, *Resiliency in Action*, pp. 15–23.
29. A.S. Masten, 'Ordinary magic: resilience processes in development', *American Psychologist*, 56 (2001), 227–38; Masten *et al.*, 'Resilience in development', pp. 117–31.
30. Luthar, *Resilience and Vulnerability*.
31. Werner and Smith, *Vulnerable but Invincible*; Werner and Smith, *Journeys*.
32. A.S. Masten and W.J. Curtis, 'Integrating competence and psychopathology: pathways towards a comprehensive science of adaptation in development', *Development and Psychopathology*, 12 (2000), 529–50; Masten *et al.*, 'Resilience in development', pp. 117–31.
33. A. Masten, 'Ordinary magic', 228.
34. A.S. Masten and J.D. Coatsworth, 'The development of competence in favourable and unfavourable environments', *American Psychologist*, 53 (1998), 205–20; S.S. Luthar *et al.*, 'The construct of resilience: a critical evaluation and guidelines for future work', *Child Development*, 71 (2002), 543–62; E.L. Cowen, 'Psychological Wellness: Some Hopes for the Future'

in D. Cicchetti *et al.* (eds), *The Promotion of Wellness in Children and Adolescents* (Washington, DC 2000), pp. 477–503; Benard, *Resiliency*.
35. A.S. Masten, 'Ordinary magic: resilience processes in development', *American Psychologist*, 56, 3 (2001), 238.
36. A.S. Masten and W.J. Curtis, 'Integrating competence and psychopathology: pathways towards a comprehensive science of adaptation in development', *Development and Psychopathology*, 12 (2000), 529–50.
37. S.S. Luthar and E. Zigler, 'Vulnerability and competence: a review of research on resilience in childhood', *American Journal of Orthopsychiatry*, 6 (1991), 6–22; R. Gilligan, 'Adversity, resilience and young people: the protective value of positive school and spare time experiences', *Children and Society*, 14 (2000), 37–47; K. Reivich and A. Shatté, *The Resilience Factor* (New York 2002); Rutter, 'Genetic Influences', pp. 489–509; B. Benard, 'The Foundations of the Resilience Paradigm' in Henderson, *Resilience in Action*, pp. 3–7.
38. S.S. Luthar, 'Resilience in development: a synthesis of research across five decades' in D. Cicchetti and D.J. Cohen (eds), *Risk, Disorder, and Adaptation* (New York 2006); T.M. Yates, B. Egeland and L.A. Sroufe, 'Rethinking Resilience: A Developmental Process Perspective' in Luthar, *Resilience and Vulnerability*, pp. 243–66.
39. S.S. Luthar and L. Bidwell Zelato, 'Research on Resilience: An Integrative Review' in Luthar, *Resilience and Vulnerability*, pp. 510–50.
40. M.E.P. Seligman *et al.*, *The Optimistic Child* (New York 1995); Cyrulnik, *Talking of Love*; J.M. Patterson, 'Understanding family resilience', *Journal of Clinical Psychology. Special Issue: A Second Generation of Resilience Research*, 58 (2002), 233–246; Rutter, 'Genetic Influences', pp. 489–509; Yates *et al.*, 'Rethinking Resilience', pp. 243–66; C. Peterson and M.E.P. Seligman, *Character Strengths and Virtues: A Handbook and Classification* (Washington, DC 2004); B. Benard, 'The foundations of the resilience paradigm' in Henderson, *Resilience in Action*, pp. 3–7.
41. K. Weed, D. Keogh and J. Borkowski, 'Stability of resilience in children of adolescent mothers', *Applied Developmental Psychology*, 27 (2006), 61.
42. N. Garmezy and K. Nuechterlein, 'Invulnerable children: the fact and fiction of competence and disadvantage', *American Journal of Orthopsychiatry*, 42 (1972), 327–9; N. Garmezy and M. Rutter, *Stress, Coping and Development in Children* (New York 1983); N. Garmezy *et al.*, 'The study of stress and competence in children', *Child Development*, 55 (1984), 97–111.
43. Masten, 'Ordinary magic', 227–38.
44. J. Kim-Cohen *et al.*, 'Genetic and environmental processes in young children's resilience and vulnerability to socio-economic deprivation', *Child Development*, 75, 3 (2004), 651–68.
45. Henderson, *Resiliency in Action*.

46. K. Reivich, J.E. Gillham and T.M. Chaplin, 'From helplessness to optimism' in Goldstein and Brooks, *Handbook of Resilience*.
47. J. Taub and M. Pearrow, 'Resilience through violence prevention in schools' in Goldstein and Brooks, *Handbook of Resilience*.
48. B. Daniel and S. Wassell, *Assessing and Promoting Resilience in Vulnerable Children* (London and Philadelphia 2002).
49. J. Kim-Cohen *et al.*, Genetic and environmental processes in young children's resilience and vulnerability to socio-economic deprivation', *Child Development*, 75, 3 (2004), 651–68.
50. Luthar, *Resilience and Vulnerability*.
51. CCDF, *Applying the Construct of Resilience to Career Development: Lessons in Curriculum Development* (Montreal 2007).
52. E.L. Cowen, 'Psychological wellness: some hopes for the future' in D. Cicchetti *et al.* (eds), *The Promotion of Wellness in Children and Adolescents* (Washington, DC 2000), pp. 477–503; Goldstein and Brooks, 'Why study resilience?', pp. 3–16.
53. Cicchetti *et al.*, *The Promotion of Wellness*.
54. J.W. Curtis and C.A. Nelson, 'Towards Building a Better Brain: Neurobehavioural Outcomes, Mechanisms and Processes of Environmental Enrichment' in Luthar, *Resilience and Vulnerability*, pp. 463–88.
55. A. Siebert, *The Resiliency Advantage: Master Change, Thrive under Pressure, and Bounce Back from Setbacks* (San Francisco 2005).
56. A.R. Nicholls *et al.*, 'Mental toughness in sport: achievement level, gender, age, experience, and sport type difference', *Personality and Individual Differences*, 47 (2009), 73–5.
57. M. Rutter *et al.*, 'Attainment and adjustment in two geographical areas: the prevalence of psychiatric disorder', *British Journal of Psychiatry*, 126 (1975), 493–509.
58. Fergusson and Horwood, 'Resilience to childhood adversity', pp. 130–55.
59. J.D. Coatsworth and L. Duncan, *Fostering Resilience: A Strengths-Based Approach to Mental Health* (Pennsylvania 2003).
60. Luthar and Zelato, 'Research on Resilience', pp. 510–50.
61. E. Morale, *Approaches Based on Resilience* (Paris 2007), p. 4.
62. Cyrulnik, *Resilience*, pp. 146–51.

EILEEN DOYLE, MEd, PhD, is a consultant and former lecturer at NUIM. Since 1991 she has contributed to the Education Management Programmes and the MEd in guidance and counselling in TCD. She is the author of *Leading the Way: Managing Voluntary Secondary Schools* (2000).

Professor John Valentine Rice (1935–2006) An Appreciation

SUSAN M. PARKES

Val Rice was appointed Professor of Education at Trinity College Dublin in 1966. He had recently returned from studying for a doctorate in education in Harvard and brought innovative and challenging ideas to the TCD School of Education. A scholar and philosopher, he was to raise the academic standards of the School and develop an extensive programme of educational research, largely through the introduction of a master in education degree programme in 1970. The 1960s and 1970s was a period of rapid change and expansion in Irish education, following the report, *Investment in Education*, in 1965, the introduction of the O'Malley scheme of free secondary education in 1967 and the establishment of the Regional Technical Colleges in 1969. Rice saw the task of the School of Education as one of responding quickly to the changing needs of the education system and of offering leadership in teacher education.

A full-time higher diploma in education for secondary teachers was introduced in 1968 and the number of students taking the course rose to 150. The two- or three-year master in education programme was the first in the country to offer academic and professional development for potential leaders in the education system and the number of graduates taking higher degrees by research also increased. In 1975 the School began to offer a bachelor in education degree course for primary teachers in association with three colleges of education and later two four-year concurrent BEd degree courses for secondary teachers, one in home economics and the other in music education. The full-time staff of the School rose from four in 1966 to sixteen by 2000, five of whom been had elected to fellowship in the College. The School became an active member of the faculty of Arts (humanities) and contributed widely to College life.

Val Rice was a native of County Kerry and held degrees from both St Patrick's College Maynooth and University College Cork. He worked for some time in the Department of Finance and was awarded a Fulbright Scholarship to study at Harvard. As a philosopher, Rice was a great admirer of the educational ideas of John Henry Newman and his belief in the value of a liberal education and of academic freedom was to be the cornerstone of his university career. He enjoyed lecturing to both undergraduates and graduate students in educational philosophy and introduced many a sceptic to the values and pleasures of his subject. A meticulous supervisor of research students, Rice set high standards in academic writing and presentation, but was always a caring and concerned pastor of his students.

Elected to fellowship in TCD in 1970 and to senior fellowship in 1997, Val was a founder member of the Irish Federation of University Teachers (IFUT) and served on various committees in College. As an art collector, he kept a keen eye on the preservation of the old buildings and on the planning of the new ones in College. Living in Leixlip, he became involved in many environmental campaigns to save the Liffey Valley for future generations, and he and his wife Ellen were generous hosts, opening their house to many student parties, at which, with encouragement, Val could be persuaded to play the piano.

When I arrived back in College as a junior lecturer in the School of Education in 1966, fresh from school-teaching, Professor Rice had just arrived. There was excitement in the air regarding the innovative step of appointing a young Catholic man with American experience to the chair of education in Trinity. We were a very small department, consisting of only four full-time members of staff. There were about sixty students taking the higher diploma in education course, and about forty students from the Church of Ireland Training College in Kildare Place, who attended lectures in arts and education during their two-year diploma course for national-school teaching. There was already a well-established tradition in the School of working with both primary and secondary teachers, which had been an important feature of the department through the years.

In 1966, the School occupied four rooms on the second floor of House No. 5. A little hand was painted at the bottom of the stairs, pointing upwards to indicate our presence. Coal fires were lit every morning, and the one secretary was accustomed to working in the professor's room. There were only two other full-time members of staff, plus the professor, Dr Clive Williams, an education psychologist who later had a distinguished career at the University of Aberystwyth, and Mrs Anita Little, who had been what was called 'assistant to the Professor' since the 1930s. She was a remarkable and wise person who guided generations of students (and myself) in the mysteries of teaching and school supervision. She used to address Professor Rice as 'My dear boy', which shows how young he seemed to her.

Life was easy-going in those first days: higher-diploma lectures did not begin until 4 pm, as many of the 'Dip' students were teaching full-time in schools. We used to play croquet after lunch in what was then the Fellows' Garden. The new Berkeley Library was being built and there were huts everywhere. I well remember preparing my first set of lectures, sitting in one of these Library huts, keeping just a week ahead of the students. Lecture term in those days did not begin until about 25 October, so, being used to a full school timetable, I wondered, as many a junior freshman student does, what I was supposed to *do* (Clive Williams used to say, 'We are paid *to think*'). Anyway, at his suggestion I spent two afternoons checking the books in the small departmental library, which was on three shelves in No. 5. I thought to myself that I never seen such a dull set of books, but little did I know, in my youthful ignorance, that I was in fact looking at the history of the School of Education: at the books on philosophy of education, history, psychology, intelligence testing, pedagogy and school organization, which had formed the basis of the education courses since 1905. I had entered into a whole new world of study, full of interest and challenge, and the School of Education was about to take off and develop to meet the needs of the rapidly expanding Irish education system of the 1960s and 1970s.

In those early days we worked as a team under Val's leadership, planning and discussing new educational ideas and experimenting with new teaching methods. New secondary schools and colleges were being opened and there was opportunity to develop new curricula and assessment procedures. Education students were radical, reading books such as Everitt Reimer's *School is Dead* or Neil Postman's *Teaching as a Subversive Activity*, while Ivan Ilich's *Deschooling Society* provided controversial material for many a discussion group. The higher diploma party was a major social event and most of the students got teaching jobs at the end of the year. The recruitment of MEd students gave the staff the opportunity to undertake research, to specialize and to lecture at a higher level, and thus the links between theory and practice were strengthened. The enthusiasm and commitment of staff and students were infectious, and we were privileged to be part of such a vibrant department.

Educational research was developed under Val Rice's leadership and an innovative research project in teaching and learning, funded by the Department of Education in the 1970s, was the beginning of a rich output of doctoral and masters' degree theses. Later, a School of Education journal, *Studies in Education* (edited by the late Dr Daniel Murphy), was published to bring the School's research work to a wider readership.

Professor Rice's sudden death in 2006, just a year after his retirement, was a great shock to all of us, as his presence had towered over the School for nearly forty years. He left a legacy not only in the many students whom he inspired to strive for excellence and service in education, but also in his ideals of the value of education as being one of the most important responsibilities of mankind and worthy of the highest standards of achievement.